OLD ELM ON BOSTON COMMON.

of the city of Boston and vicinity at the date of Lee's arrival

JESSE LEE

March 12, 1758 - September 12, 1816

(This portrait is not taken from life.)

A SHORT HISTORY OF THE METHODISTS

by

JESSE LEE

limited facsimile edition
of 600 copies

Rutland, Vermont
Academy Books
1974

ISBN 0-914960-04-0
Library of Congress Card No. 74-84416
Printed in the United States of America

10-12 Cleveland Ave.
Rutland, VT 05701

A

SHORT HISTORY

OF THE

METHODISTS,

IN THE

UNITED STATES OF AMERICA;

BEGINNING IN 1766, AND CONTINUED TILL 1809.

TO WHICH IS PREFIXED,

A BRIEF ACCOUNT

OF

THEIR RISE IN ENGLAND,

IN THE YEAR 1729, &c.

BY JESSE LEE,

Author of LEE'S LIFE, *and* CHAPLAIN TO CONGRESS.

The LORD hath done great things for us, whereof we are glad. Pſ.126,3
Come thou with us, and we will do thee good; for the Lord hath spoken good concerning Israel. Numb 10,29
We will go with you, for we have heard that God is with you. Zach 8,23

BALTIMORE,

PRINTED BY MAGILL AND CLIME, BOOK-SELLERS, 224, BALTIMORE-STREET.

1810.

PREFACE.

MR. WESLEY, in a letter to a friend in America, which was written a few weeks before he died, says, "I have given a distinct account of the work of God, which has been wrought in Britain and Ireland, for more than half a century. We want some of you to give us a connected relation, of what our Lord has been doing in America, from the time that Richard Boardman accepted the invitation, and left his country to serve you."

In compliance with this request I have written the best account I could. Withal, it has long been the wish of many of the Methodist preachers and people in America, that some account of the rise and progress of the Methodists in these United States should be published, for the information of the world in general, and of our own societies in particular. And I believe no preacher born in America has had a better opportunity of being thoroughly acquainted with the Methodists than I have. When I became a member of the Methodist Society early in the Spring of 1774, there were but 1160 members in the whole of the United States. I continued four years as a private member; and five years more as a class-leader, exhorter and local preacher; and have since been regularly travelling and preaching for upwards of 26 years. I have also travelled extensively from St. Mary's River in Georgia, to Passamaquoddy Bay in the District of Maine.

As no person has yet appeared willing to engage in this work, I have thought good, by the advice, and with the consent of many of our preachers, to publish the following SHORT HISTORY; in which I have been as careful as possible to state dates and facts, such as I think will be for the information and consolation of pious people.

The materials from which I have chiefly compiled this work, are the Minutes of the Annual and General Conferences. The Societies having been formed by the labours of the preachers, they have also been preserved as one body, united by one spirit, by the blessing of God, by our rules and regulations formed at those conferences. The origin, increase, and establishment of the Societies, must therefore be sought for chiefly in these records.

I have inserted all the Minutes of importance. 1. Those which relate to Doctrines. 2. The rules by which the preachers are called to, and directed in, the work of the Ministry. 3. Those which were made at different times for the regulation, and well-ordering of the societies. And, 4. Those which concern strangers, or persons not of our society. I have noticed these things at the times and places when they occurred.

I have also taken notice of the increase and decrease of Methodism; and in some cases have spoken of the places where the greatest revivals have been: and also of particular declensions, and the causes which produced them.

I have consulted every author that I could find, which I thought would afford information on this subject; especially Wesley's Journals, his Ecclesiastical History, and his Life, written by Dr. Coke and Mr. Moore, and that by Dr. Whitehead. Also, the Methodist Memorial, published by Mr. Atmore. Mr. William Myles's Chronological History of, and Mr. Joseph Benson's Apology for, the people called Methodists. Mr. Francis Asbury's Journals, bound, and unbound. And the Magazines published by the Methodists.

Also, Mr. Freeborn Garrettson's Travels, and William Waters's Life, published by himself.—I have also read over more than 2000 pages of my own manuscript Journals, and consulted many of the travelling and local preachers, in order to ascertain historical facts, and to find out useful things which have never yet been published.

There has been, in general, very many errors and imperfections in the Minutes of the Annual Conferences; but I have used my utmost endeavours to avoid those errors, and to send into the world the truth, the whole truth, and nothing but the truth. In order that every one may understand what the principles, doctrines, and discipline of the Methodists are, and what is the economy and government of their Church and Society. I also wish the Methodists to see what great things the Lord has done for them, and for their fathers and friends before them.

I desire to shew to all our societies and friends, that the doctrines which we held and preached in the beginning, we have continued to support and maintain uniformly to the present day. We have changed the economy and discipline of our church at times, as we judged for the benefit and happiness of our preachers and people; and the Lord has wonderfully owned and prospered us. It may be seen from the following account, how the Lord has, from very small beginnings, raised us up to be a great and prosperous people. It is very certain, that the goodness of our doctrine and discipline, our manner of receiving preachers, and of sending them into different circuits, and the frequent changes among them from one circuit to another, not allowing them in general to stay more than one year in a station or circuit, and in no case more than two years, has greatly contributed to the promotion of religion, the increase of our societies, and the happiness of our preachers.

I have in some cases stated things which took place among us, that were not approved of by all the preachers, and that were afterwards given up. I have likewise made mention of some of the errors of the conferences and COUNCILS; and of the preachers who continued among us, as well as those who separated from us: that it may be seen and understood, that I have not written with partiality, and thereby kept back things necessary to be known.

I am sorry to say, that some of the preachers who separated from us, became bitter enemies to us, and wrote and spoke many things against us which were not true: which things did no honour to the inventors or retailers of them.

I have been particular in collecting the names of all the travelling preachers who have been itinerants, and have been so entered on the annual minutes, with the dates when they began to travel, and also when they stopped; shewing at the same time, by certain marks, whether they were expelled or located; or whether they died in the work, or left the connection.

Withal, I have set down in it's proper place, an account of the number of members in society for each year, with the increase or decrease of every year from the beginning of Methodism in the United States to the present year, as far as I have been able to ascertain it.

Whatever defects are found in this history, (as there will likely be some) I hope will be considered as owing to the want of better information; as some improper information may have been obtained from some imperfect publications. I sincerely wish that it may be rendered a blessing to those who read it, and to the Methodists in particular.

May the Lord redeem us from all iniquity, and make us meet to be partakers with the saints in light for Christ's sake. Amen.

JESSE LEE.

Petersburg, Virginia.
October 28, 1809

CONTENTS.

CHAPTER I.

CONTENTS.

A

SHORT HISTORY

OF THE

METHODISTS, &c.

CHAPTER I.

Of the rise of the Methodists in England in 1729, to the beginning of Methodism in the United States of America, in 1766.

THE Rev. John Wesley, (by the grace of God the Father and Founder of Methodism, and second son of the Rev. Samuel Wesley), was born June 17, old style, 1703. In the year 1720, he entered a student in Christ Church College, Oxford, and soon after took his degree of bachelor of arts.

Sept. 19, 1725, he was ordained a deacon, by Dr. Potter, at that time bishop of Oxford.

Shortly after he preached his first sermon, at South Leigh, within two miles of Witney in Oxfordshire.

March 17, 1726, he was elected Fellow of Lincoln College, Oxford.

February 14, 1727, he took his degree of Master of Arts.

September 22, 1728, he was ordained Priest, by the same bishop.

Of the *name* of Methodist, as applied to Mr. Wesley and his followers, the following account is given. Mr. John Wesley, and by his advice and example his brother Charles, when at Oxford had become deeply serious. They received the sacrament weekly, and prevailed with two or three more young men to do the same. These young men occasionally met together, for the purpose of assisting and encouraging each other in their studies and religious duties ; they also regulated their employments by certain rules. This regularity procured them the distinguishing epithet of *Methodists*. This title was given in the first instance to Mr. Charles Wesley, by a fellow of Merton College, in allusion to an ancient college of physicians at Rome, who began to flourish about the time of Nero, and continued several ages ; they were remarkable for putting their patients under regimen, and were therefore termed *methodists*. This is the most accurate account ; for when Mr. Wesley speaks of this appellation, he mentions it only in very general terms, without attempting to state at what period of the society it was first given. ,' The exact regularity of their lives, as well as studies," says he, "occasioned a young gentleman of Christ's Church to say, ' There is a new set of Methodists sprung up.' The name was new and quaint, so it took immediately, and the Methodists were known all over the university." It would seem, then, from the above account, that the name was given to the young gentleman in consequence of the remarks of the fellow of Merton College ; and Mr. Wesley in his Journal refers to it after the name had become pretty general. One thing is certain, the name was first given at Oxford in the year 1729.

Thus the society began and continued, till Mr. John Wesley went to Epworth to assist his father as his curate. In his absence, June 16, 1729, Mr. Charles Wesley, and one or two more, began again to meet to assist each other. In Nov. 1729, when Mr. John Wesley returned from Epworth, the whole management of the society devolved upon him. The society at that time consisted of the following persons—Mr. John Wesley, fellow of Lincoln college; Mr. Charles Wesley, student of Christ's church; Mr. Richard Morgan, commoner of Christ's church; and Mr. Kirkman, of Merton college. The next year, two or three of Mr. John Wesley's pupils desired the liberty of meeting with them, and afterwards one of Mr. Charles Wesley's pupils. In 1732, Mr. Benjamin Ingham, of Queen's college, and Mr. Broughton, of Exeter, were added to their number. In April in the same year, Mr. Clayton, of Brazen-Nose college, with two or three of his pupils, were added. It was by his advice that they began to observe the fasts of the ancient church, every Wednesday and Friday. About the same time Mr. James Harvey, one of Mr. John Wesley's pupils, was added to the society. And in the year 1735, Mr. George Whitefield, of Pembroke college, joined them. At that time they were fourteen or fifteen in number, all of one heart and of one mind. They formed rules for the regulation of their *time* and their *studies*; for reading the *scriptures*, and *self-examination.*—They also visited the *sick*, and the *prisoners*, and received the Lord's Supper once a *week*.

Mr. John Wesley gives the following account of the rise of Methodism. "In 1729, my brother and I, by reading the Bible, saw inward and outward holiness therein; followed after it, and incited others so to do. In 1737, we saw that this holiness comes by faith, and that men are justified before they are sanctified—But still holiness was our point."

In the beginning of the year 1735, Mr. Wesley for the first time preached extempore, which practice is now followed by all the Methodist preachers. In the latter part of this year Mr. Wesley and his brother Charles consented to leave their native country, and to come over to America as missionaries to the Indians; and on the 14th day of October 1735, they set off. After a passage of more than three months, they landed on the 6th of February 1736, over against Tybee, near Savannah, in Georgia.

In April 1736, Mr. Wesley formed a society at his own house in Savannah, and instructed them weekly in the things belonging to their peace. This he used to consider as the second rise of Methodism. But in the end of the following year, Mr. Wesley left America, and sailed from Charleston, in South-Carolina, for England on December 24th, 1737, and never more returned to America; of course that society fell through, and there was no society of Methodists formed in that town for seventy years afterwards. It was not until the year 1807 that a regular Methodist society was formed in Savannah. Mr. Charles Wesley embarked for England in July 1736, about six months after his arrival in Georgia.

May 1, 1738, Mr. Wesley and some Moravian brethren formed themselves into a religious society, which met at Fetter-lane, in London. This he calls in his Ecclesiastical History, vol. 4, page 175, the third period of Methodism. Mr. Wesley, speaking of this society, says, "Our little society began in London, when forty or fifty of us agreed to meet together every Wednesday evening, in order to a free conversation, began and ended with singing and prayer."

They also formed themselves into little bands, and drew up rules to live by, nearly, if not quite in the order of our present Band Rules.

It was not until the year 1739, that the Methodists were formed into regular societies. The rise of these societies is thus related by Mr. Wesley : "In the latter end of the year 1739, eight or ten persons came to me in London, who appeared to be deeply couvinced of sin, and earnestly groaning for redemption. They desired, as did two or three more the next day, that I would spend some time with them in prayer, and advise them how to flee from the wrath to come, which they saw continually hanging over their heads. That they might have more time for this great work, I appointed a day when they might all come together, which from thence forward they did every week, namely, on Thursday in the evening. To these, and as many more as desired to join with them, (for their number increased daily) I gave that advice which I judged most needful for them, and we always concluded our meeting with prayer suited to their several necessities." This was the rise of the Methodist society, first in London and then in other places. Such a society is no other than "a company of persons, having the form, and seeking the power of godliness ; united in order to pray together, to receive the word of exhortation, and to watch over one another in love, that they may help each other to work out their salvation." All the members of these societies were at liberty to commune in any church, or with any denomination, as they pleased.

This must be considered the fourth period in Methodism. The first at Oxford in 1792 ; the second in America, at Savannah, in 1736—the third in London, in 1738 ; and now this in 1739.

This last was properly the first regular society that was formed, on the plan which has been pursued ever since.

The first itinerant preachers who travelled under the direction of Mr. Wesley, engaged in that work in 1740. His account of it is as follows:—after mentioning that he formed the first society in 1739, he says, "After a time a young man named *Thomas Maxfield*, came and desired to help me as a son in the gospel. Soon after came a second, *Thomas Richards*; then a third, *Thomas Westall*. These severally desired to serve me as sons, and to labour when and where I should direct." We conclude that this was in the beginning of the year 1740.

THOMAS MAXFIELD, was the first Lay Preacher that travelled under the direction of Mr. Wesley.

In the latter end of the year 1740, Mr. Wesley printed a sermon against the Calvinistic notion of Predestination, and sent a copy of it to commissary Garden, at Charleston in South-Carolina, where Mr. Whitefield then was. Mr. Whitefield, having some time before embraced that doctrine, wrote a reply, and published it in America. When he returned to England in 1741, he republished this reply in London. The points in dispute were, 1, Unconditional election—2, Irresistible grace—3, Final perseverance. Each party remained firm in his opinion, and a separation of course took place between them. From that time they had different places of worship, and formed different societies. They had then two societies of Methodists, and Mr. Whitefield became the head, or leader, of the party that adhered to the Calvinistic doctrine of Predestination.

Mr. George Whitefield came first to America in May 1738; he came over a second time in 1739, and then visited New-England in 1740—afterwards he returned to England, and parted with Messrs. Wesleys in 1741.

In 1742, the societies having greatly increased, they were divided into *classes*, each class consisting of about twelve persons, who were committed to the care of one person styled the Leader.—Mr. Wesley observes on this occasion as follows :

" Feb. 15. 1742—Many of us were met together in Bristol, to consult on a proper method of paying the public debt contracted by building ; and it was agreed, 1, That every member of the society that was able, should contribute a penny a week—2. That the whole society should be divided into little companies or classes, of about twelve in each class—3. That one person in each class should receive the contribution of the rest. Thus began, says he, that excellent institution, merely upon a temporal account, from which we have reaped so many spiritual blessings : we soon fixed the same rule in all our societies."

April 9, 1742—The first *watch-night* was held in London. It is said this custom began first at Kingswood by the colliers there, who, before their conversion, used to spend every Saturday night at the Ale-house. After they were taught better, they spent that night in prayer. Mr. Wesley hearing of it, ordered it first to be once a month, at the full of the Moon ; then once a quarter, and then recommended it to all his societies.

Mr. Wesley says of it, " I was informed, that several persons in *Kingswood* frequently met together, at the school, and (when they could spare the time) spent the greater part of the night in prayer and praise and thanksgiving. Some advised me to put an end to this ; but upon weighing the thing thoroughly, and comparing it with the practice of the ancient Christians, I could see no cause to forbid it. Rather, I believed, it might be made of more general use. So I sent them word, ' I designed to watch with them on the

Friday nearest the full of the moon, that we might have light thither and back again.' I gave public notice of this the Sunday before, and withal, that I intended to preach, desiring they, and they only, would meet me there, who could do it without prejudice to their business or families. On Friday abundance of people came. I began preaching between eight and nine, and we continued till a little beyond midnight, singing, praying and praising God."

May 26, 1742—Mr. Wesley visited Birstal, in the county of York, where he met with *John Nelson*, a Lay-Preacher, who was instrumental in turning many of his neighbours from darkness to light. After some time Mr. Nelson, who heartily joined Mr. Wesley in his work, published a journal of his travels and Christian experience, which has been rendered a blessing to thousands, and is still in circulation among the Methodists in the United States.

In the year 1744, June 25, the first conference was held in London. Mr. Wesley invited the persons who attended, and also presided among them. There were six clergymen, and four travelling preachers present. The names of the clergymen were, John Wesley, Charles Wesley, John Hodges, Henry Piers, Samuel Taylor, and John Meriton. The names of the preachers were, Thomas Maxfield, John Downs, Thomas Richards, and John Burnett. From this time the conference met every year under Mr. Wesley's direction, at London, Bristol, or Leeds; but he did not annually publish the Minutes till the year 1765.

The subject of their deliberations at these conferences, were proposed in the form of questions, which were fully discussed, and then with the answers written down, and afterwards printed under the title of "Minutes of several conversations between the Rev. Mr. Wesley and others." But now they are called "The Minutes of the Conference."

On Friday, August 24, 1744, Mr. Wesley preached for the last time at Oxford, before the university. He had preached to them twice before, after he began to declare the truth in the fields and highways. He then makes this observation, "I am now clear of the blood of these men—I have fully delivered my own soul; and am well pleased that it should be the very day on which, in the last century, near two thousand burning and shining lights were put out at one stroke. Yet what a wide difference is there between their case and mine! They were turned out of house and home, and all that they had; whereas I am only hindered from preaching, without any other loss; and that in a kind of honourable manner; it being determined, that when my next turn to preach comes, they will pay another person to preach for me." And so they did twice or thrice; even to the time of his resigning his fellowship.

December 25, 1744—Mr. Wesley drew up directions for the Band Societies, and recommended them, with the Band Rules.

I will here insert the friendly *Epistle to the Reverend Mr. George Whitefield*, which was written in the year 1755, by the Reverend Charles Wesley, A. M.

COME on, my WHITEFIELD! (since the strife is past,
And friends at first are friends again at last)
Our hands, and hearts, and counsels let us join
In mutual league, t'advance the work Divine.
Our one contention now, our single aim,
To pluck poor souls as brands out of the flame;
To spread the victory of that bloody cross,
And gasp our latest breath in the Redeemer's cause.

Too long, alas! we gave to Satan place,
When party-zeal put on an angel's face,
Too long we list'ned to the coz'ning fiend,
Whose trumpet sounded, "For the faith contend!"
With hasty blindfold rage, in error's night
How did we with our fellow-soldiers fight!
We could not then our father's children know,
But each mistook his brother for his foe.
"Foes to the truth, can you in conscience spare?
"Tear them, (the tempter cry'd) in pieces, tear!"
So thick the darkness, so confus'd the noise,
We took the stranger's for the Shepherd's voice;
Rash nature wav'd the controversial sword,
On fire to fight the battles of the Lord,
Fraternal love from every breast was driv'n,
And bleeding Charity return'd to heaven.

The Saviour saw our strife with pitying eye,
And cast a look that made the shadows fly:
Soon as the day-spring in his presence shone,
We found the two fierce armies were but one;
Common our hope, and family, and name,
Our arms, our Captain, and our crown the same,
Enlisted all beneath Immanuel's sign,
And purchas'd every soul with precious blood divine.

Then let us cordially again embrace,
Nor e'er infringe the league of gospel-grace:
Let us in Jesus' name to battle go,
And turn our arms against the common foe;
Fight side by side beneath our Captain's eye,
Chace the Philistines, on their shoulders fly,
And, more than conquerors, in the harness die.

For whether I am born to "*blush above,*"
On earth suspicious of electing love,
Or you o'erwhelm'd with honourable shame,
To shout the universal Saviour's Name,
It matters not; if, all our conflicts past,

Before the great white throne we meet at last:
Our only care, while sojourning below,
Our real Faith by real Love to show:
To blast the aliens' hope, and let them see
How friends of jarring sentiments agree:
Not in a party's narrow banks confin'd,
Not by a sameness of opinions join'd,
But cemented with the Redeemer's blood,
And bound together in the heart of GOD.

Can we forget from whence our union came,
When first we simply met in JESUS' name?
The name mysterious of the GOD UNKNOWN,
Whose secret love allur'd, and drew us on
Thro' a long, lonely, legal wilderness,
To find the promis'd land of gospel peace.
True yoke-fellows, we then agreed to draw
Th' intolerable burden of the Law.
And jointly lab'ring on with zealous strife,
Strengthen'd each other's hands to work *for* Life:
To turn against the world our steady face,
And, valiant for the truth, enjoy disgrace.

Then, when we serv'd our GOD thro' fear alone,
Our views, our studies, and our hearts were one:
No smallest difference damp'd the social flame:
In MOSES' school we thought, and spake the same:
And must we, now in CHRIST, with shame confess,
Our love was greater when our light was less?
When darkly thro' a glass with servile awe,
We first the spiritual commandment saw,
Could we not then, our mutual love to show,
Thro' fire and water for each other go?
We could:—we did:—In a strange land I stood,
And beckon'd thee to cross th' Atlantic flood:
With true affection wing'd, thy ready mind,
Left country, fame, and ease, and friends behind,
And, eager all heav'n's counsels to explore,
Flew thro' the watry world and grasp'd the shore.

Nor did I linger, at my friends desire,
To tempt the furnace, and abide the fire:
When suddenly sent forth, from the high-ways
I call'd poor outcasts to the feast of grace;
Urg'd to pursue the work by thee begun,
Thro' good and ill report I still rush'd on,
Nor felt the fire of popular applause,
Nor fear'd the tort'ring flame in such a glorious cause.

Ah! wherefore did we ever seem to part,
Or clash in sentiment, while one in heart?
What dire device did the old Serpent find,
To put asunder those whom God had join'd?
From folly and self-love Opinion rose,
To sever friends who never yet were foes;
To baffle and divert our noblest aim,
Confound our pride, and cover us with shame;
To make us blush beneath her short-lived pow'r,
And glad the world with one triumphant hour.

But lo! the snare is broke, the captive's freed,
By Faith on all the hostile powers we tread,
And crush thro' Jesus' strength the Serpents head.
Jesus hath cast the curst Accuser down,
Hath rooted up the tares by Satan sown:
Kindled anew the never-dying flame,
And re-baptiz'd our souls into his Name.
Soon as the virtue of his Name we feel,
The storm of strife subsides, the sea is still,
All nature bows to his benign command,
And two are one in his Almighty hand.
One in his hand, O may we still remain,
Fast bound with love's indissoluble chain;
(That adamant which time and death defies,
That golden chain which draws us to the skies!)
His love the tie that binds us to his throne,
His love the bond that perfects us in one;
His love (let all the ground of friendship see)
His only love constrains our hearts t'agree,
And gives the rivet of Eternity!

1749.—This year Mr. Wesley began to compile the Christian Library, and completed it in fifty volumes duodecimo. He published it under the following title: "A Christian Library, consisting of Extracts from, and Abridgments of, the choicest pieces of Practical Divinity, which have been published in the English tongue."

1760.—In this year a great revival of religion took place among the Methodists. Many persons, men and women, professed to be cleansed from all unrighteousness and made perfect in love in a moment; often while hearing the word, but more frequently while at prayer, or while others were praying for them. Mr. Wesley thus speaks of it: "Here began that glorious work of sanctification, which had been nearly at a stand for twenty years. From time to time it spread, first through various parts of Yorkshire, afterwards in London, then through most parts of England; next to Dublin, Limerick, and through all the south and west of Ireland; and wherever the work of sanctification increased, the whole work of God increased in all it's branches. Many were convinced of sin, many justified, and many backsliders healed."

1763.—The conference was held in London, on the 19th of July. All the minutes of the former conferences, respecting discipline, were now for the first time published. It appears from their minutes that a great deal of business was done in a few days. I will enter one of their questions and answers, respecting their taking a preacher into the travelling connection.

Q. What method may we use in receiving a helper?

A. A proper time for doing this is at a conference, after solemn fasting and prayer. We may then receive him as a probationer, by giving him the minutes of the conference inscribed thus :

" *To A. B.*

" You think it your duty to call sinners to repentance. Make full proof hereof, and we shall be glad to receive you as a fellow-labourer.

" Observe, you are not to ramble up and down, but to go where the Assistant directs, and there only.

" Let him then read, and carefully weigh what is contained therein, and see whether he can agree to it or not. If he can, let him come to the next conference, where, after examination, fasting and prayer, he may be received into full connection with us, by giving him the minutes, inscribed thus :

" So long as you freely consent to, and earnestly endeavour to walk by these rules, we shall rejoice to acknowledge you as a fellow labourer."

From this it may be seen, that Mr. Wesley and the conference at that time, only required a probationary state of one year, in order to be admitted into full connection among the travelling preachers.

However, in 1784, the conference thought proper to lengthen out the time of their probation to four years, before the young preachers could be admitted into full connection.

At that time all the travelling preachers were called helpers, *i. e.* helpers of Mr. Wesley ; some were *Assistants*, and others *Preachers.*

1764.—Mr. Myles says, " In the beginning of this year, Mr. Erskine re-published in Scotland Mr. Hervey's Eleven Letters, and spread them with all his might. They prejudiced the Scotch against the Methodists' doctrine, and hindered the prosperity of the work. These letters did no harm in England. Mr. Wesley and Mr. Sellon wrote masterly answers to them. It was afterwards known, that a Mr. Cudworth, a violent Antinomian, had written the most virulent passages in these letters."

Having considered a few particulars respecting the beginning and progress of Methodism in *Europe*, I come now to the beginning of Methodism in the United States of *America*.

CHAPTER II.

From the beginning of the first Society in New-York in 1766, to the first Conference, which was held in America in 1773.

Previous to the year 1766, some of the members of the Methodist Society from Europe, settled in the United States (then British colonies) but were scattered about as sheep having neither fold nor shepherd. In the beginning of the year 1766 the first permanent Methodist society was formed in the city of New-York. *Mr. Philip Embury*, an Irishman, began to hold meetings in his own house, and to sing and pray with as many as would assemble with him. Soon after that, he collected and joined a few of them together in society, chiefly of his own countrymen. In about three months after, Mr. *White*, and Mr. *Sause*, from Dublin, joined with them.

They then rented an empty room in their neighbourhood adjoining the barracks, in which they held their meetings for a season: yet but few thought it worth their while to assemble with them in so contemptible a place. Some time after that, captain Thomas Webb, (*a*) barrack-master at Albany, found them out, and preached among them in his regimentals. The novelty of a man preaching in a scarlet coat, soon brought great numbers to hear, more than the room could contain. Some more of the inhabitants joining the society, they then united and hired a rigging loft to meet in, that would contain a large congregation. There Mr. Embury used to exhort and preach frequently.

(a) Captain Webb was a lieutenant in the army that conquered Canada, and took it from the French. He lost one eye in the battle on the plains of Abraham, at the taking the city of Quebec.

There are a few persons still living in New-York, who formerly met with the society in the rigging-loft; and are pleased at the recollection of what the Lord did for them in their little society, when they were weak and ignorant in the things of religion; but were united together in christian love and fellowship, and were willing to be despised for the sake of their Lord and master.

Not long after the society was formed in New-York, *Robert Strawbridge*, from Ireland, who had settled in Frederick county, in the state of Maryland, began to hold meetings in public, and joined a society together near Pipe Creek. Mr. Strawbridge was a useful man, and zealous in the cause of God; and spent much of his time in preaching the gospel in different places before any regular preachers were sent over by Mr. Wesley to this country.

The first Methodist meeting house that was built in the United States, was that in New-York. By the influence of captain Webb, the society purchased a lot of ground in John-street, for the purpose of building a house for public worship.—The house was built in 1768, and was sufficiently large to hold twelve or fourteen hundred people. On the 30th day of October, 1768, it was first opened for divine service, and Mr. Embury preached the dedication sermon. This was about twelve months before we had any circuit preachers in America.

There was another meeting house built by Mr. Strawbridge and his society, near Pipe Creek in Maryland, called the Log Meeting-House, which was erected for the use of the first Methodist society that was formed in that county.

The new meeting house in the city of New-York, was first called *Wesley's Chapel*, which name it bore for several years after the itinerant preachers came to this country.

In 1769, Mr. Wesley says in his Ecclesiastical History, vol. 4, page 261, "Tuesday, August 1, our conference began at Leeds. On Thursday I mentioned the case of our brethren at New-York. For some years past, several of our brethren from England and Ireland, (and some of them preachers,) had settled in North America, and had in various places formed societies, particularly in Philadelphia and New-York. The society at New-York had lately built a commodious preaching-house, and now desired our help, being in great want of money, but much more of preachers. Two of our preachers, Richard Boardman and Joseph Pillmore, willingly offered themselves for the service; by whom we determined to send over fifty pounds, as a token of our brotherly-love."

Mr. Boardman and Mr. Pillmore came over to Amcrica from that conference, and landed at Gloucester Point, six miles below Philadelphia, on the 24th day of October. These were the first regular itinerant Methodist preachers that ever came to these United States. Mr. Boardman had been an itinerant preacher in Europe for six years, and Mr. Pillmore for four years, before they came to this country as missionaries, a work for which they were well qualified, and in which they were owned and honoured of God, and made a blessing to thousands.

Soon after the two preachers mentioned above had arrived at Philadelphia, Mr. Robert Williams came over. He had been a local preacher in England, and had received a permit from Mr. Wesley to preach in America, under the direction of the regular missionaries. Mr. Williams, however, was not sent over by Mr. Wesley.—

His coming to America was partly owing to temporal business, and, withal, feeling a particular desire to preach the gospel in America, he had given his word to a Methodist man in Ireland, that if he (Mr. Ashton) would come over to live in America, he would accompany him across the Atlantic. Mr. Williams was an Englishman, but not a travelling preacher at that time. At length he heard that Mr. Ashton had embarked for America, and, according to his promise, he hurried down to the town near to which the ship lay, sold his horse to pay his debts, and taking his saddle-bags on his arm, set off for the ship, with a loaf of bread and a bottle of milk, and no money to pay his passage. His good friend Ashton provided for him and paid his passage, and they came over together. As soon as Mr. Williams landed he went to New York, where he preached in Wesley's Chapel, before either of the other itinerant preachers came to that city. Although Mr. Williams had come to this country of his own accord, the preachers and people encouraged him in his labours in spreading the gospel. On the first of November he visited Mr. Pillmore in Philadelphia, and then went on to Maryland.

As soon as Mr. Boardman and Mr. Pillmore came to Philadelphia, they began their ministerial labours; and soon began to preach on the commons, or in the fields, in the open air, where some thousands of people gathered together to hear the word of the Lord. At the close of the month in which they landed Mr. Pillmore wrote a letter to Mr. Wesley, of which the following is an extract:

Philadelphia, Oct. 31, 1769.

Reverend Sir,

"By the blessing of God we are safe arrived here after a tedious passage of nine weeks.

"We were not a little surprized to find captain Webb in town, and a society of about a hundred members, who desire to be in close connection with you. This is the Lord's doing, and it is marvellous in our eyes.

"I have preached several times, and the people flock to hear in multitudes. Sunday evening I went out upon the common. I had the Stage appointed for the horse-race, for my pulpit, and I think between four and five thousand hearers, who heard with attention, still as night. Blessed be God for field-preaching! When I began to talk of preaching at five o'clock in the morning, the people thought it would not answer in *America:* however I resolved to try, and had a very good congregation.

"Here seems to be a great and effectual door opening in this country, and I hope many souls will be gathered in. The people in general like to hear the word, and seem to have some ideas of salvation by grace."

Some time after this, *John King* arrived from London. He waited on Mr. Pillmore in Philadelphia, and desired to be employed as a preacher: but having no licence from Mr. Wesley, nor any recommendation from the preachers in Europe, he could not be admitted. However, this young man determined to preach; and appointed to preach in the Potters-Field. Some of the members of the society heard him, and told Mr. Pillmore that he appeared to be a good hearted zealous young man, and wished he might be encouraged. After examination he was permitted to make a trial before the congregation; and as he appeared to be engaged for God, he received a licence from the preacher to go down to Wilmington and exhort among a few people, who were earnestly seeking the Lord. This was the beginning of his preaching in America. Afterwards he went down to Maryland, and with Robert Williams and Robert Strawbridge, began a good work in Baltimore county, and in some other parts of the state.

The preachers during the following winter, spent most of their time in Philadelphia and New-York, one of them at a time, remaining in each city, and interchanging as they thought best for themselves, and for the people under their direction.

1770.—In the course of this year, the preachers enlarged their borders, and preached considerably in thestate of New-Jersey; and went beyond New-York as far as West-Chester, and New-Rochelle, preaching the Gospel to many attentive hearers.

The Rules by which the societies were then governed, were the same that Mr. Wesley had previously drawn up in England, and have with very little alteration been continued among us ever since, and are as follows:

The nature, design, and general rules of our united societies.

1. In the latter end of the year 1739, eight or ten persons came to me in London, who appeared to be deeply convinced of sin, and earnestly groaning for redemption. They desired (as did two or three more the next day) that I would spend some time with them in prayer, and advise them how to flee from the wrath to come; which they saw continually hanging over their heads. That we might have more time for this great work, I appointed a day when they might all come together, which from thence forward they did every week, namely on *Thursday* in the evening. To these, and as many more as desired to join with them, (for their number increased daily) I gave those advi-

ces from time to time, which I judged most needful for them: and we always concluded our meetings with prayer suited to their several necessities.

2. This was the rise of the UNITED SOCIETY, first in London, and then in other places. Such a society, is no other than *a company of men* having the form and seeking the power *of godliness, united in order to pray together, to receive the word of exhortation, and to watch over one another in love, that they may help each other to work out their salvation.*"

3. That it may the more easily be discerned, whether they are indeed working out their own salvation, each society is divided into smaller companies, called Classes, according to their respective places of abode. There are about twelve persons in every class: one of whom is stiled *The Leader.*—It is his business,

I. To see each person in his class once a week at least, in order

1. To enquire how their souls prosper.
2. To advise, reprove, comfort or exhort, as occasion may require.
3. To receive what they are willing to give, towards the relief of the poor.

II. To meet the ministers and the stewards of the society once a week, in order,

1. To inform the minister of any that are sick, or of any that walk disorderly, and will not be reproved.
2. To pay to the stewards what they have received of the several classes in the week preceding.

4. There is one only condition previously required of those who desire admission into these societies, *a desire to flee from the wrath to come*, i. e. *a desire to be saved from their sins.* But where-

ever this is really fixed in the soul, it will be shewn by it's fruits. It is therefore expected of all who continue therein, that they should continue to evidence their desire of salvation,

First—By doing no harm, by avoiding evil of every kind; especially that which is most generally practised: such as

The taking the name of God in vain;

The prophaning the day of the Lord, either by doing ordinary work thereon, or by buying or selling.

Drunkenness, buying or selling spirituous liquors; or drinking them, unless in cases of necessity.

Fighting, quarrelling, brawling, brother *going to law* with brother, returning evil for evil, or railing for railing, the *using many words* in buying or selling.

The *buying or selling of goods that have not paid the duty.*

The *giving or taking things on usury*, i. e. unlawful interest:

Uncharitable or *unprofitable* conversation; particularly speaking evil of magistrates or of ministers:

Doing to others as we would not they should do unto us:

Doing what we know is not for the glory of God: As

The *putting on of gold or costly apparel*:

The *taking such diversions* as cannot be used in the name of the Lord Jesus:

The *singing* those *songs*, or *reading* those *books*, which do not tend to the knowledge or love of God:

Softness and needless self-indulgence:

Laying up treasure upon earth:

Borrowing without a probability of paying; or

taking up goods without a probability of paying for them.

5.—It is expected of all who continue in these societies, that they should continue to evidence their desire of salvation:

Secondly, By doing good, by being in every kind merciful after their power, as they have opportunity, doing good of every possible sort, and as far as is possible, to all men:

To their bodies, of the ability which God giveth, by giving food to the hungry, by cloathing the naked, by visiting or helping them that are sick, or in prison.

To their souls, by instructing, reproving or exhorting all we have any intercourse with; trampling under foot that enthusiastic doctrine, that "we are not to do good, unless *our hearts be free to it.*"

By doing good, especially to them that are of the household of faith, or groaning so to be; employing them preferably to others, buying one of another, helping each other in business; and so much the more, because the world will love it's own and them only.

By all possible *diligence* and *frugality*, that the gospel be not blamed.

By running with patience the race that is set before them, *denying themselves, and taking up their cross daily*; submitting to bear the reproach of Christ, to be as the filth and off-scouring of the world: and looking that men should *say all manner of evil of them falsely for the Lord's sake.*

6.—It is expected of all who continue in these societies, that they should continue to evidence their desire of salvation:

Thirdly, By attending upon all the ordinances of God: such are

The public worship of God:
The ministry of the word, either read or expounded:
The supper of the Lord;
Family and private prayer;
Searching the scriptures, and
Fasting, or abstinence.

7.—These are the general rules of our societies, all which we are taught of God to observe, even in his written word, which is the only rule, and the sufficient rule both of our faith and practice. And all these we know his Spirit writes on every truly awakened heart. If there be any among us who observe them not, who habitually break any of them, let it be made known unto them who watch over that soul, as they that must give an account. We will admonish him of the error of his ways: we will bear with him for a season. But then, if he repent not, he hath no more place among us. We have delivered our own souls.

JOHN WESLEY.
CHARLES WESLEY.

These are the general rules which were first introduced among us, and which have continued among us from the beginning; and they have been admired, not only by the Methodists themselves, but also by most religious people of other denominations.

It will be necessary to insert here the rules of the Band societies.

Three, four, or five true believers, who have confidence in each other, form a Band. Only it is to be observed, that in each of these bands all must be men, or all women; and all married or all single.

Rules of the Band Societies, Drawn up December 25, 1738.

"The design of our meeting is to obey that command of God, *Confess your faults one to ano-*

ther, and pray one for another, that you may be healed.

To this end we agree,

1. To meet once a week, at the least.

2. To come punctually at the hour appointed, without some extraordinary reason.

3. To begin (those of us who are present) exactly at the hour with singing or prayer.

4. To speak, each of us in order, freely and plainly the true state of our souls, with the faults we have committed in thought, word, or deed, and the temptations we have felt since our last meeting.

5. To end every meeting with prayer, suited to the state of each person present.

6. To desire some person among us to speak HIS own state first, and then to ask the rest in order, as many and as searching questions as may be, concerning their state, sins, and temptations.

Some of the questions proposed to every one before HE is admitted among us, may be to this effect:

1. Have you the forgiveness of your sins?

2. Have you peace with GOD, through our LORD JESUS CHRIST?

3. Have you the witness of GOD'S Spirit with your Spirit, that you are a child of GOD?

4. Is the love of GOD shed abroad in your heart?

5. Has no sin, inward or outward, dominion over you?

6. Do you desire to be told of your faults?

7. Do you desire to be told of all your faults, and that plain and home?

8. Do you desire, that every one of us should tell you, from time to time, whatsoever is in HIS heart concerning you?

9. Consider! Do you desire we should tell you

whatsoever we think, whatsoever we fear, whatsoever we hear, concerning you?

10. Do you desire, that in doing this we should come as close as possible, that we should cut to the quick, and search your heart to the bottom?

11. Is it your desire and design to be on this and all other occasions entirely open, so as to speak every thing that is in your heart, without exception, without disguise, and without reserve?

Any of the preceding questions may be asked as often as occasion offers: the five following at every meeting.

1. What known sins have you committed since our last meeting?

2. What temptations have you met with?

3. How was you delivered?

4. What have you thought, said, or done, of which you doubt whether it be sin or not?

5. Have you nothing you desire to keep secret?

Directions given to the Band Societies. December 25, 1744.

You are supposed to have the *Faith that overcometh the world.* To you therefore it is not grievous,

I. Carefully to abstain from doing evil; in particular,

1. Neither to *buy* nor *sell* any thing at all on the Lord's day.

2. To taste no spirituous liquor, *no dram* of any kind, unless prescribed by a physician.

3. To be *at a word* both in buying and selling.

4. To *pawn nothing.*

5. Not to *mention the fault* of any *behind his back*, and to stop those short that do.

6. To wear no *needless ornaments*, such as rings, ear-rings, necklaces, lace, ruffles.

7. To use no *needless self indulgence*, such as

taking snuff or tobacco, unless prescribed by a physician.

II. Zealously to maintain good works; in particular,

1. To *give alms* of such things as you possess, and that to the uttermost of your power.

2. To *reprove* all that sin in your sight, and that in love, and meekness of wisdom.

3. To be patterns of *diligence* and *frugality*, of *self denial*, and taking up the cross daily.

III. Constantly to attend on all the ordinances of God; in particular,

1. To be at church, and at the Lord's table every week, and at every public meeting of the bands.

2. To attend the ministry of the word every morning, unless distance, business, or sickness prevent.

3. To use private prayer every day, and family prayer, if you are the head of a family.

4. To read the Scriptures, and meditate thereon, at every vacant hour. And,

5. To observe, as days of fasting or abstinence, all *Fridays* in the year."

In the course of this year, 1770, Mr. George Whitefield passed through Philadelphia, on his way to the North, and calling on our preachers who were in the city, he expressed to them his great satisfaction at finding them in this country, where there was such a great call for faithful labourers in the vineyard of their Lord. From thence Mr. Whitefield went on through all the New England states; and on his return he preached his last sermon in Exeter, in New-Hampshire state, on the top of a hogshead by the meeting house, the house being too small to contain the congregation. His text was 2. Cor. 13, 5....*Examine yourselves whether ye be in the faith.* He spake with much animation; and after meeting he rode to Newburyport in the state of Massachusetts; but on the road he complained of a shortness of breath, occasioned by the asthma. But said "Another pulpit sweat or two will cure me." That night he rested but poorly. The next morning his complaint was much worse; he prayed devoutly for the world in general, and for the orphans at his Orphan House in Georgia in particular; and withal requested, that if his work was done, that the Lord would take him to himself.—Soon after which he died on his knees, on September 30, 1770, which was exactly 30 years to a day from the first time that he ever preached in that town. The first time he ever travelled through that part of the country was in the year 1740. In his journal of this journey he says, "*Tuesday*, Sept. 30, preached at *Ipswich about* 10 in the morning, to some thousands;—the Lord gave me freedom, and there was a great melting in the congregation. Dined, set out and reached *Newbury*, another large town, twelve miles distant from *Ipswich*, about 3. Here again the Lord accompanied the word with his power. The meeting-house was very large, many ministers were present, and people were greatly affected. Blessed be God, his divine power attends us more and more. Took ferry immediately after sermon; went with Mr. *Cotton*, minister of the place, who came to meet me in a chaise to Hampton, another great town, nine miles from *Newbury*."

Mr. Whitefield had often felt his soul so much comforted in preaching in the Presbyterian meeting-house, in Newburyport, that he told his friends long before his death, that if he died in that part of the world, he wished to be buried under the pulpit of that house. The people who remembered his former request, had it now in their power to grant it; and they prepared a vault in the ground, under the pulpit, where they laid his body. I myself went into the vault to see the body after it had lain there twenty years; and was much surprised to find the greater part of it firm, and hard: a small part of it only had putrified.

Mr. Whitefield had separated from the Wesleys in 1741, but always retained a particular love for them, and requested that John Wesley should preach his funeral sermon. As soon as Mr. Wesley received the news of Mr. Whitefield's death, being desired by Mr. Whitefield's executors, he performed that labour of love, on Sunday Nov. 18, at the Tabernacle: his text was Numb. 23, 10. *Let me die the death of the righteous, and let my last end be like his.*

Mr. Whitefield died in the fifty-sixth year of his age. He had crossed the Atlantic 13 times in order to preach the gospel which was more than any other minister had done before him.

Mr. Whitefield's labours as an Itinerant preacher had been greatly blessed to the people in *America*; and thereby the way was opened for our preachers to travel and preach the gospel in different parts of the country. And in most places where the people were lively in religion, they were fond of having Itinerant preachers to visit them.

1771.—Mr. *Francis Asbury*, and Mr. *Richard Wright*, were sent by Mr. Wesley, to *America*, and they landed at Philadelphia on the 27th day of October, after a passage of fifty five days. Mr. Asbury had been a travelling preacher four years, and Mr. Wright one year, previous to their coming over.

They soon began to extend their labours farther into the country, and did not spend their time in the cities as the other preachers had done. Mr. *Asbury* spent most of his time among the people in the country, and formed societies in different places. He preached his first sermon in New-York Nov. 13. He then went into the country, and on the 24th day of the same month he went for the first time to *West-Chester* and preached, then at *West-Farmes, East-Chester, New-Rochelle, Rye* and *Mairnock*. He soon found that their labours were more visibly owned of God in the country, than in the cities.

In the latter part of this year, some of the preachers visited Delaware and Maryland states, and preached sometimes on the Western shore, and sometimes on the Eastern shore of Maryland.

The first Methodists that came to the Eastern Shore of Maryland, were two private christian men belonging to Mr. Strawbridge's society, who came over to John Randal's, in Kent county, and talked to the family, and prayed with them: by which means there were some religious impressions made on the minds of some of the family. From that time the preachers were desired to come over and help them. Mr. *Strawbridge* came himself, and preached with them: sometime afterwards, old Robert Williams made them a visit, and preached among them a few times, and in Dec. following, which was on the 12th day, in 1772, Mr. Asbury preached in Kent county for the first time. From that time those people have been much favoured with preaching by the Methodists; and that county has ever since been famous for a number of solid, steady Methodists.

In April there was laid a plan for Mr. Joseph Pillmore to travel to the South, and Mr. Boardman to visit the North.—Mr. Pillmore travelled and preached through Maryland to Norfolk, in Virginia; and left Norfolk in the begining of 1773, and travelled through the lower parts of Virginia, and North Carolina to Charleston in South Carolina;

and from thence to Savannah in Georgia, and then to the Orphan House, which was begun by Mr. Whitefield, in March 1740. After which he returned again to the North sometime inthe following spring.—Mr. Boardman went as far to the North as Boston, and then returned to New-York.

In the first part of the year 1772, Mr. Robert Williams made his first visit to Norfolk, in Virginia, and without any previous notice being given, he went to the court house, and standing on the steps of the door, and beginning to sing, the people collected together; and after prayer, he took his text and preached to a considerable number of hearers, who were very disorderly; as they all thought the preacher was a mad man: and while he was preaching the people were laughing, talking, and walking about in all directions. The general conclusion was, that they never heard such a man before: for they said, Sometimes he would preach, then he would pray, then he would swear, and at times he would cry. The people were so little used to hearing a preacher say hell, or Devil in preaching, that they thought he was swearing, when he told them about going to hell, or being damned if they died in their sins. As he was believed to be a mad-man, none of them invited him to their houses. However he preached at the same place the next day, when they found out he was not insane, and they were glad to get him to their houses. This may be considered as the beginning of Methodism in Virginia. And it was not long before a Methodist Society was formed in the town of Norfolk.

In October, Mr. *Asbury* received a letter from Mr. Wesley, appointing him to be the assistant in America.

Mr. Wesley being the founder of the society, was considered as the head; and all the preachers were considered as helpers to Mr. Wesley in their different stations.

In this country, they formerly stood in three grades, 1, Helpers, 2, Assistants, 3, General Assistants. The *Helper*, was the young preacher in each circuit where there were generally two preachers in a circuit. The *Assistant*, was the oldest preacher in the circuit, who had the charge of the young preacher, and of the business of the circuit. The *General Assistant*, was the preacher who had the particular charge of all the circuits, and of all the preachers, and appointed all the preachers to their several circuits, and changed them as he judged to be necessary, for the good of the preachers, or the benefit of the people. For we are well convinced that it is not good for a preacher, or a society, to keep the same preacher long in one place. His being called a *General Assistant*, also signified that he was to assist Mr. Wesley in carrying on the work of God in a general way, without being confined to a particular circuit, as another preacher.

During this time the preachers regulated their business at the different *Quarterly Meetings*, one of which began on Tuesday the 23d of December, on the Western Shore of Maryland, where they enquired, "How are the preachers stationed?" Three on the *Eastern Shore*, two in *Frederick*, and Mr. Asbury in *Baltimore*. They then asked, "Will the people be contented without our administering the sacraments?" John King was neuter; Mr. Strawbridge plead for the ordinances, and so did the people, who appeared to be much biassed by him. But Mr. Asbury would not agree to it at that time.

The next Quarterly Meeting for the same circuit was held on the 30th day of March following, when several questions were proposed, which tended to unite the travelling preachers together I will mention five of them.

Q. 1. Does not dram-drinking too much prevail among our people.

Q. 2. Do none contract debts without due care to pay them ?

Q. 3. Are the band meetings kept up ?

Q. 4. Is there nothing immoral in any of our preachers ?

Q. 5. What preachers travel now, and where are they stationed ?

It was then urged that none must break our rules under the penalty of being excluded from our connexion. All was settled in the most amicable manner.

At that time it was customary to have the Quarterly Meeting on Tuesday, and to preach, settle their business and hold a love-feast, and some times a watch night. After a while it became a custom in country places for the Quarterly Meeting to continue for two days together. After further trial, it was thought best to have the Quarterly Meetings on Saturday and Sunday ; which is now the constant practice in most places. One weighty reason for this last plan was, that many of the slaves could not attend these meetings, except on the Lord's day ; another reason was, that many of the wealthy people would come to hear us on the Sabbath, at such meetings, who would not be at the trouble of coming to meeting on any other day: and lastly, many of the poor people, especially those of our own society, could not spare time, or procure horses to come to such meetings unless they were on the Sabbath.

1773. In the beginning of this year, Robert Williams came to Petersburg in Virginia, and began to preach first in the town, and then through various parts of the country. He was the first Metho-

-dist preacher that ever came into that part of Virginia. He was a plain, artless, indefatigable preacher of the gospel, and often proved the goodness of his doctrine, by his tears in public, and by his life and conduct in private. His manner of preaching was well calculated to awaken careless sinners, and to encourage penitent mourners. He spared no pains in order to do good. He has frequently went to church to hear the established clergy, and as soon as divine service has ended, he has went out of the Church, and standing on a stump, block, or log, has begun to sing, pray, and then preach to hundreds of people. It was common with him after preaching to ask most of the people that he spake with, some question about the welfare of their souls ; and to encourage them to serve God. Soon after he began to preach through the country from Petersburg into the north part of North Carolina, the fruit of his labours began to appear, and souls were awakened and brought to the knowledge of God. And the name of *Robert Williams*, still lives in the minds of many of his spiritual children.

Previous to the coming of Mr. Williams into that part of Virginia, there had been a gracious revival of religion by the means of Mr. Jarratt's preaching ; who was a clergyman of the church of England, so called at that time. In the year 1770, and 1771, there was a considerable out-pouring of the spirit, at a place called White Oak. It was there that Mr. Jarratt first formed the people into a society, that they might assist and strengthen each other. The good effects of this were soon apparent ; convictions were deep and lasting ; and not only knowledge, but faith, and love, and holiness continually increased.

In the year 1772, the revival was more considerable, and extended in some places, for fifty or sixty miles round, and many sinners were truly converted to God.

The revival of religion which first began under the ministry of Mr. Jarratt, was greatly increased by the labours of the Methodist preachers, who, uniting with Mr. Jarratt in the same blessed work, were greatly owned and honoured of God and had the pleasure of seeing the work of the Lord prospering greatly in their hands.

CHAPTER III.

From the first Conference in 1773, to the Conference in 1779.

1773.—In the spring of this year, Mr. Wesley sent two more preachers to America, viz. Thomas Rankin, and George Shadford, who landed in Philadelphia, on the third day of June. Mr. Rankin had been a travelling preacher for eleven years; and Mr. Shadford had travelled five years. Mr. Rankin began to travel in 1762, and of course had travelled longer than any of the other preachers in the United States. From that time Mr. Rankin had the superintendancy of the Methodist connection in America, and was stiled the *General Assistant.*

Immediately after Mr. Rankin's arrival in Philadelphia he called the travelling preachers together, and on the 14th of July, 1773, the first conference that was ever held in America, began in Philadelphia. There were six or seven travelling preachers at it, most of whom were Europeans. William Waters of the Western shore of Maryland began to travel this year; and he was the first travelling preacher that was raised up among the Methodists in America.

The minutes of that conference were taken down in writing, as were the minutes of all the succeeding conferences for several years after; and none of the annual minutes were published until the year 1785. From that time our minutes have been published annually. However, in the year 1795 we had all the minutes from 1773 to that time published, and bound in one book. In the preface of this book it is said, "Many of our travelling preachers have expressed a desire to have the minutes of our yearly conferences published, in the order in which they have occurred; and are of opinion that a book of this kind would be pleasing, and entertaining; especially to the travelling and local preachers; wherein may be seen the growth of Methodism. This little publication contains in substance, a brief history of the rise and progress of the travelling ministry, and the success of their labours through the United States."

The minutes of this conference, were introduced as follows.

"Minutes of some conversations between the preachers in connection with
The Revd. Mr. John Wesley."

The following queries were proposed to every preacher:

1. Ought not the authority of Mr. Wesley and the English conference, to extend to the preachers and people in America, as well as in Great-Britain and Ireland?

A. Yes.

2. Ought not the doctrine and discipline of the Methodists, as contained in the English minutes to be the rule of our conduct, who labour in the connection with Mr. Wesley?

A. Yes.

3. If so, does it not follow, that if preachers deviate from the minutes, we can have no fellowship with them till they change their conduct?

A. Yes.

The following rules were agreed to, by all the preachers present:

1. Every preacher who acts in connection with Mr. Wesley and the brethren who labour in America, is strictly to avoid administering the ordinances of baptism and the Lord's supper.

2. No person or persons to be admitted to our love-feasts oftener than twice or thrice, unless they

become members; and none to be admitted to the society meetings more than three times.

3. None of the preachers in America to reprint any of Mr. Wesley's books, without his authority (when it can be got) and the consent of their brethren, &c.

It was also recommended to all our people, and especially to those in Maryland and Virginia to attend the church, and to receive the ordinances there.

These regulations were made at that conference, with a few others of but little consequence to the world in general, and the preachers were much united together in love and brotherly affection.

At that time, the Methodists in America considered themselves as much under the direction of Mr. Wesley, as were the European Methodists; for they were dependant on him to send them preachers, and such directions as he thought best. Of course the preachers agreed to submit to Mr. Wesley's authority, and to abide by his doctrine and discipline as established in England. This resolution entered into by the preachers was both wise and prudent; and tended to keep them united together; and afterwards, it had the same good effects amongst the private members.

The conference also agreed, that none of our preachers should administer the ordinances of baptism or the Lord's supper. The necessity of this rule appeared in the conduct of Mr. Strawbridge, a local preacher, who had taken on him to administer the ordinances among the Methodists without the consent of their preachers, who at that time were all lay-preachers. We were only a religious society, and not a church: and any member of any church, who would conform to our rules, and meet in a class, had liberty to continue in their own church.

But, as the most of our society had been brought up in the church of England (so called) and especially those of Maryland and Virginia, it was recommended to them to attend on the service of that church, and to partake of the ordinances at the hands of the ministers: for at that time the Church people were established by law in Maryland and Virginia; and the ministers were supported by a tax on the people. In many places for a hundred miles together, there was no one to baptize a child, except a minister of the established church; the greatest objection to this plan therefore was, that by far the greatest part of them were destitute of religon.

As it was thought improper to have many people among us where we were speaking of our experiences and of the deep things of God, a rule was adopted, "That no person should be admitted into our Love-feasts, more than twice or thrice, except he becomes a member." This prudent rule has continued among us ever since.

The rule formed for putting a stop to the printing of Mr. Wesley's books without his authority, and the consent of the preachers in this country, was well enough. Previous to the formation of this rule, Robert Williams, one of the preachers, had reprinted many of Mr. Wesley's books, and had spread them through the country, to the great advantage of religion. The sermons which he printed in small pamphlets, and circulated among the people, had a very good effect, and gave the people great light and understanding in the nature of the new birth, and in the plan of salvation: and withal, they opened the way in many places for our preachers to be invited to preach where they had never been before. But notwithstanding the good that had been done by the circulation of the books, it now became necessary for the preachers to be all united in the same cause of printing and selling our books, so that the profits arising therefrom, might be divided among the preachers, or applied to some charitable purpose.

At that time there were ten travelling preachers, and six circuits, which were as follows; New-York, New-Jersey, Philadelphia, Baltimore, Norfolk, and Petersburg. The two last were in Virginia. The number of members in society were 1160, In the following places:

New-York,	180	Maryland,	500
New-Jersey,	200	Virginia,	100
Philadelphia	180		
			1160

During this year there was a considerable revival of religion on the Eastern shore of Maryland, especially in Kent county, where many souls were awakened and brought to the knowledge of God. There was a class formed also in New-Rochelle this year, about twenty-five miles north of New-York. There was some revival also in Baltimore; and in November the society at Fell's Point engaged to build a meeting-house, and agreed with a man to do the brick work of the house. The first meeting-house that was built by the Methodists in Baltimore, was that at Fell's Point. At present, (1809,) we have five meeting-houses in Baltimore: four for the white people, and one for the black people.

In the beginning of the year 1774, John King, an Englishman, came first to the south parts of Virginia, where his labours were made a blessing to many people. He was a sensible, zealous preacher, and was very useful while he continued to travel.

1774.—In February, this year, the Methodists engaged to build a meeting-house in Baltimore town, and on the eighteenth day of April the foundation of the house was laid in *Lovely-lane.* The first quarterly meeting that was ever held in the town of Baltimore was on Tuesday the third of May in this year.

The first meeting-house that was ever built by the Methodists on the Eastern shore of Maryland, was in Kent county, about nine miles below Chester town, in the spring 1774, and was called Kent meeting-house. Many of the wicked neighbours were violently opposed to the building of that house; and after the workmen had prepared the frame in order to raise it the next day, some evil designing men came in the night, and broke the rafters to pieces, to prevent the house from being raised. But the workmen went on nevertheless, and the Lord prospered his work among the people, and there has been an established society in that place ever since.

1774.—The second conference was held this year in Philadelphia, on the 25th day of May. There were six questions asked at that conference.

Q. 1. *Who are admitted this year?* i. e. into full connection. There were five.

Q. 2. *Who are admitted on trial this year?* There were seven.

Q. 3. *Who are assistants this year?* There were nine.

Q. 4. *Are there any objections to any of the preachers?*

A. They were examined one by one.

Q. 5. *How are the preachers stationed this year?*

Q. 6. *What numbers are there in society?*

A. 2073.

This year we had ten circuits; last year we had but six.

The three following circuits were formed since the last conference, namely, *Chester*, *Kent*, and *Frederick*. Two other circuits were changed; New Jersey was divided and called *Trenton*, and *Greenwich*; and Petersburgh in Virginia was changed and called *Brunswick*. We had seventeen travelling preachers this year. Last year we had only ten.

This year there were added to the society 913 members.

At that conference the preachers agreed that every travelling preacher should be allowed £6 Pennsylvania currency a quarter; which was $64 a year, and his travelling expences.

As Thomas Rankin was the general assistant, he was to be supported where he spent his time: he was appointed for Philadelphia, and Mr. Asbury in New York.

In the beginning of this year on Sunday the 2d of January, after commending the Americans to God, Mr. Boardman and Mr. Pillmore embarked at New York for England. Mr. Boardman lived about eight years afterwards, and died in peace.

In the beginning of this year, 1774, Robert Williams began to form societies in Virginia, and made out a plan for a six weeks circuit, which extended from Petersburgh, to the south over Roanoke River, some distance into North Carolina. From the conference, three preachers came to that circuit, John King, John Wade, and Isaac Rollings: these preachers were blessed among the people and were made a blessing to them in their turn; and in the latter part of the year, there was a most remarkable revival of religion in most parts of the circuit. Christians were much united, and much devoted to God; and sinners were greatly alarmed, and many of them truly changed both in heart and life. The preachers had not only large congregations to hear them in the day time, but also in the night when meetings were appointed. Indeed, the Lord wrought wonders among us during that year.

In 1775, the third conference was held on May 17, in Philadelphia. Two preachers were sent over from England, viz. James Dempster, and Martin Rodda: Mr. Rodda had been travelling twelve years, and Mr. Dempster ten years. The conference took in three preachers besides the two from Europe.

It was planned at the conference, for some of the preachers to change in three, and others in six months; the preachers saw that it would be best for themselves and for the people to have frequent changes of gifts, and of congregations. And we still know the good effects of having strangers to preach, and strangers to hear.

Hanover circuit in Virginia was formed this year, and preachers sent to it; but in the minutes it was included in Brunswick circuit.

This year the preachers at the conference concluded to have a yearly collection in the classes, for the benefit of the ensuing conference: they also concluded to have a general fast in the societies, on the 18th of July, for the prosperity of the work of God, and for the peace of America.

At that time the revolutionary war between us and England was fast approaching; and the Americans shewed a *firm* and *fixed* determination to contend for their *rights* and *liberty*.

This year Mr. Asbury was appointed to Norfolk, and landed there on the 29th day of May, and continued in that station about five months; and then went up to Brunswick circuit, where he arrived on the second of November.

In the course of this year there was a gracious work of God in several places; but in none to equal that which took place in Brunswick circuit, where George Shadford was travelling at that time. It was quite common for sinners to be seized with a trembling and shaking, and from that to fall down on the floor as if they were dead: and many of them have been convulsed from head to foot, while others have retained the use of their tongues so as to pray for mercy, while they were lying helpless on the ground or floor.

The christians too were sometimes so overcome with the presence and love of God, as not to be able to stand on their feet. It was truly affecting to see them collecting round the penitent sinners, and praying for them one after another, and sometimes two or three together at the same time, until some of the mourners would get converted; and then to see the young converts leaping up with streaming eyes, and catching in their arms those that were nearest to them, and calling upon all present to praise God for what he had done for their souls. In that revival there were some things which might be called imprudent; yet there were so many souls brought to God, that it was thought to be dangerous to try to stop the irregularities, for fear of stopping that gracious work which the Lord was so strangely carrying on. There were above 600 members added to the society in that circuit in the course of that year.

Robert Williams, who was the first Methodist preacher that came to that part of Virginia, had married and left the travelling connection: but on the 26th day of September he died between Norfolk and Suffolk in Virginia, at the place where he had been living with his wife. Although he is dead, he yet speaketh to many of his spiritual children, while they remember his faithful preaching, and his holy walk.

Mr. Jarratt, the church Clergyman, was very useful in that revival of religion; and his heart was closely united to the Methodists. He would frequently preach, meet the classes, hold love-feasts, and administer the Lord's supper among them. He was an eye witness of this work; and as it was the greatest revival of religion that had ever been known in that part of the country, I think it will be a satisfaction to many people, to give them some further account of it.

1775.—In the latter end of this year, there was as great a revival of religion in the south parts of *Virginia*, as perhaps was ever known in country places in so short a time; but it became still more considerable in January 1776. Mr. G. Shadford then preached in *Virginia*; and while the ears of the people were opened by novelty, God sent his word home upon their hearts. Many sinners were powerfully convinced, and cried for mercy. The news of convictions and conversions were common; and the people of God were inspired with new life and vigour, by the happiness of others. But in a little time they were made thoroughly sensible, that they themselves stood in need of a deeper work of grace in their hearts, than they had yet experienced: and entreated God with strong cries and tears, to save them from the remains of inbred sin; and so to "circumcise their hearts," that they might "love him with all their hearts," and serve him with all their strength.

In almost every assembly might be seen signal instances of divine power; more especially in the meeting of the classes. The shaking among the dry bones was increased from week to week. Numbers of old and grey headed, of middle aged persons, of youth, yea, of little children, were the subjects of this work. There were instances of the latter of eight or nine years old. Some of the children were exceedingly happy in the love of God, and spoke of the whole process of the work of God, of their convictions, the time when, and the manner how they obtained deliverance, with such clearness as might convince an atheist, that this was nothing but the great power of God.

Many who had long neglected the means of grace, now flocked to hear, not only the preachers, but also the exhorters and leaders. And whether there was preaching or not, the Lord's power was still among the people. And it was found that prayer meetings were singularly useful in promoting the work of God.

This out-pouring of the spirit extended itself, more or less, through most of the circuits, which takes in a circumference of between four and five hundred miles; and the work went on with a pleasing progress till the beginning of May; when a quarterly meeting was held at Boisseau's, (commonly called Bushill's) chapel, about twelve miles from Petersburg. At that meeting the windows of heaven were opened indeed, and the rain of divine influence continued to pour down for more than forty days.

The second day of the quarterly meeting, a love-feast was held. As soon as it began, the power of the Lord came down on the assembly, and it seemed as if the whole house was filled with the presence of God. A flame kindled and ran from heart to heart. Many were deeply convinced of sin; many mourners were filled with consolation, and many believers were so overwhelmed with love, that they could not doubt but God had enabled them to love him with *all* their heart.

When the love feast was ended, the doors were opened, and many who had stayed without, came in, and beholding the anguish of some, and the rejoicing of others, were filled with astonishment, and not long after, with trembling apprehensions of their own danger, several of them prostrating themselves before God, cried aloud for mercy.

The multitude that attended on this occasion, returned home alive to God, and spread the flame through their respective neighbourhoods, which ran from family to family, so that within four weeks, several hundred found the peace of God; and scarce any conversation was to be heard, but concerning the things of God. In many large companies one careless person could not be seen; and the far greater part seemed perfectly happy in a clear sense of the love of God.

This work in a very short time spread through *Dinwiddie*, *Amelia*, *Brunswick*, *Sussex*, *Prince George*, *Lunenberg*, and *Mecklenburg* counties.

The work was so great on the last day of the quarterly meeting, that they continued in the meeting house till night, and then sent for candles, and continued till some time in the night before they broke up. I left them about the setting of the sun, and at that time their prayers and cries might have been heard a mile off.

It has been frequently observed, that there was never any remarkable revival of religion, but some degree of enthusiasm was mingled with it. This work was not quite free from it. But it never rose to any considerable height, nor was it of long continuance. In some meetings there was not that order observed, which could have been wished. Some of the assemblies resembled the congregation of the *Jews* at laying the foundation of the second temple in the days of *Ezra*. Some wept for grief; others shouted for joy; so that it was hard to distinguish one from the other. So it was here. The mourning and distress were so blended with the voice of joy and gladness, that it was hard to distinguish the one from the other. But the voice of joy prevailed, the people shouted with a great shout, so that it might be heard afar off.

The work of God thus increased on every side, and more preachers were soon wanting. And the Lord raised up several young men, who were exceeding useful as local preachers.

In the course of the summer, Mr. Thomas Rankin came to Virginia, and on the last day of June he preached for the first time at Boisseau's (i. e. Bushill's) chapel, where Mr. Shadford met him, and they had preaching in the forenoon, and at four o'clock in the afternoon; but before the last sermon was ended such a power descended, that many fell to the floor, and seemed to be filled with the presence of God. The Chapel was full of people, and many were without that could not get in. Look which way one would, they might behold streaming eyes, and faces bathed in tears: and but little could be heard, except groans and strong cries to God for mercy.

It might be truly said, *This is none other than the house of God! this is the gate of heaven!* Husbands and wives were inviting each other to go with them to heaven; parents and children also, were intreating each other. In short, those who were happy in God themselves, were for bringing all their friends to him in their arms. This mighty effusion of the spirit continued for more than an hour, in which time many were awakened, some found peace with God, and others experienced perfect love. The preachers attempted to speak or sing again and again; but their voices were soon drowned. Mr. Rankin commanded them to be silent; but all in vain, and it was with difficulty that they persuaded the people as night drew on to retire to their own homes.

On the 14th of July, which was two weeks after, Mr. Rankin preached again at the same place, i. e. at Bushill's chapel. He gave us a good discourse in the forenoon, and tried to keep the people from making any noise while he was speaking, and at the close of the meeting, he thanked the people for their good behaviour, and told them he was much better pleased with them at that time, than he was when among them before. He then went to a friend's house to get his dinner, and was to return and preach again in the afternoon. As soon as he was gone, the people felt at liberty, and began to sing, pray and talk to their friends, till the heavenly flame kindled in their souls, and sinners were conquered, and twelve or fifteen souls were converted to God, before the preacher returned from his dinner; and many of the people were sorry that he returned at all, knowing that he was not fond of so much noise. It was with much difficulty that he prevailed on them to be quiet enough for him to begin to preach. He gave us a good discourse, and I was pleased with it. Yet the people did not hold in till he was done, but some of them began to cry and pray aloud for mercy on their poor souls. He tried again to stop them; but he could not. After that he sat down, and asked Mr. Shadford, who had been preaching among them for some months before, to speak to them, which he did with pleasure, and in a little time cried out in his usual manner; "Who wants a Saviour? the first that believes shall be justified." In a few minutes the house was ringing with the cries of broken hearted sinners, and the shouts of happy believers. It was an awful time indeed; and several souls were justified, and many christians were lost in wonder, love and praise.

On Tuesday and Wednesday, the 30th and 31st days of July, a quarterly-meeting was held at Mabury's dwelling house in *Brunswick* (now Greensville) county. No meeting-house in *Virginia* could have held the people. We had a large arbour in the yard, which would shade from the sun, two or three thousand people. The first day was a blessed season; but the second day was a day never to be forgotten. We held the love-feast under the arbour in the open air; the members of society took their seats, and other people stood all around them by hundreds. The place was truly awful, by reason of the presence of the Lord. Many of the members spake; and while some declared how the Lord had justified them freely, others declared how, and when the blood of Jesus had cleansed them from all sin. So clear, so full, and so strong was their testimony, that while some were speaking their experience, hundreds were in tears, and others vehemently crying to God, for pardon or holiness.

Such a work of God as that was, I had never seen, or heard of before. It continued to spread through the south parts of *Virginia*, and the adjacent parts of *North-Carolina*, all that summer and autumn.

When the returns of the members were made to conference this year, there had been added to the society in *Brunswick* circuit 811 members.

But if we include *Hanover* circuit, and Carolina, which had been united to *Brunswick*, there had been added in one year 1800 members.

I have spoken largely of this revival of religion; but my pen cannot describe the one half of what I saw, heard and felt. I might write a volume on this subject, and then leave the greater part untold.

1776.—On the 21st day of May the fourth Conference was held in Baltimore. This was the first time that the preachers ever held a conference in that town. At that time there were four new circuits added, three of which were in *Virginia, Fairfax, Hanover*, and *Pittsylvania*. The other was called *Carolina*, as it lay in the state of *North Carolina*. The two circuits which had been formed in the state of *New-Jersey*, were now put together, and called *New-Jersey* in the minutes.—*Norfolk* was left out of the minutes altogether, on account of the war, which had so distressed the town, that we could not keep a preacher in that station.

There were twenty-five itinerant preachers appointed to the different circuits this year; the conference had admitted on trial eleven young preachers.

This conference appointed a day of fasting, to be on the 26th of July.

On the 4th day of July, 1776, the United States of America were declared by Congress to be *Free and Independent States*.

The Methodists met with some particular persecutions this year. Mr. Asbury says on the 20th day of June, "I was fined near Baltimore five pounds for preaching the gospel." It was with great difficulty that our preachers could travel their circuits, on account of the war which was spreading through the land. What made the matter worse than it would otherwise have been, was, our head preachers were all from Europe, and some of them were imprudent in speaking too freely against the proceedings of the Americans.

Mr. Asbury being afflicted, did not attend the conference that was held in Baltimore.

1777.—The fifth conference was held at Deer-Creek meeting-house, in Harford county in Maryland, on the 20th day of May. There were two new circuits taken in at that time, namely, *Sussex* and *Amelia*, in Virginia. Both of them were taken off from *Brunswick* ; and some new places were taken into the plan. There were two more circuits taken on the minutes which had been left off the year before, viz. *Norfolk* and *Chester*. In all, there were fifteen circuits this year, and thirty-five travelling preachers to travel in them. There was no preacher appointed to *New-York*, the place being so much distressed by the war, that the preachers could not travel in safety.

This year there were added to the society 2047 members, and thirteen young preachers were taken on trial to travel the circuits.

It was not customary, at that time, to give an account of the preachers that died, or of those who stopped travelling ; so that we cannot tell at what time some of them stopped travelling, or the cause of their stopping.

The war raged and spread much in the course of this year, and the conference appointed the 25th of July to be observed as a fast-day among our societies—and the preachers came to the following resolution, " That they would take no step to detach themselves from the work of the ministry, for the ensuing year." They further say, " We purpose, by the grace of God, to take no step that may separate us from our brethren, or from the blessed work in which we are engaged."

They also determined not to preach any more funeral sermons, except it was over such persons as they might have good reason to believe died in the fear and favour of God.

Some of the British preachers who were at that conference, intended to return to England ; but they agreed to stay and continue preaching among the Americans, until their way should be quite open and clear for them to return to their native country. About the middle of September, Mr. Rankin and Mr. Rodda left the continent, and sailed for Europe. But some time before they embarked, Mr. Rodda had taken some imprudent steps in favour of the Tories; a company of them having collected together in Delaware state, below Philadelphia. Mr. Rodda's conduct brought many sufferings, and much trouble, on the Methodist preachers and people.

Notwithstanding the opposition that the preachers met with in their labours, there was a gracious revival of religion in many places; but the greatest was in *Brunswick* circuit, and the two circuits that were lately taken from it, *Sussex* and *Amelia*. And there was a very gracious work in *North-Carolina*, where we had but one circuit in all the state.

There was a decrease in the members in several circuits to the north, principally owing to the spreading of the war in those parts; where the preachers found great difficulties in keeping their stations, and some were forced to be given up; so that some of the Classes were entirely given up.

It might be well said during this year, that *without were fightings, and within were fears.* War, and the shedding of blood, was heard of in all directions: armies marching back and forth, one after another; and in many places the people were in great confusion, so that religion was almost banished from some neighbourhoods where it had been pretty lively. Some of our societies in the north, suffered more from that quarter than we did in the south parts of *Virginia*. But the Lord took care of his own work, and his own people.

1778.—The sixth conference was in *Leesburg*, in *Virginia*, on the 19th day of May ; at which time they added six new circuits. Four of them were in Virginia, *Berkley*, *Fluvanna*, *James-City*, and *Lunenburg*. And in *North-Carolina*, the preachers divided the one that was there before, so as to form three circuits, and they were now called *Roanoke*, *Tar-River*, and *New-Hope*.

Five of the old circuits were left out this year, namely, *New-York*, *Philadelphia*, *Chester*, *Frederick*, and *Norfolk*. Some of these circuits could not be attended to, on account of the war, and some of them were in the possession of the British.

We had seventeen circuits this year, and twenty-nine preachers to travel in them. There were ten young preachers received on trial.

The form of the annual minutes was changed this year, and the second question was, "What preachers remain on trial ?" Whereas it used to be, "What preachers are admitted on trial ?"

In the return of members this year, we found we had lost in numbers 873. This was the first time that we came short of the old number given in the preceding year. This decrease was wholly owing to the breaches made upon many societies and circuits by the distresses of war ; and some of our preachers had scruples of conscience about taking the oath of allegiance in the different states where they laboured, and of course were forced to leave their stations.

As paper money was much depreciated, the preachers concluded to allow each travelling preacher eight pounds Virginia money a quarter, or thirty-two pounds per year. They also appointed the last Friday in August for a day of fasting and prayer.

This was a year of distress, and uncommon troubles. The war on one hand, and persecution on the other, the preachers were separated from their flocks, and all conspired to increase the burden of christians.

In the beginning of March, G. Shadford left his friends, after he had kept a day of private fasting and prayer with Mr. Asbury, in order to know the will of God. He then said he saw his way clear to return to England. Mr. Asbury saw it best to abide in America; so they parted, and each one acted as he thought right.

On the fifth day of March, Mr. Asbury began to lye by at Thomas White's, in the Delaware state, where he shut himself up. Speaking of himself he says, "On conscientious principles I was a non-juror, and could not preach in the state of Maryland; and therefore withdrew to the Delaware state, where the clergy were not required to take the state oath: though with a clear conscience, I could have taken the oath of the Delaware state, had it been required; and would have done it, had I not been prevented by a tender fear of hurting the scrupulous consciences of others."

Notwithstanding Mr. *Asbury* was shut up in a friend's house, he looked forward, and hoped for the time to come when he might again visit his brethren, and be of some service to the scattered flock; among whom he had laboured almost seven years.

Some of our preachers were brought into difficulties and sufferings this year; in the month of April, Joseph Hartley, one of our travelling preachers from Virginia was apprehended in Queen-Ann's county, on the Eastern Shore of Maryland, for preaching the gospel; he gave bond and security to stand his trial at court. He was then obliged to desist from preaching in that county; but he would attend his appointments, and after singing and prayer he would stand on his knees and exhort the people; till his enemies said they had as lieve he should preach on his feet as on his knees. After that he went to Talbot county and preached, and the people took him and shut him up in *Jail.* But he was not silent there; for he frequently preached through the grates, or window, to the listening crowd who stood on the outside of the prison. His preaching took such hold on the minds of the hearers, that some of them were deeply awakened, and began to seek the Lord in earnest. Some of the inhabitants said, if the preacher was not turned out of jail, he would convert all the town. After a while he was turned out, and set at liberty; but they had kept him too long, for religion had began to revive, and soon after that it prospered greatly in that place. And from that day to the present time, religion has prospered in that town.

Freeborn Garretson, another of our travelling preachers, was much persecuted. One day while he was riding in Queen-Ann's county, on the Eastern shore of Maryland, about the beginning of July in the same year, J. Brown met him, and taking his horse by the bridle, began to beat Mr. Garretson over the head and shoulders with a stick, and continued to beat him for some time; and then called to the servants in the field to come and help him. But Mr. Garretson getting loose from him, gave his horse the whip, and rode off as fast as he could: Brown mounted his horse and pursued him, and taking a near way, he overtook him, and making another stroke at him, by some means Garretson was thrown off his horse, and falling very hard, was stunned and nearly killed; but providentially for him, a woman came along the road, and finding him in that condition, bled him, and he revived; and being taken to a house, he sat up and exhorted the people with freedom.

CHAPTER IV.

From the year 1779, to the time of our being formed into a regular church, in 1784.

1779.—On the 18th day of May, the seventh conference was held at the *Broken-back church* in *Fluvanna* county in *Virginia.* Previous to this conference, the preachers in the northern states held a preparatory conference at *Thomas White's*, in Delaware state, in order that their sentiments might be carried by brother *William Waters*, to the conference in *Virginia:* for it was judged to be improper for brother *Asbury* to leave his solitary retreat, to go to *Virginia.* However the conference determined that brother *Asbury* ought to act as *general assistant* in America.

At the preparatory conference (so called) the preachers concluded for every exhorter, and local preacher, to go by the directions of the assistants, where, and only where they were appointed to labour.

There were two new circuits taken in at this conference, namely, *Matichen* and *Delaware.* The name of one circuit in *Virginia* was changed from Lunenburg to *Mecklenburg*; and some of the circuits which had been left out of the minutes last year, were inserted in the minutes for this year, viz. *Philadelphia, Chester*, and *Frederick. James-City* circuit was left out of the annual minutes for this year. We had twenty circuits in all; and forty-four preachers were sent to them, to travel and preach among the people.

We had a large addition of members to the society this year. In the different circuits we added 2482 members. In some places the work of

God spread rapidly, and bore down all before it. But in many places the societies were thrown into great disorder and confusion, by reason of the war which continued to rage through the land. Many of the men were drafted, and taken into the army, and many people left their homes to keep out of the way of the enemy, and to save their property, by carrying it with them.

The form of the annual minutes was changed this year in a few points: and the first question stands thus: "Who are admitted on trial?" the first question used to be, *who are admitted into connection?*

Another question was "what shall be done with the preachers who were upon trial last year?" Answer. "Let them continue upon trial until next conference." Before this conference, it had been a constant practice to take a preacher upon trial for one year only, and then admit him into full connection. But from that time, it has been a constant practice even to the present day, to keep a young preacher on trial for two years at least, before he is admitted into full connection. And at the expiration of two years, if the conference have doubts concerning the piety, gifts, or usefulness of the preacher, they continue him on trial for three years, or a longer time, as they may judge best.

But if the preacher is approved of, and there is no objection to him, after he is entered the first year, admitted on trial, he is entered the second year, remaining on trial; and after he has travelled two years, he is entered, admitted into full connection, and becomes a regular member of the conference.

For the first time the following question was asked: "Who desist from travelling?" Answer. "Robert Cloud, William Duke." Previous to this year, no account had been taken of those preachers who had left the travelling connection, or as it was termed, "desisted."

The preachers this year agreed to consider all the Methodist preachers who take money by subscription, as persons excluded from the Methodist connection.

In the course of this year there were great troubles and distresses in the Methodist connection, both among preachers and private members; owing to an unhappy division which took place among the travelling preachers. Many of our travelling preachers in *Virginia* and *North-Carolina*, seeing and feeling the want of the instituted means of grace among our societies; (and there being but few church ministers in that part of the country, and most part of them strangers to heart-felt religion) concluded, that if God had called them to preach, he had called them also to administer the ordinances of baptism and the Lord's Supper. They met together at the conference held at the *Broken Back* church this year, and after consulting together, the conference chose a committee for the purpose of ordaining ministers. The committee thus chosen, first ordained themselves, and then proceeded to ordain and set apart other preachers for the same purpose, that they might administer the holy ordinances to the church of Christ. The preachers thus ordained, went forth preaching the gospel in their circuits as formerly, and administered the sacraments wherever they went, provided the people were willing to partake with them. Most part of our preachers in the south, fell in with this new plan; and as the leaders of the party were very zealous, and the greater part of them very pious men, the private members were influenced by them, and pretty generally fell in with their measures. However, some of the old Methodists would not commune with them; but steadily adhered to their former customs.

The preachers north of *Virginia*, were opposed to this step so hastily taken by their brethren in the south, and made a stand against it, believing that unless a stop could be put to this new mode of proceeding, a separation would take place among the preachers and the people. There was great cause to fear a division, and both parties trembled for the ark of God, and shuddered at the thought of dividing the church of Christ. The preachers in the south were very successful in their ministerial labours, and many souls were brought to God in the latter part of that year; and the christians were very lively in religion. These things all united to confirm the preachers in the belief, that the step they had taken was owned and honoured of God. And at that time there was very little room to hope that they would ever recede from their new plan, in which they were so well established. But after all they consented, for the sake of peace, and the union of the body of Methodists, to drop the ordinances for a season till Mr. Wesley could be consulted.

1780.—On the 24th day of April, the eighth conference met in *Baltimore*, where the northern preachers only attended; for the *Virginia* preachers had a conference appointed in that state. The proceedings of both must be considered together, as it respects the general work.

At the conference which was held in *Baltimore*, and that which was held in *Virginia*, there were three new circuits taken in: one in Delaware state called *Sussex*, and one on the eastern shore of *Maryland*, called *Dorset*; and one in *North Carolina*, called *Yadkin*. Some of the old circuits were left out of the minutes, and we had only twenty circuits this year, which was the same number that we had the year preceding. We had thirty-six preachers to travel in the above number of circuits. They admitted fourteen young preachers on trial.

At this conference it was concluded on, 1st, for all the preachers to change circuits at the end of six months. 2d, That all the assistants should see to the settling of all our meeting houses by trustees; and for regular deeds to be taken for the houses. 3d, That all the preachers should take a written license from the conference, certifying that they were either assistants or helpers in connection with the Methodists, and that these certificates should be signed by Mr. Asbury in behalf of the conference.

It was also concluded on, that every local preacher and exhorter should have a license every quarter (if required,) to speak in public, and that none of them should attempt to speak in public without such license.

They also made a rule for all our preachers to rise at four o'clock in the morning, or at farthest at five o'clock.

They also agreed for the first time to allow the wives of our travelling preachers as much money for each quarter (if they needed it) as was allowed to the preachers.

They also advised for our quarterly meetings in future to be held on Saturdays and Sundays, where it was convenient. Before this plan was adopted, the quarterly meetings were generally held on the week days.

They also concluded to have a fast day in each circuit on the Friday after each quarterly meeting.

The conference disapproved of the practice of distilling spirits out of grain, and they agreed to disown our friends who would not renounce the practice.

They concluded that the preachers should meet the black people in class; and appoint white men to lead them, and not let them stay late at meeting, nor allow them to meet by themselves.

The conference took under consideration the subject of slavery, and required all the travelling preachers who belonged to the Baltimore conference to promise that if they held slaves they would set them free. They went farther, and said, that they believed that keeping of slaves was contrary to the laws of God, of man, and of nature, and that it was hurtful to society, and contrary to the dictates of conscience, and pure religion. They then say, "We pass our disapprobation on all our friends who keep slaves."

It is evident that the preachers in this case went too far in their censures; and their language in their resolves was calculated to irritate the minds of our people, and by no means calculated to convince them of their errors.

The whole of the conference that met in Baltimore agreed in disapprobating the conduct of the preachers in Virginia, in respect to their ordination, and their administering the ordinances, and concluded that they did not look upon the Virginia preachers as *Methodists* in connection with Mr. *Wesley*, and that conference; neither could they consider them as such unless they came back to their former standing, and to their elder brethren.

The Baltimore conference then appointed brother Asbury, brother William Waters, and brother Freeborn Garrettson to attend the conference in Virginia, and to inform the preachers in that conference of what had been determined on in the Baltimore conference; and to let them know withal that the only condition upon which they could be united was, that they (the Virginia preachers) should suspend the administration f the ordinances for one year; and then all the preachers to meet together at the next annual conference to be held in *Baltimore*.

In the spring of the year, some time in April, Mr. *Asbury* left his quiet retreat in Delaware state, where he had been lying by, (and for the most part of the time at Thomas White's) for two years and one month; and then met with the preachers in conference at Baltimore, as has been already mentioned. He then visited his brethren in Virginia, and attended the conference at the Manakin town, which began on the 8th day of May, 1780. At that time Mr. Asbury had to exert all his powers, and to use all possible prudence in order to bring about a settled peace and union among all the preachers. The most influential preachers in that separation in favour of the ordinances, were Philip Gatch, John Dickins, and James O'Kelly. These men were much respected for their usefulness in the ministry.

After much contention, and distress, Mr. *Asbury* proposed to the southern preachers a plan for union which was this; that they should not administer the ordinances for a twelve-month, and that they should all then meet together in conference at Baltimore—And in the course of the year they would write to Mr. Wesley in England, and lay their situation before him and get his advice. The plan took with the Virginia preachers, and they consented to the proposal. By this prudent step a division was prevented, and a blessed union restored. The preachers pretty generally went from that conference to their circuits, with thankful hearts that the breach was healed, and union restored to the connection.

A few of the preachers were so fond of their new self made ordination, that it was with some reluctance that they gave it up, and submitted to the proposed plan for union.

Mr. *Asbury* then travelled through the different circuits in the south parts of *Virginia*, and from thence into *North Carolina*, through Roanoak, Tar River, and New-Hope circuits; and by his being often with the preachers, and among the people in the south, the devisive spirit died away; and the preachers and people by degrees became more reconciled to the old plan, and to the old preachers; and peace and harmony were once more established throughout the connection.

Notwithstanding the difficulties which were found among the preachers on account of the ordinances, there was a gracious revival of religion in many places this year, and especially on the Eastern Shore of *Maryland*. Yet in many places the circuits and societies were so much interrupted by the armies, both of our friends and of our enemies, which were marching through the country, that we had not as many members in society at conference, as we had the year before. Indeed, some of the circuits were wholly forsaken, and no return of the members could be made.

There were some heavy persecutions this year also. Freeborn Garrettson says, that on the 25th day of February, he was judged, and condemned in Dorchester county, on the Eastern Shore of *Maryland*, for preaching the gospel; and two days after he was thrust into Cambridge prison, and the keys were taken away to prevent his friends from administering unto him.

If a person was disposed to persecute a Methodist preacher, it was only necessary to call him a *Tory*, and then they might treat him as cruelly as they pleased. For in many places existing laws were little regarded. But the Lord stood by us and protected us from being destroyed.

1781—On the 24th day of April, the ninth conference met in Baltimore. But previous to this, a few preachers on the Eastern Shore, held a *little conference* in Delaware state, near Choptank, to make some arrangements for those preachers who could not go with them, and then adjourned (as they called it) to Baltimore; so upon the whole it was considered but one conference, at which six new circuits were taken in. The circuit in New Jersey being divided into two, one was called *West-Jersey*, and the other *East-Jersey*. In Pennsylvania was taken in, one called *York*. In Maryland three, *Somerset*, *Talbot*, and *Calvert*; and one in Virginia called *Isle of Wight*. We had at that time 25 circuits, and 54 travelling preachers to supply them.

At this conference there were 20 young preachers admitted upon trial, and sent into the circuits. We had added 2035 members to the society in the course of the year. The Lord wonderfully favoured the travelling preachers, so that we spread our borders, and our numbers increased abundantly.

At this conference, most part, if not all the travelling preachers who were present, resolved, and to give the greater sanction, they subscribed their names, to the resolution to discountenance a separation among either preachers or people. They also agreed that they would preach the old Methodist doctrine, and inforce the discipline which was contained in the *Notes*, *Sermons* and *Minutes* published by Mr. Wesley.

It was also again determined, not to take a young preacher into full connection before he had travelled two years, excepting one who is especially and generally approved of.

It was agreed upon to admit members into society upon trial for three months, before they could be considered as regular members. And in case any member had been once turned out of society, and wished to be re-admitted, they should first evidence their repentance, and then generally be recommended by the society, before they could be received.

It was also advised, that the preachers should often read the rules of the societies, the character of a Methodist, and the plain account of christian perfection. Also, that every assistant preacher should give in writing to his successor, a circumstantial account of the circuit at large, and particularly of the societies and local preachers. And further, that he should inform the societies of the sum of money that ought to be raised for the preachers' quarterage; and that he should press it on them to give according to their several abilities.

For the first time a rule was formed for settling disputes among our members in their dealings with each other, and the following plan was adopted. "Let the assistant preacher at quarterly meeting consult the stewards, in appointing proper persons to examine into the circumstances, and determine the case, and let the parties abide by their decision, or else be excluded from the society." It was found necessary after some years, to alter this rule, and instead of requiring the preacher and stewards to appoint men to settle the disputes, it was advised that each of the persons concerned, when directed by the preacher, should choose his man, and these two should choose a third, who should form the committee; all of them being members of our society—and their decision to be final.

It was also agreed on to have four general fast days throughout all our societies in the course of twelve months: namely, on the first Thursdays in June, September, January and April.

There were five preachers who desisted from travelling this year, John Dickins, Daniel Ruff, Isham Tatum, Greenberry Green and William Moore.

The greatest revival of religion among us this year, appeared to have been on the Eastern Shore of Maryland, and in some parts of Delaware State: where there were many, very many precious souls brought into the liberty of the children of God.

There was also a blessed revival of religion in *Virginia*, and in some parts of *North Carolina*: but the war was so distressing in those parts, that the preachers could not constantly attend their circuits; and many of the societies were dispersed, and prevented from assembling together. Many of the male members were drafted, and when the militia were called out, they had to go into the army to fight, in the defence of their country. Some of them lost their lives, and some made shipwreck of the faith, and but few of them returned home with as much religion as they formerly possessed. Some of the Methodists were bound in conscience not to fight; and no threatenings could compel them to bear arms or hire a man to take their places. In consequence of this, some of them were *whipped*, some were fined, and some imprisoned; others were sent home, and many were much persecuted. The societies had much to discourage them, and but little to help them forward in religion. Yet, notwithstanding all their difficulties, they stood fast as one body, and waxed stronger and stronger in the Lord.

During this year, the societies and circuits in *Virginia*, were more interrupted by the war, than they had ever been before. The British army moved in various directions, and there were many battles fought in the state ; which kept the people constantly alarmed, and prevented them from meeting at their usual times and places. And most of the times when they did assemble for divine worship, their conversation was principally turned upon the times, and the distresses of themselves and their friends. Before meeting would begin, and as soon as it was closed, the enquiry was what is the news of the day ? One would say my son is killed; another my husband is wounded, or taken a prisoner, or sick and likely to die, &c. These things greatly hindered the progress of religion in the south of *Virginia ;* yet in some places there was a pleasing prospect.

This year Cornwallis and the *British* army were captured by the *Americans* at *York Town* in Virginia, in the month of October.

1782—The tenth conference was held : which began at Ellis's Chapel, in Sussex county in *Virgina*, on the 27th day of April, and adjourned to Baltimore on the 21st day of May.

The work had so increased and spread, that it was now found necessary to have a conference in the south every year, continuing the conference in the north as usual. Yet as the conference in the north was of the longest standing, and withal composed of the oldest preachers, it was allowed greater privileges than that in the south ; especially in making rules, and forming regulations for the societies. Accordingly, when any thing was agreed to in the Virginia conference, and afterwards disapproved of in the Baltimore conference, it was dropped. But if any rule was fixed and determined on at the Baltimore conference, the preachers in the south were under the necessity of abiding by it. The southern conference was considered at that time as a convenience, and designed to accommodate the preachers in that part of the work, and to do all the business of a regular conference, except that of making or altering particular rules.

At this time they took in two new circuits, according to the minutes; *Lancaster*, in Pennsylvania, and *South Branch* in Virgina. They also admitted on trial thirteen young preachers; and there was an addition to the society of 1246 members. We had 26 circuits, and 59 preachers to travel in them.

The form of the minutes was altered in some points this year; and the questions were stated as follows:

Q. 1. What preachers are admitted into full connection?

Q. 2 What preachers remain on trial?

Q. 3. What preachers are admitted on trial?

Q. 4. Who act as assistants?

Q. 5. Are there any objections to any of the preachers?

Q. 6. How are the preachers stationed?

Q. 7. How are the preachers to change after six months?

Q. 8. What numbers are there in society? Ans. 11,785.

There were twenty-two questions asked and answered; and the last was, "When and where shall our next conferences be held?"—This was the first time that this question was ever found on the minutes. It was now settled and fixed to have two *conferences* in each year.

One of the questions was, "What shall be done to revive the work?" Ans. "Hold evening meetings, and preach in the morning in convenient places."

There was a new regulation made at this time, that the preachers might more certainly receive their quarterage.

All the gifts received by the preachers, whether it be money or clothing, shall be brought to the quarterly meeting, and be valued by the preachers and stewards: and the preacher who has received the gifts shall be considered as having received so much of his quarterage: and if he is still deficient, he shall carry an account of such deficiency to the next conference, that if possible he may have it made up; out of the profits arising from the sale of books, and the yearly collections.

In order to guard more effectually against disorderly travelling preachers, it was agreed, that there should be written at the bottom of every certificate given to the preachers, at conference, "The authority which this conveys, is limited to the next conference."

To guard more effectually against disorderly local preachers, they agreed to write at the bottom of their certificates, "This conveys authority no longer than you walk uprightly, and submit to the direction of the assistant preacher."

And to guard against disorderly members, it was concluded, that no member of our society should remove to another part of the country, without a certificate from the assistant preacher. And if they did not carry with them such a certificate, they should not be received into society.

The 19th question was a very important one, as follows: "*Do the brethren in conference unani-*

mously choose brother Asbury to act according to Mr. Wesley's original appointment, and preside over the American conference and the whole work? A. Yes.

It was agreed we should have the next conference in *Virginia*, on the first Tuesday in May following; and the conference in the north in *Baltimore*, on the last Wednesday in the same month.

The general fast days were continued to be held on the first Thursday in June, September, January and April.

The minutes were concluded thus, "Every assistant preacher must so order his circuit, that either himself or one of his helpers may travel with Mr. Asbury in the circuit."

As Mr. D. Jarratt, a church minister of Dinwiddie county, in *Virginia*, had paid particular attention to the Methodist preachers and people, this conference expressed themselves in the following manner: "The conference acknowledge their "obligations to the Rev. Mr. Jarratt, for his kind "and friendly services to the preachers and people, from our first entrance into *Virginia*: and "more particularly for attending our conference "in *Sussex*, both in public and private; and we "advise the preachers in the south to consult "him, and to take his advice in the absence of "brother Asbury."*

* Mr Jarratt was one of the most pious clergymen that I was acquainted with, and his attachment to the Methodists was very great, and never abated until the Methodists broke off from the Church of England in 1784, and formed themselves into a regular church. His mind then began to be somewhat turned against them; and in some cases he shewed too much warmth in his opposition. But through the greater part of his life, he was a man of great calmness, and of a candid and liberal sentiment towards other denominations. He died in peace on the 30th of January 1801, in the 69th year of his age. Mr. John Coleman

There was however a great revival of religion this year, in the north of *Virginia*, and in some parts of *Maryland*. Some of our preachers left their circuits to keep out of the way of the enemy: but others having more courage, continued to travel as usual, and to trust the Lord with their bodies as well as their souls.

Considering all things, our societies were greatly blessed, and the number of our members greatly increased: and notwithstanding we were scattered, and in some places suffered loss, yet taking the whole connection throughout, we were highly favoured of the Lord.

In 1783, the eleventh conference began at Ellis's meeting house, Sussex county, *Virginia*, on the 6th day of May, and adjourned to *Baltimore* to the 27th day of the same month.

At this time we took in eleven circuits, which are as follows. In Maryland, *Caroline* and *Annamessex*: in Virginia, *Alleghany*, *Cumberland* and *Holstein*: in North Carolina, *Guilford*, *Caswell*, *Salisbury*, *Marsh*, *Bertie* and *Pasquotank*. We also took in two of the old stations which had been left out of the minutes for some years, on account of the war, i. e. *Norfolk* and *New York*.

We had thirty-five circuits, and eighty-two preachers to travel in them. We added to the society this year 1955 members. We took nineteen young preachers upon trial, so that all the circuits were well supplied.

once a travelling Methodist preacher, but now a minister of the Protestant Episcopal Church, published in 1806, a book called Jarratt's Life: and if what he published be *true*, and Mr. Jarratt did write the letters just as they are published, they shew that *he* was more severe in his spirit against the Methodists, than they who knew him ever thought him to be The book, as far as it speaks of the Methodists, does no credit to the writer or publisher of it. If Mr. Jarratt had been living when the book was printed, I am persuaded he would never have consented for the private letters to have been published.

At this conference the preachers fell upon a new plan, in order to provide a support for the preachers' wives: they required such circuits as they thought able, to raise a certain sum of money for the support of the preachers' wives in other circuits. The minute stands thus: Q. "What sum is to be raised for the support of the preachers' wives? A. North circuits £200, south circuits £60." The wives to be provided for, the circuits which were to raise the money, the sum to be raised, and the particular sum to be given to each preacher's wife, were all specified in the minutes. This plan was quite new, and some of the leading men in particular circuits did not approve of it; and thought it unreasonable that they should raise money for a woman they never saw; and whose husband had never preached among them.

But the Methodist cause is but one in every place; and he who loves his neighbour as himself, will feel for every circuit, every preacher, and every preacher's family.

There was a new minute formed respecting our local preachers who held *slaves*, where the laws of the state would admit of their being free. It says, "We will try them another year, in the mean time let every assistant deal faithfully and plainly with them, and report to the next conference. It may then be necessary to suspend them."

The following was one of the questions, "Shall our friends be permitted to make spiritous liquors, sell, or drink them in drams? A. By no means; we think it wrong in it's nature and consequences; and desire all our preachers to teach the people by precept and example to put away this evil."

At that time it was but seldom known that a Methodist preacher drank spiritous liquors, unless in cases of extreme necessity.

The conference appointed two days for public thanksgiving throughout our connection, for the peace which was established between the United States of *America*, and the *British* nation: for our temporal and spiritual prosperity, and for the glorious revival of the work of God which had taken place among us. The first thanksgiving day was to be on the first Thursday in July, and the second was to be on the first Thursday in October. They also appointed two fast days, the first to be held on the first Friday in the following January; and the second, on the first Friday in April.

They then concluded, that all the assistants, and the preachers to be received into full connection, should attend the next conference.

There were three preachers who desisted from travelling this year, namely, Richard Garrettson, Micajah Debruler, and Samuel Watson.

The revolutionary war being now closed, and a general peace established, we could go into all parts of the country without fear; and we soon began to enlarge our borders, and to preach in many places where we had not been before. We soon saw the fruit of our labours in the new circuits, and in various parts of the country, even in old places where we had preached in former years with but little success.

One thing in particular, that opened the way for the spreading of the gospel by our preachers was this: during the war, which had continued seven or eight years, many of the members of our societies had, through fear, necessity, or choice, moved into the back settlements, and into new parts of the country: and as soon as the national peace was settled, and the way was open, they solicited us to come among them; and by their earnest and frequent petitions, both verbal and written, we were prevailed on, and encouraged to go among them: and they were ready to receive us with open hands and willing hearts, and to cry out *Blessed is he that cometh in the name of the Lord.*

The Lord prospered us much in the thinly settled parts of the country, where, by collecting together the old members of our society, and by joining some new ones with them, the work greatly revived, and the heavenly flame of religion spread far and wide.

The intercourse being now open between us and *England*, we thought there was danger of preachers or members coming from that country, to preach or live among us, whose characters might not be good. In order that we might not be imposed upon, the following regulation was adopted.

Q. " *How shall we conduct ourselves towards the European Methodists, should they come to this continent?*

A. We will not receive them without a letter of recommendation, the truth of which we have no reason to doubt."

In the latter part of this year, Mr. Wesley in *England*, wrote a letter to *America*, which agreed with the last minute; the following is an extract from that letter.

Bristol, October 3, 1783.

1. Let all of you be determined to abide by the methodist doctrine, and discipline, published in the four volumes of sermons, and the notes upon the New Testament, together with the large minutes of the conference.

2. Beware of preachers coming from *Great Britain* or *Ireland*, without a full recommendation from me. Three of our travelling preachers here eagerly desired to go to *America*; but I could

not approve of it by any means; because I am not satisfied that they thoroughly like either our discipline or doctrine: I think they differ from our judgment, in one or both. Therefore, if these or any others come without my recommendation, take care how you receive them.

3. Neither should you receive any preachers, however recommended, who will not be subject to the *American* conference, and cheerfully conform to the minutes both of the *English* and *American* conferences.

4. I do not wish our *American* brethren to receive any, who make any difficulty of receiving *Francis Asbury* as the general assistant.

Undoubtedly the greatest danger to the work of God in *America*, is likely to arise either from preachers coming from Europe, or from such as will arise from among yourselves, speaking perverse things, or bringing in among you new doctrines, particularly Calvinian. You should guard against this with all possible care, for it is far easier to keep them out than to thrust them out.

I commend you all to the grace of God, and am your affectionate friend and brother,

JOHN WESLEY.

In 1784, the twelfth conference began at Ellis's chapel, in *Virginia*, on the 30th day of April, and ended in Baltimore, on the 28th of May. It was considered as but one conference, although they met first in *Virginia*, and then adjourned to Baltimore, where the business was finished.

This year we took in seven new circuits; four of them were in Virginia, *Amherst*, *Bedford*, *Hampton*, and *Accomack*; the other three were in the north part of our connection, which were *Juniata*, *Trenton*, and *Long-Island*. We also admitted on trial twelve young preachers, and added to the society 1248 members. We had now forty-six circuits, and eighty-three travelling preachers.

There were four preachers who desisted from travelling this year, David Abbott, James Thomas, James Mallory and John Coleman.*

A new question was introduced into our minutes this year, which was thus;

Q. *What preachers have died this year?*

A. Henry Medcalf and William Wright.

This was a new plan, and it was a very proper and profitable one. By it we might know when our preachers left the world. Previous to this we had taken no account in our minutes of the death of any of our travelling preachers. And notwithstanding we now mentioned the names of those who had died, yet there was nothing said about their deaths or their characters. It might be proper therefore here to observe, that Henry Medcalf was considered as a man deeply rooted and grounded in the faith, and very much devoted to God; and I was informed, that when he was near his end, he got out of his bed, and kneeling down, he there died upon his knees.

We had twenty-four questions and answers on our minutes this year, and some of them are well worth noticing at this time.

Q. *What can be done towards erecting new Chapels, and discharging the debts on those already built?*

A. Let the assistant preacher offer a yearly subscription through the circuit, and insist on every member that is able, to give something; let them subscribe the first quarter, and pay the second; and let the money be applied by two general stewards.

Q. *How shall we prevent superfluity in dress among our people?*

* Mr. Coleman published Jarratt's Life.

A. Let the preachers carefully avoid every thing of this kind in themselves; and let them speak frequently and faithfully against it in all our societies.

It was also determined, that if any of our friends buy slaves with no other intention than to hold them as slaves, after being previously warned they should be turned out of society. And they were not permitted to sell a slave on any condition whatever. And if the local preachers would not free their slaves in those states where the laws would allow of it, they should be suspended, except in *Virginia*, and there they should be tried another year.

However good the intention of the preachers might be in framing these rules, we are well assured that they never were of any particular service to our societies. Some of the slaves, however, obtained their freedom in consequence of these rules.

Q. *How shall we reform our singing?*

A. Let all our preachers who have any knowledge of singing by note, improve it, and sing by rule, and keep close to Mr. Wesley's tunes and hymns.

The conference then adopted the directions which Mr. Wesley had written in the latter part of the preceding year, and formed a rule to take in the substance of that letter.

We agreed, that if any European Methodist preachers should come over recommended by Mr. Wesley, and would be subject to the *American* conference, preach the Methodist doctrine, keep the circuits they were appointed to, and be subject to Francis Asbury as general assistant, while he stands approved by Mr. Wesley and the conference, we will receive them; but if they walk contrary to the above directions, no appointment shall prevent them from being excluded from our connection.

There was a plan laid also for keeping four fast days in the year in each circuit; and the preachers were directed to write on each Class-paper, "The first Friday after every quarterly meeting is to be observed as a day of fasting and prayer."

It was a custom among the Methodists formerly, to observe all Fridays in the year as days of fasting or abstinence; but this custom is not strictly attended to by our societies at present.

We had a gracious revival of religion this year in many of the frontier circuits, and the way was opening fast for us to enlarge our borders, and to spread the gospel through various places where we had never been before. The call of the people was great, for more labourers to be sent into the harvest.

Note—Here end the minutes that were formerly taken and kept in manuscript, and not printed until 1795. After this all our annual minutes were printed every year. In the following part of this history, the printed minutes will be attended to as they came out year after year.

CHAPTER V.

From the first general Conference in 1784, *to the end of the year* 1786.

The Methodists had until this time one *form* both of worship and discipline in every part of the world; but the independence of these United States of *America*, confirmed by the peace of 1783, occasioned an extraordinary change in this respect. During the war our societies were deprived of the ordinances of *baptism, and the Lord's supper:* for the ministers of the church of England had mostly left their parishes: some of them were silenced, others left off preaching, because they could not procure a maintenance by it; and many more went into the British dominions. From the time of the peace no ecclesiastical authority of any kind was either exercised or claimed by any person or persons whatsoever. In this situation, we desired Mr. Wesley's advice and assistance; and as he observes, "his scruples being at an end, he conceived himself at perfect liberty to exercise that right which he doubted not God had given him."

At the British conference held at Leeds in July 1784, Mr. Wesley declared his intention of sending Dr. *Coke* and some other preachers to *America.* Mr. *Richard Whatcoat*, and Mr. *Thomas Vasey* offered themselves as missionaries for that purpose, and were accepted. But before they sailed, Mr. *Wesley* wrote to Dr. *Coke* then in *London*, desiring him to meet him in *Bristol*, to receive fuller powers; and to bring the Rev. Mr. *Creighton* with him. The Dr. and Mr. *Creighton* accordingly met him in Bristol; where Mr.

Wesley with the assistance of Dr. *Coke*, and Mr. *Creighton*, ordained *Richard Whatcoat* and Mr. *Thomas Vasey*, presbyters for *America*: and, did afterwards ordain Dr. *Coke* a superintendant, giving him letters of ordination, under his hand and seal. Previous to this Dr. *Coke* had been ordained a presbyter by a bishop of the church of England.

Dr. *Coke*, with Messrs. *Whatcoat* and *Vasey* sailed for *America*, in the month of September, and landed at *New York* on the third day of November.

By these preachers, Mr. *Wesley* wrote a letter to us in *America*, to be printed and circulated among us; the following is the letter.

Bristol, *September* 10, 1784.

To Dr. *Coke*, Mr. *Asbury*, and our brethren in *North America*.

"1. By a very uncommon train of providences, many of the provinces of *North America* are totally disjoined from the British empire, and erected into Independent States. The English government has no authority over them either civil or ecclesiastical, any more than over the states of *Holland*. A civil authority is exercised over them, partly by the Congress, partly by the state assemblies But no one either exercises or claims any ecclesiastical authority at all. In this peculiar situation some thousands of the inhabitants of these States, desire my advice: and in compliance with their desire; I have drawn up a little sketch.

"2. Lord KING's account of the primitive church convinced me many years ago, that bishops and presbyters are the same order, and consequently have the same right to ordain. For many years I have been importuned from time to time, to exercise this right, by ordaining part of our travelling preachers. But I have still refused, not only for peace sake, but because I was determined, as little as possible to violate the established order of the national church to which I belonged.

"3. But the case is widely different between England and North America. Here there are bishops who have a legal jurisdiction. In America there are none, and but few parish ministers. So that for some hundred miles together there are none either to baptize, or administer the Lord's supper. Here therefore my scruples are at an end: and I conceive myself at full liberty, as I violate no order, and invade no man's right, by appointing and sending labourers into the harvest.

"4. I have accordingly appointed Dr. *Coke* and Mr. *Francis Asbury*, to be joint *superintendants*, over our brethren in North America. As also *Richard Whatcoat*, and *Thomas Vasey*, to act as *elders* among them, by baptising and administering the Lord's Supper.

"5. If any one will point out a more rational and scriptural way of feeding and guiding those poor sheep in the wilderness, I will gladly embrace it. At present I cannot see any better method than that I have taken.

"6. It has indeed been proposed, to desire the *English* bishops to ordain part of our preachers for *America*. But to this I object, 1. I desired the Bishop of *London* to ordain one only; but could not prevail. 2. If they consented, we know the slowness of their proceeding; but the matter admits of no delay. 3. If they would ordain them *now*, they would likewise expect to govern them. And how grievously would this entangle us? 4. As our *American* brethren are now totally disentangled both from the state, and from the *English* hierarchy, we dare not entangle them again, either with the one or the other. They are now at full liberty, simply to follow the scriptures and the primitive church. And we judge it best that they should stand fast in that liberty, wherewith God has so strangely made them free." JOHN WESLEY.

At the same time Mr. Wesley prepared a liturgy little differing from that of the Church of England, or rather revised the Common Prayer Book, leaving out certain parts, and altering some of the ceremonies, and some of the psalms, and making the morning and evening service much shorter than it was before. He advised all the travelling preachers to use it on the Lord's day in all the congregations, reading the Litany only on Wednesdays and Fridays, and to pray extempore on all other days. He also advised the *Elders* to administer the Supper of the Lord on every Lord's day.

As soon as Dr. *Coke* landed in America, he laid his plan to meet Mr. *Asbury* as soon as possible, and travelling from *New-York* to *Philadelphia*, and then down into the *Delaware* state, he met with Mr. *Asbury* at *Barratt's* Chapel on the 14th day of the same month. They then consulted together about the plan which Mr. *Wesley* had adopted, and recommended to us. After the business was maturely weighed, and sufficient time was taken to consult some more of the preachers who were present on that day, it was judged advisable to call together all the travelling preachers in a general conference to be held in *Baltimore* at christmas.

Mr. Freeborn Garrettson undertook to travel to the south, in order to give notice to all the travelling preachers of this intended meeting.

But being fond of preaching by the way, and thinking he could do the business by writing, he did not give timely notice to the preachers who were in the extremities of the work; and of course several of them were not at that conference.

December 27th, 1784—The thirteenth conference began in *Baltimore*, which was considered to be a general conference, in which *Thomas Coke* and *Francis Asbury* presided.

At this conference we formed ourselves into a regular church, by the name of *The Methodist Episcopal Church*; making at the same time the Episcopal office elective, and the elected superintendant amenable to the body of ministers and preachers.

Mr. *Asbury* was appointed a *superintendant* by Mr. *Wesley*, yet he would not submit to be ordained, unless he could be voted in by the conference: when it was put to vote, he was unanimously chosen. He was then ordained *Deacon*, then *Elder*, and afterwards *Superintendant*, before the end of the conference. At the request of Mr. Asbury when he was about to be ordained a Superintendant, Mr. Otterbine, a German minister, who was a pious man, assisted in his ordination by the laying on of his hands with the other ministers.

At this conference there were 13 preachers elected to the Elder's office, and most of them were ordained—their names were,

Freeborn Garrettson,*	James O. Cromwell,*
William Gill,	John Tunnel
Le Roy Cole,	Nelson Reed,
John Hagerty,	Jeremiah Lambert,†

* Mr. Garrettson, and Mr. Cromwell, were ordained for Nova-Scotia, and were sent there immediately afterwards.

† Mr. Lambert, was ordained for Antigua, in the West-Indies.

Reuben Ellis,
James O'Kelly,
Richard Ivey,
Beverly Allen,*
Henry Willis.†

They also elected three Deacons, John Dickins, Caleb Boyer, and Ignatius Pigman. Mr. Boyer was not present.

Being now formed into a church, a regular plan of proceeding was laid, and a form of discipline drawn up. In the minutes of this conference there were eighty one questions with answers, a few of which I shall take notice of: If any one wishes to see the whole, he may read the minutes of that general conference.

This being the beginning of the Methodist Episcopal Church, it will be necessary to take particular notice of those regulations or rules, which were formed at that time, especially such as had not been previously practised by us.

Q. 2. "What can be done in order to the futur union of the Methodists?"

A. "During the life of the Reverend Mr. Wesley, we acknowledge ourselves his Sons in the Gospel, ready in matters belonging to church-government, to obey his commands. And we do engage after his death, to do every thing that we judge consistent with the cause of religion in *America*, and the political interest of these states to preserve and promote our Union with the Methodists in *Europe*."

This engagement to obey Mr. Wesley's commands "in matters belonging to church-government" was afterwards the cause of some uneasiness: which will be noticed in it's proper place.

Q. 3. "As the ecclesiastical as well as civil

* Mr. Allen was not ordained until the conference held at Green Hill's, in North-Carolina, in the latter part of April 1785

† Mr. Willis was not at the conference; but was ordained a few weeks afterwards, by the Bishop and one Elder only.

affairs of these United States have passed through a very considerable change by the revolution, what plan of church-government shall we hereafter pursue?"

A. "We will form ourselves into an Episcopal church under the direction of superintendants, elders, deacons, and helpers, according to the forms of ordination annexed to our liturgy, and the form of discipline set forth in these minutes."

Q. 4. "What may we reasonably believe to be. God's design in raising up the Methodist preachers?"

A. "To reform the continent, and to spread scriptural holiness over these lands."

The following rules were formed respecting strangers, or persons not of our society.

Q. 11. "How often shall we permit strangers to be present at the meeting of the society?"

A. "At every other meeting of the society in every place, let no stranger be admitted. At other times they may; but the same person not above twice or thrice."

Q. 12. "How often shall we permit strangers to be present at our Love-feasts?"

A. "Let them be admitted with the utmost caution; and the same person on no account above twice, unless he becomes a member."

Q. 16. "How shall we prevent improper persons from insinuating into the society?"

A. 1. "Give tickets to none till they are re commended by a leader, with whom they have met at least two months on trial.

2. Give notes to none but those who are recommended by one you know, or till they have met three or four times in a class."

Q. 17. "When shall we admit new members?"

A. "In large towns, admit them into the society on the Sunday following the quarterly meeting. Then also read the names of those that are excluded."

In country places, it has always been a custom to admit persons into our society, at any time when the circuit preacher who has the charge of the circuit is present.

Q. 18. "Should we insist on the rules concerning dress?"

A. "By all means. This is no time to give any encouragement to superfluity of apparel. Therefore give no tickets to any, till they have left off superfluous ornaments. Allow no exempt case, not even of a married woman. Better one suffer than many. Give no ticket to any that wear high heads, enormous bonnets, ruffles or rings."

There was a rule formed respecting marrying, which runs thus: "Many of our members have married with unawakened persons. Q. What can be done to put a stop to this? A. Let every preacher publicly inforce the Apostle's caution, *be not unequally yoked together with unbelievers.* 2. Let him openly declare, whoever does this will be expelled the society. Let all be exhorted to take no step in so weighty a matter without advising with the most serious of their brethren."

This rule continued with but little alteration, until the general cenference in 1804. It was then altered by a small majority of votes; and no one is expelled from our society at present, for marrying persons without religion. Formerly the rule was "whoever marries an unawakened person *will be expelled:*" now it stands, "Will be put back on trial for six months." If any of our members now (1809) marries a person who has the form, and is seeking the power of godliness, there is no objection; but if the person does not come up to this description, such offending member is to be put back on trial for six months.

Q. 23. "May our ministers or travelling preachers drink spiritous liquors?"

A. "By no means, unless it be *medicinally.*"

Q. 27. "To whom is the *Superintendant* amenable for his conduct?"

A. "To the conference: who have power to expel him for improper conduct, if they see it necessary."

N. B. No person shall be ordained a *Superintendant, Elder* or *Deacon,* without the consent of a majority of the conference, and the consent and imposition of hands of a *Superintendant;* except in the following instance:

Q. 29. "If by death, expulsion or otherwise, there be no Superintendant remaining in our church, what shall we do?"

A. "The conference shall elect a Superintendant, and the Elders or any three of them shall ordain him according to our liturgy."

Another rule was, "that if a Superintendant ceases from travelling without the consent of the conference, he shall not thereafter exercise any ministerial function whatsoever in our church." The same rule was also made for the Elders and Deacons, in case they should cease to travel without the consent of the conference.

There were twelve rules formed for a helper, which are proper, and worth attending to by all our preachers; they are as follow:

1. "Be diligent. Never be unemployed. Never be triflingly employed. Never *while away* time: neither spend any more time at any place than is strictly necessary."

2. "Be serious. Let your motto be, holiness to the Lord. Avoid all lightness, jesting and foolish talking."

3. "Converse sparingly and cautiously with women: particularly with young women."

4. "Take no step toward marriage without first consulting with your brethren."

5. "Believe evil of no one: unless you see it done, take heed how you credit it. Put the best construction on every thing. You know the judge is always supposed to be on the prisoner's side.

6. "Speak evil of no one: else *your* word especially would eat as doth a canker: keep your thoughts within your own breast, till you come to the person concerned.

7. "Tell every one who is under your care, what you think wrong in his conduct and temper, and plainly, as soon as may be, else it will fester in your heart. Make all haste to cast the fire out of your bosom.

8. "Do not affect the gentleman.—A preacher of the gospel is the servant of all.

9. "Be ashamed of nothing but sin: not of fetching wood (if time permit) or drawing water: not of cleaning your own shoes, or your neighbour's.

10. "Be punctual. Do every thing exactly at the time. And do not *mend* our rules, but *keep* them: not for wrath, but for conscience sake.

11. "You have nothing to do but to save souls. Therefore spend and be spent in this work. And go always, not only to those that want, but to those that want you most.

"Observe. It is not your business to preach so many times, and to take care of this or that society; but to save as many souls as you can; to bring as many sinners as you possibly can to repentance, and with all your power to build them up in that holiness without which they cannot see the Lord! And remember! a Methodist preacher is to mind *every* point, great and small, in the Methodist discipline! Therefore you will need all the sense you have, and to have all your wits about you!

12. "Act in all things, not according to your own will, but as a son in the gospel. As such, it is your part to employ all your time in the manner which we direct: partly in preaching and visiting from house to house: partly in reading, meditation and prayer. Above all, if you labour with us in our Lord's vineyard, it is needful you should do *that part* of the work which we advise, at *those times and places* which we judge most for his glory."

In some cases we had been imposed on by strange preachers, who, coming among us under the character of Methodist preachers, had been encouraged to preach for a season, even till they were found out to be bad men. It was now thought proper to guard against such impostors; and the following rule was formed. "Let no person be employed as a travelling preacher, unless his name be printed in the minutes of the conference preceding, or a certificate be given him under the hand of one of the superintendants; or, in their absence, of three assistants. And for this purpose, let the minutes of the conference be always printed."

From that time all the minutes of the conferences have been printed regularly every year.

Q. 37. "What shall be the regular annual salary of the *elders, deacons* and *helpers?*"

A. "$64 and no more?" And for each preacher's wife $64. And for each preacher's child, if under the age of six years, there shall be allowed $16; and for each child of the age of six, and under the age of eleven years, $21 33 cts."

This rule for allowing a support for the children was not pleasing to our societies in general; and as there were many objections raised against it, the conference in 1787 resolved, that no allowance should be made in future for the children of our married preachers.

And there was no regular provision made for them after that, until the year 1800, when the general conference settled an allowance for the children, which still continues in our discipline.

There were also some rules drawn up respecting the emancipation of slaves, which were in substance as follows: "Every member in our society who has slaves, in those states where the laws will admit of freeing them, shall, after notice given him by the preacher, within twelve months, (except in Virginia, and there within two years) legally execute and record an instrument, whereby he sets free every slave in his possession, those who are from forty to forty-five, immediately, or at farthest at the age of forty-five. Those who are between the ages of twenty-five and forty, immediately, or within the course of five years. Those who are between the ages of twenty and twenty-five, immediately, or at farthest at the age of thirty. Those who are under the age of twenty, as soon as they are twenty-five at farthest.—And every infant, immediately on it's birth.

"Every person concerned, who will not comply with these *rules*, shall have liberty quietly to withdraw from our society within the twelve months following, the notice being given him as aforesaid. Otherwise the assistant shall exclude him in the society.

"No person holding slaves, shall in future be admitted into society, or to the Lord's supper, till he previously comply with these rules concerning slavery.

"Those who buy or sell slaves, or give them away, unless on purpose to free them, shall be expelled immediately."

These rules were but short lived, and were offensive to most of our southern friends; and were so much opposed by many of our private members, local preachers, and some of the travelling preachers, that the execution of them was suspended at the conference held in June following, about six months after they were formed; and they were never afterwards carried into full force. However, some parts of them have been retained among us; but they have been changed and altered, until the last general conference in 1808; at which time the greater part of the rule about slavery was abolished, and no part of it was retained respecting private members. The part retained in our discipline, only relates at present to our travelling preachers, and such other persons as are to be brought forward to official stations in our church. I shall therefore take no further notice of the rules about slavery which were made at various times for twenty-four years. i. e. from the Christmas conference in 1784, to the last general conference held in 1808. For a long experience has taught us, that the various rules which have been made on this business have not been attended with that success which was expected.

The directions given concerning the administration of the Lord's supper, were 1, "Let it be recommended to the people to receive it *kneeling*: but they may receive it *standing* or *sitting*. 2. Let no person who is not a member of our society be admitted to the communion without a sacrament ticket, which ticket must be changed every quarter."

The direction given about baptism was, "Let every adult person, and the parents of every child to be baptized, have their choice either of *immersion* or *sprinkling*."

It is also said, "We will on no account whatsoever, suffer any *elder* or *deacon* among us to receive a *fee* or *present* for administering the ordinance of marriage, baptism, or the burial of the dead; *freely* we receive, and *freely* we give."

After a few years, it was thought best to take a *present* for performing the marriage ceremony; and for the money so received to be given in to the stewards of the circuit, to be applied to the making up of the preacher's quarterage; but in case the preachers of the circuit received their quarterage without it, then the money so received, should be brought to the next conference, and be applied to the making up of the deficiencies of the preachers. But there was another alteration made in 1800, and each preacher was then allowed to take for marrying people, what they chose to give him, and to keep it, without giving any account of it: which custom has prevailed ever since.

There were some further directions given to the preachers which respect visiting families, and instructing the children: "Go into every *house* in course, and teach *every one* therein, young and old, if they belong to us, to be christians inwardly and outwardly. Make every particular plain to their understanding; fix it in their memory; write it on their heart. In order to this, there must be *line upon line, precept upon precept.* What patience, what love, what knowledge is requisite for this!"

" But what shall we do for the *rising generation?* Who will labour for them? Let him who is zealous for God and the souls of men begin *now*.

1. " Where there are ten children whose parents are in society, meet them at least an hour every week.

2. " Talk with them every time you see any of them at home:

3. " Pray in earnest for them:

4. " Diligently instruct and vehemently exhort all parents at their own houses:

5. " Preach expressly on education. " But I have no gift for this." Gift or no gift, you are to do it, else you are not called to be a *Methodist* preacher: Do it as you can, till you can do it as you would. Pray earnestly for the gift, and use the means for it."

Q. 57. " How shall we guard against *formality* in *singing?*

A. 1. " By choosing such hymns as are proper for the congregation: 2. By not singing too much at once; seldom more than five or six verses: 3. By suiting the tune to the words: 4. By often stopping short and asking the people, " Now! Do you know what you said last? Did you speak no more than you felt?" 5. Do not suffer the people to sing too slow. This naturally tends to formality. 6. In every large society let them learn to sing. And let them always learn our own tunes first. 7. Let the women constantly sing their parts alone. Let no man sing with them unless he understands the notes, and sings the bass. If you cannot sing yourself, choose a person or two in each place to pitch the tune for you. Exhort every one in the congregation to sing, not one in ten only. If a preacher be present, let no singer give out the words."

Another minute was this. Q. "What shall we do with those members of our society who wilfully and repeatedly neglect to meet their class?

A. 1. "Let the assistant or helper visit them, whenever it is practicable, and inform them, if they continue to neglect they will be *excluded.*

2. "If they do not amend, let the assistant exclude them in the society, informing it, that they are laid aside for a breach of our rules of discipline, and not for immoral conduct."

At this conference there was a regular plan laid for raising money to support, or help our preachers and their families. It was called the "Preachers' Fund." For the money was to be collected from the travelling preachers, and applied to the support of the preachers.

Q. 72. "How can we provide for superannuated preachers, and the widows and orphans of preachers?"

A. 1. "Let every travelling preacher contribute two dollars yearly at the conference.

2. "Let every one, when first admitted as a travelling preacher, pay two dollars and sixty-seven cents.

3. "Let this money be lodged in the hands of the treasurers.

4. "Let there be three treasurers; three clerks, each of whom shall keep a separate account; and three inspectors, who shall annually lay before the conference an exact state of the fund.

5. "Let these nine form a committee for the management of the fund. Three of whom shall be competent to proceed on any business, provided one be a treasurer, another an inspector, and a third a clerk.

6. " Out of this fund let provision be made, first for the worn out preachers, and then for the widows and children of those that are dead.

7. " Every worn out preacher shall receive, if he wants it, $ 64 a year.

8. " Every widow of a preacher shall receive yearly, if she wants it, $ 53 and 33 cts.

9. " Every child of a preacher shall receive once for all, if he wants it, $ 53 and 33 cts.

10. " But none shall be entitled to any thing from this fund, till he has paid $ 6 67 cts.

11. " Nor any who neglects paying his subscription for three years together, unless he be sent by the conference out of these United States, &c."

This fund afforded relief to a good many of our preachers in the time of distress; and most part of the preachers were subscribers to it. The regulations were changed afterwards in some particulars, but the fund continued in operation until we established the chartered fund in 1796. Then all the stock of the preachers' fund was thrown into the chartered fund, which was incorporated in 1797 in Philadelphia. After that time there was some alteration made in the application of the money given annually by the preachers.

The annual subscriptions of the travelling preachers, to the preachers' fund, was to be reserved for extraordinary cases, which the chartered fund might not reach. Some time after that, the subscriptions were dropped altogether, and have never since been revived.

The 75th question was, " Is there any exception to the rule " let the men and women sit apart?" A. There is no exception. Let them sit apart in all our chapels."

This rule has been established among the *Methodists* from the beginning, and every departure therefrom, has been deemed a departure from the order and discipline of the *Methodists.*

At this time the prayer book, as revised by Mr. Wesley, was introduced among us; and in the large towns, and in some country places, our preachers read prayers on the Lord's day: and in some cases the preachers read part of the morning service on Wednesdays and Fridays. But some of the preachers who had been long accustomed to pray extempore, were unwilling to adopt this new plan. Being fully satisfied that they could pray better, and with more devotion while their eyes were shut, than they could with their eyes open. After a few years the prayer book was laid aside, and has never been used since in public worship.

The Superintendants, and some of the Elders, introduced the custom of wearing gowns and bands, but it was opposed by many of the preachers, as well as private members, who looked upon it as needless and *superfluous.* Having made a stand against it, after a few years it was given up, and has never been introduced among us since.

The Methodists were pretty generally pleased at our becoming a church, and heartily united together in the plan which the conference had adopted. And from that time religion greatly revived.

I will here insert some of the Articles of Religion which were received at that conference. There were twenty-five articles in all; but I shall insert only twelve of them.

N. B. The whole of the articles may be seen in the Methodists' form of discipline.

ARTICLES OF RELIGION.

I. *Of Faith in the Holy Trinity.*

There is but one living and true God, everlasting, without body or parts; of infinite power, wisdom, and goodness; the Maker and Preserver of all things both visible and invisible. And in unity of this Godhead there are three Persons of one substance, power, and eternity; the Father, the Son, and the Holy Ghost.

II. *Of the Word, or Son of God, who was made very Man.*

The Son, who is the Word of the Father, the very and eternal God, of one substance with the Father, took man's nature in the womb of the blessed Virgin; so that two whole and perfect natures, that is to say, the Godhead and Manhood, were joined together in one Person, never to be divided, whereof is one Christ, very God, and very man, who truly suffered, was crucified, dead, and buried, to reconcile his Father to us, and to be a sacrifice, not only for original guilt, but also for actual sins of men.

III. *Of the Resurrection of Christ.*

Christ did truly rise again from the dead, and took again his body, with all things appertaining to the perfection of man's nature, wherewith he ascended into Heaven, and there sitteth until he return to judge all men at the last day.

IV. *Of the Holy Ghost.*

The Holy Ghost, proceeding from the Father and the Son, is of one substance, majesty, and glory, with the Father and the Son, very and eternal God.

V. *Of the Sufficiency of the Holy Scriptures for Salvation.*

Holy Scripture containeth all things necessary to salvation: so that whatsoever is not read therein, or may be proved thereby, is not to be required of any man, that it should be believed as an article of the faith, or be thought requisite or necessary to salvation. In the name of the Holy Scripture we do understand those Canonical books of the Old and New Testament, of whose authority was never any doubt in the church.

VIII. *Of Free-Will.*

The condition of man after the fall of Adam is such, that he cannot turn and prepare himself by his own natural strength and works to faith, and calling upon God: Wherefore we have no power to do good works pleasant and acceptable to God, without the grace of God by Christ preventing us, that we may have a good will, and working with us, when we have that good will.

IX. *Of the Justification of Man.*

We are accounted righteous before God, only for the merit of our Lord and Saviour Jesus Christ, by faith, and not for our own works or deservings: wherefore, that we are justified by faith only, is a most wholesome doctrine, and very full of comfort.

X. *Of Good Works.*

Although good works, which are the fruits of faith, and follow after justification, cannot put away our sins, and endure the severity of God's judgment; yet are they pleasing and acceptable to God in Christ, and spring out of a true and lively faith, insomuch that by them a lively faith may be as evidently known, as a tree discerned by it's fruit.

XII. *Of Sin after Justification.*

Not every sin willingly committed after justification, is the sin against the Holy Ghost, and unpardonable. Wherefore the grant of repentance is not to be denied to such as fall into sin, after justification: after we have received the Holy Ghost, we may depart from grace given, and fall into sin, and by the grace of God rise again, and amend our lives. And therefore they are to be condemned who say they can no more sin as long as they live here, or deny the place of forgiveness to such as truly repent.

XIII. *Of the Church.*

The visible Church of Christ is a congregation of faithful men, in which the pure word of God is preached, and the Sacraments duly administered according to Christ's ordinance, in all those things that of necessity are requisite to the same.

XXII. *Of the Rites and Ceremonies of Churches.*

It is not necessary that rites and ceremonies should in all places be the same, or exactly alike; for they have been always different, and may be changed according to the diversity of countries, times, and men's manners, so that nothing be ordained against God's word. Whosoever, through his private judgment, willingly and purposely doth openly break the rites and ceremonies of the church to which he belongs, which are not repugnant to the word of *God*, and are ordained and approved by common authority, ought to be rebuked openly, that others may fear to do the like, as one that offendeth against the common order of the church, and woundeth the consciences of weak brethren.

Every particular church may ordain, change, or abolish rites and ceremonies, so that all things may be done to edification.

XXIII. *Of the Rulers of the United States of America.*

The President and Congress, the General Assemblies, the Governors, and the Councils of State, *as the Delegates of the People*, are the rulers of the United States of America, according to the division of power made to them by the Constitution of the United States, and by the Constitutions of their respective States. And the said States are a sovereign and independent nation, and ought not to be subject to any foreign jurisdiction.

1785—The business of the conference being over, the preachers soon set out for their different stations. About the middle of February, Mr. *Freeborn Garrettson*, and Mr. *James O. Cromwell* embarked for *Nova Scotia*, for which place they had been ordained and appointed. It was a dangerous voyage for that season of the year; but after many difficulties they came to the desired *Haven*. They were owned and honoured of God in that country; and by their labours, souls were awakend and converted; and societies were formed. At the close of the revolutionary war, some of the Methodists had gone to *Nova Scotia* and settled in the *British* province, and were longing and praying for labourers to be sent into that part of the Lord's vineyard, who were ready at the arrival of our brethren to cry out as others had likewise done, "Blessed is he that cometh in the name of the Lord."

In the latter part of February, Messrs. *Asbury*, *Henry Willis*, and myself, went in company to *Charleston*, in *South-Carolina;* and were all taken in to lodge at Mr. Edgar Wells's, who was a merchant, but not religious. We applied for the use of an old meeting house, which formerly belonged to the Baptists, but had not been occupied for some years. We obtained liberty to preach in it and advertised in the newspapers, (it being Saturday night) that we would preach there the next day.

On Sunday, the 27th day of February, I preached the first sermon in Charleston, which may be considered the first Methodist sermon that was ever preached in the city, with a view of continuing preaching in that place. Mr. Pillmore had preached there some years before, as he was passing through the country.

At this first meeting, Mr. *Wells*, at whose house we put up, was awakened, and felt the need of religion. Mr. *Willis* preached in the afternoon, and I preached again at night, and again the next night; after which I left the city. Mr. *Asbury* continued in the city a few days, and then left Mr. *Willis* there as a stationed preacher; by whose labours a society was soon formed, and has continued until the present day.

After the arrival of Dr. Coke in the latter part of the past year, he and Mr. Asbury consulted about the propriety of building a school or college, and at length began to solicit donations for that purpose. The business was brought before the conference which met at Christmas, and it was agreed to, and steps were taken in order to go on with the work. At the close of the conference a plan for erecting the college was published, and signed by the two *Superintendants*, and was as follows:

"*A plan for erecting a college, intended to advance religion in* America, *to be presented to the principal members and friends of the Methodist Episcopal Church.*

"The college is to be built at *Abingdon* in *Maryland*, on a healthy spot, enjoying a fine air and very extensive prospect. It is to receive for education and board the sons of the elders and preachers of the Methodist church, poor orphans, and the sons of the subscribers, and of other friends. It will be expected that all our friends who send their children to the college, will, if they be able, pay a moderate sum for their education and board: the rest will be taught and boarded, and, if our finances will allow of it, cloathed *gratis*. The institution is also intended for the benefit of our young men who are called to preach, that they may receive a measure of that improvement which is highly expedient as a preparative for public service. A teacher of the languages with an usher will be provided, as also an English master to teach with the utmost propriety, both to read and speak the English language: nor shall any other branch of literature be omitted, which may be thought necessary for any of the students; above all, especial care shall be taken that due attention be paid to the religion and morals of the children, and to the exclusion of all such as continue of an ungovernable temper. The college will be under the presidentship of the superintendants of our church for the time being: and is to be supported by yearly collections throughout our circuits, and any endowments which our friends may think proper to give and bequeath, consistently with the laws of the respective States, in which they are made. The buildings, if it please God, will be begun in next June, and the subscribers are desired to send in their subscriptions, as far as it is convenient, to any of our ministers or preachers in the intermediate space: but wherever it is inconvenient, we will most cheerfully wait the subscriber's time.

Three objects of considerable magnitude, we have in view in the erection of this college.

The first is a provision for the sons of our married ministers and preachers.

The wisdom and love of God have now thrust out a large number of labourers into his harvest: men who desire nothing on earth but to promote the glory of God, by saving their own souls and those that hear them. And those to whom they minister spiritual things, are willing to minister to them of their carnal things; so that they *have food to eat, and raiment to put on,* and are content therewith.

A competent provision is likewise made for the wives of married preachers; and an allowance over and above for their little children.

Yet one considerable difficulty lies on those that have boys, when they are grown too big to be under their mother's direction. Having no father to govern and instruct them, they are exposed to a thousand temptations. To remedy this, is one motive that induces us to lay before our friends the present plan, that these little ones may have all the instruction they are capable of, together with all things necessary for the body.

In this view, our college will become one of the noblest charities that can be conceived. How reasonable is the institution? Is it fit that the children of those who leave wife and all that is dear, to save souls from death, should want what is needful either for soul or body? ought we not to supply what the parent cannot, because of his labours in the Gospel? How excellent will be the effect of this institution? The preacher, eased of this weight, can the more cheerfully go on in his labour. And perhaps many of these children may hereafter fill up the place of those that shall *rest from their labours.*

The second object we have in view, is the education and support of poor orphans, and surely we need not enumerate the many happy consequences arising from such a charity. Innumerable blessings concenter in it; not only the *immediate* relief of the objects of our charity, but the ability given them, under the providence of God, to provide for themselves through the remainder of their lives.

The last, though perhaps not the least object in view, is the establishment of a seminary for the children of our competent friends, where learning and religion may go hand in hand: where every advantage may be obtained which may promote the prosperity of the present life, without endangering the morals and religion of the children through those temptations, to which they are too much exposed in most of the public schools. This is an object of importance indeed: and here all the tenderest feelings of the parent's heart range on our side.

But the expence of such an undertaking will be very large: and the best means we could think of at our late conference to accomplish our design was, to desire the assistance of all those in every place, who wish well to the work of God; who long to see sinners converted to God, and the kingdom of Christ set up in all the earth.

All who are thus minded, and more especially our own friends who form our congregations, have an opportunity now of shewing their love to the gospel. Now promote, as far as in you lies, one of the noblest charities in the world. Now forward, as you are able, one of the most excellent designs that ever was set on foot in this country. Do what you can to comfort the parents, who give up their all for you, and to give their children cause to bless you. You will be no poorer for what you do on such an occasion. God is a good pay-master. And you know, in doing this you *lend unto the Lord: in due time he shall repay you.*

THOMAS COKE.
FRANCIS ASBURY.

Baltimore, January 3, 1785.

We have already been favoured with subscriptions, amounting to £1057 17*s.* sterling."

Dr. Coke then went to *Abingdon*, and made some engagements for the land as a scite for the college, and for materials for the building; and the work was begun without delay; and many of our friends gladly assisted, by giving liberally toward the support of the institution.

The college was built on an eminence in Abingdon, and was of the following dimensions, 108 feet in length from east to west, and 40 feet in breadth, from north to south; and stood on the summit and centre of six acres of land.

The house was divided into rooms as follows, at the west end there were two rooms on the lower floor, each 25 by 20. The second and third stories the same. The rooms in the east end were of the same size with those in the west.

In the middle of the lower floor was the college hall, 40 feet square, and over that on the second floor, two school rooms; and on the third floor two bed chambers. At the ends of the hall were places for four sets of stair cases, two at each end, with proper doors opening on the stair cases.

The college was built of brick, and from the top of it there was an extensive prospect, both of the bay, and of the adjacent country. As soon as the house was in order for the school to begin, even before any of the rooms were finished, a few scholars were collected, and a master provided to teach them; but the college was to be opened in form at a future day.

On the 8th, 9th, and 10th days of December 1787, the college was opened, and Mr. Asbury preached each day; the dedication sermon on Sunday from 2 Kings, 4, 40. "O thou man of God, there is death in the pot."

The two superintendants called the college after their own names, *Cokesbury College.*

When the college was built, it was well understood, that the whole management of it was to be under the direction of the conference. But after some years Mr. Asbury consented for it to be incorporated, which was done, and done without the consent of all the conferences. And the trustees who were named in the act of incorporation had the management of the institution among themselves, and the conference was deprived of all the power of making rules or giving orders for the future welfare of the children.

This step was disliked by many of our friends; who from that time concluded that the institution would not prosper. And the business was not well conducted afterwards. On the 4th day of December 1795, the college took fire by some means, but we cannot tell how, and was all burnt down; and the library was consumed with the house.

It was but little upwards of ten years from the time the house was begun, until it was burnt: and there has been no attempt made to rebuild it, from that time till now.

In 1785 we had three conferences. The fourteenth conference was held at Green Hill's, in North-Carolina, on the 20th of April. The fifteenth conference was held at Mr. Mason's, in Brunswick county, in Virginia, on the 1st day of May. The sixteenth conference was held in Baltimore on the 1st day of June.

This was the first time that we had more than one regular conference in the same year. For a few years before this, we had two conferences in the same year, but they were considered only as one, first begun in one place, and adjourned to another. Now there were three, and no adjournment. I have therefore considered the conferences as but one in the year, and have numbered them accordingly; but from this time I shall consider the number of the conferences as I find them in the minutes.

This year, and the two succeeding years, the minutes were called, "Minutes of the General Conference of the Methodist Episcopal Church in America."

The business of the three conferences was all arranged in the minutes as if it had all been done at one time and place. And for the first time we had the annual minutes printed; which practice we have followed ever since.

This year at the three conferences we took in seven new circuits; one was in the state of

Georgia, called *Georgia;* and three were in South-Carolina, by the names of *Charleston, Georgetown,* and *Broad River.* There was one in North Carolina, by the name of *New River;* one in Virginia, called *Lancaster,* and one in Maryland, called *St. Mary's.*

There were three more places taken on our minutes; two of them were in Nova Scotia, *Shelburne,* and *Fort Rosway.* And one called *Antigua,* in the West Indies. The three places last mentioned at that time belonging to the American conference, and for the first we now sent preachers to them.

We admitted twenty-eight young preachers on trial. We had fifty-two circuits in all, and one hundred and two preachers. We added to the society three thousand and twelve members this year; including those in Nova Scotia and in Antigua. The whole number of members was mentioned this year in the minutes, without telling us how many there were in each circuit.

We had three old preachers located this year, namely Samuel Row, James G. Martin, and James Morris. And one was laid aside or expelled, *Le Roy Cole.*

This year, for the first time we gave a short sketch in our annual minutes, of the characters of our preachers who died in the work: which was as follows:

Q. "Who have died this year?"

A. "1. *Caleb B. Peddicord,* a man of sorrows, and like his master, acquainted with grief; but a man dead to the world, and much devoted to God.

"2. *George Mair,* a man of affliction, but of great patience and resignation, and of an excellent understanding."

The form of the minutes of conference was changed this year, and all the *Elders,* who were directed to take the oversight of several circuits, were set to the right hand of a bracket, which inclosed all the circuits and preachers of which he was to take charge.

This may be considered as the beginning of the presiding elder's office; although it was not known by that name at that time; yet, in the absence of a *Superintendant*, this *Elder* had the directing of all the preachers that were inclosed in the bracket against which his name was set.

As soon as the conference in Baltimore was over, Dr. Coke sailed for Europe. The Dr. was much respected in the United States; but he met with some opposition in the south parts of *Virginia*, owing to his imprudent manner of preaching against slavery. No doubt but the Dr. thought at that time he was doing right: but afterwards, when he printed his journal in England, he acknowledged that he was wrong in preaching publicly against slavery in Virginia, where the practice was tolerated by law.

There was a great revival of religion this year in most parts of the connection, both in North and South. On the Eastern Shore of Maryland the work was great, and many souls were brought into the liberty of the children of God.

Some of the new circuits in the south were greatly blessed, and religion prospered among the people very much.

The *Broad River* circuit which we took in this year, was partly formed by James Foster, a local preacher, who had once been in the travelling connection. After he located and lost hie wife, he moved into South-Carolina, and there he preached and laboured among the people for a considerable time, before any travelling preacher went into that part of the country. Several Methodist families had removed from Virginia into those parts, and they united and held their class meetings regularly, and the Lord made it a blessing to some of their neighbours: they then petitioned our conference to send them some travelling preachers; which at last we did, and by taking in the places where the local preacher used to preach, and adding a few more new places, there was a good circuit formed at once.

In 1786, we had three conferences. The seventeenth conference was held at Salisbury in North-Carolina, on the 21st of February. The eighteenth conference was held in Virginia, at Laine's chapel, on the 10th day of April. The nineteenth conference was held at Baltimore on the 8th day of May.

At these conferences we took in five new circuits. Two in South-Carolina, *Santee*, and *Bee Dee*: one in North-Carolina, *Newbern*: one in New-Jersey, called *Newark*: and one in Kentucky, called after the state, *Kentucky*.

We admitted on trial twenty-three young preachers. Seven hundred and ninety-one members were added to the society this year.

Jeremiah Lambert died this year, who was an *Elder*, and had been travelling six years. The year before he died, he was sent to Antigua, in the West Indies; but finding himself declining, he returned to Maryland, where he died. His character is thus stated in the minutes, "A man of sound judgment, clear understanding, good gifts, genuine piety, and very useful, humble and holy: diligent in life, and resigned in death; much esteemed in the connection, and justly lamented.

James Thomas, a young man, died also: he was a pious man, of good gifts; blameless in his life, and much resigned in his death.

William Glendenning, (according to the minutes) desisted from travelling this year. By some means he lost his reason: which his own words will prove.

As his case was rather extraordinary, I will give some account of his stopping, &c. in his own words; taken from a book written by himself, and published in Philadelphia in 1795, entitled, "The life of William Glendenning."

He says in page 11 and 12, "In 1784, I travelled in *Brunswick*, in the state of Virginia, where my mind got more and more darkened, and I lost sight of my reconciled God, and all spiritual comforts departed from me." Page 13, at the christmas conference this year, "They wanted me to go as a missionary to *Nova Scotia*; which I refused with warmth." However, he was proposed for the elder's office, and he says page 14, "I was rejected from the eldership. The reason assigned was, *that I wanted gifts.*" Afterwards, "While Mr. Asbury was at prayer, I felt all light of divine mercy, as in a moment, take it's flight from me. My soul then sunk into the depths of misery and despair." Page 15, "I stopped travelling in the month of June 1785." Page 16, "I staid first at the house of Robert Jones in Sussex county, Virginia."

Page 18, "About the last of November the same year, I was removed to *Leonard Smith's*, in North-Carolina;" page 19, "and in about six weeks I was removed to *John Hargrove's.*" Page 21, "When I would be in the fields, I would for hours together be blaspheming in the most horrid manner."

He wrote to the general conference in 1792, wishing to be united with us, &c. The conference believed him to be beside himself at that time, and would not receive him.

We had fifty-six circuits this year; and one hundred and sixteen travelling preachers, which was a good supply of labourers.

This year we sent preachers to Kentucky for the first time; *James Haw*, and *Benjamin Ogdon* went to that new settled country, and laboured with great success, and were prospered in their endeavours to build up the redeemer's kingdom. They collected a good many societies together in the course of that year; and many people in the Western country will have cause to bless God for the coming of those preachers into that part of the world.

At the conference at Laine's meeting in Virginia, there was a proposal made for preachers to go to Georgia, and if any one felt freedom to offer themselves as missionaries for that service, they were requested to speak: several persons offered, more than could be spared. It was concluded that two only should go, and Thomas Humphris, and John Major were accepted. They went forth in the name of the Lord, and were made a blessing to many of the inhabitants of Georgia. They formed a circuit up and down the Savannah river and round by Little river, and the town of Washington, and in the course of that year they collected together and joined into society four hundred and fifty members. Mr. Major continued in Georgia about two years, and died in peace.

This was a prosperous year with our societies; many were added to us, and joined among us; and the work of the Lord revived in general where we laboured, and in some places, souls were gathered in by scores. Many of the old christians took a fresh start, and the holy fire kindled and spread from heart to heart.

CHAPTER VI.

From the begining of 1787, to the end of 1791, the year in which Mr. John Wesley died.

In 1787, we had three conferences. The twentieth conference was held at Salisbury in North-Carolina on the 17th day of March. The twenty-first conference was held at Rough Creek church in Virginia, on the 19th day of April. The twenty-second conference was held at Baltimore on the 1st day of May.

At these conferences we took in ten new circuits: one in Georgia; the old circuit being divided, and the name changed, the divisions were now called *Burk* and *Augusta*. We took in two in South-Carolina, *Cainhoy* and *Edistò*. In Virginia we took in *Greenbrier*, *Bath* and *Ohio*. We also took in *Clarksburg*, *Nolachuckie* and *Cumberland*. In New York state, we took in *New Rochelle*.

We admitted on trial thirty-four young preachers; and added to the society 7082 members, according to the minutes; but strictly speaking, we had an increase of 8592 members. In our minutes for the past year we had taken in the numbers from Nova Scotia and Antigua; but this year we left them off, and did not take them into the numbers; and they amounted to 1510. This year for the first time the numbers in society were taken in each state separately.

We had now sixty-five circuits in the United States, and 131 travelling preachers.

At the Baltimore conference the preachers complained of Dr. Coke, because he had taken upon himself a right which they never gave him, of altering the time and place of holding our conferences, after it had been settled and fixed on at the previous conference. Another complaint was brought against him for writing improper letters to some of our preachers, such as were calculated to stir up strife and contention among them.

At that time the Dr. saw that the preachers were pretty generally united against him; he acknowledged his faults, begged pardon, and promised not to meddle with our affairs again when he was out of the United States. He then gave in writing a certificate to the same purpose, which is as follows:

" The certificate of Dr. Coke to the conference.

" I do solemnly engage by this instrument, that I never will, by virtue of my office, as superintendant of the Methodist church, during my absence from the United States of America, exercise any government whatever in the said Methodist church during my absence from the United States. And I do also engage, that I will exercise no privilege in the said church when present in the United States, except that of ordaining according to the regulations and law, already existing or hereafter to be made in the said church, and that of presiding when present in conference, and lastly that of travelling at large. Given under my hand the second day of May in the year 1787.

Witnesses, THOMAS COKE."

John Tunnil,
John Hagerty,
Nelson Reed.

The preachers then agreed to forgive what was past, provided this condition should be expressed in the minutes; which was done thus:

Q. " Who are the superintendants of our church for the United States ?"

A. "Thomas Coke (when present in the states) and Francis Asbury."

At this conference it was agreed, that no married preacher should demand more money than the allowance for himself and his wife.

In the month of April this year, Mr. Freeborn Garrettson left Nova-Scotia, and returned to the United States; and from that time he has continued in his own native country. Mr. Wesley had given directions for brother F. Garrettson to be ordained a superintendant for Nova Scotia; but when the business was taken under consideration, some of the preachers insisted that if he was ordained for that station, he should confine himself wholly to that place for which he was set apart; and not be at liberty to return again to this part of the country. Mr. Garrettson did not feel freedom to enter into an obligation of that kind, and chose rather to continue as he was; and therefore was not ordained.

Mr. Wesley also directed that Richard Whatcoat should be ordained a joint superintendant with Mr. Asbury. When this business was brought before the conference, most of the preachers objected, and would not consent to it. The reasons against it were, 1, That he was not qualified to take the charge of the connection. 2. That they were apprehensive that if Mr. Whatcoat was ordained, Mr. Wesley would likely recall Mr. Asbury, and he would return to *England*.

Dr. Coke contended that we were obliged to receive Mr. Whatcoat, because we had said in the minutes taken at the Christmas conference, when we were first formed into a church in 1784, "During the life of the Rev. Mr. Wesley, we acknowledge ourselves his sons in the gospel, ready in matters belonging to church government, to obey his commands."

Many of the members of that conference argued that they were not at the conference when that engagement was entered into, and they did not consider themselves bound by it. Other preachers who had said they were "Ready to obey his commands," said they did not feel ready *now* to obey his command. The preachers at last agreed to depart from that engagement which some of the elder brethren had formerly entered into, and in the next printed minutes, that engagement was left out.

They had made the engagement of their own accord, and among themselves, and they believed they had a right to depart therefrom, when they pleased, seeing it was not a contract made with Mr. Wesley, or any other person, but an agreement among themselves. It was further argued, that Mr Wesley while in England, could not tell what man was qualified to govern us, as well as we could who were present, and were to be governed. We believed also, that if Mr. Wesley was here himself, he would be of the same opinion with us.

We then wrote a long and loving letter to Mr. Wesley, and requested him to come over to America and visit his spiritual children.

This step of receding from the above engagement, was afterwards considered by some disaffected persons, as improper. If there was any thing improper in the business, it was in entering into the engagement, and not in departing from it.

In the course of this year Mr. Asbury reprinted the general minutes; but in a different form from what they were before. The title of this pamphlet was as follows:

"A form of discipline for the ministers, preachers, and members of the Methodist Episcopal Church in America; considered and approved at a conference held at Baltimore, in the state of Maryland, on Monday the 27th day of December, 1784. In which the Reverend Thomas Coke, L. L. D. and the Reverend Francis Asbury, presided. Arranged under proper heads, and methodized in a more acceptable and easy manner."

In this discipline there were thirty-one sections, and sixty-three questions, with answers to them all.

The third question in the second section, and the answer, read thus.

Q. Is there any other business to be done in conference?

A. The electing and ordaining of Bishops, Elders and Deacons.

This was the first time that our Superintendants ever gave themselves the title of Bishops in the minutes. They changed the title themselves without the consent of the conference; and at the next conference they asked the preachers if the word *Bishop* might stand in the minutes; seeing that it was a scripture name, and the meaning of the word *Bishop*, was the same with that of *Superintendant.*

Some of the preachers opposed the alteration, and wished to retain the former title; but a majority of the preachers agreed to let the word *Bishop* remain; and in the annual minutes for the next year the first question is, "Who are the bishops of our church for the United States?"

In the third section of this form of discipline, and in the sixth page, it is said, "We have constituted ourselves into an *Episcopal Church,* under the direction of *bishops, elders, deacons* and *preachers,* according to the form of ordination annexed to our prayer book, and the regulations laid down in this form of discipline. From that time the name of bishop has been in common use among us, both in conversation, and in writing.

The last SECTION is as follows, "As it has been frequently recommended by the preachers and people, that such books as are wanted, be printed in this country, we therefore propose,

1. That the advice of the conference shall be desired concerning any valuable impression, and their consent be obtained before any steps be taken for the printing thereof.

2. That the profits of the books, after all the necessary expences are defrayed, shall be applied, according to the discretion of the conference, towards the college, the preachers' fund, the deficiencies of the preachers, the distant missions, or the debts on our churches."

From that time we began to print more of our own books in the United States than we had ever done before; and the principal part of the printing business was carried on in *New-York.*

We had a remarkable revival of religion this year. The heavenly flame spread greatly in various directions. Such a time for the awakening and conversion of sinners was never seen before among the Methodists in America. The greatest revival was in the south parts of Virginia, which began in July, and continued to prosper throughout the year.

There was a remarkable revival of religion in the town of *Petersburg*, and many of the inhabitants were savingly converted; and the old christians greatly revived. That town never witnessed before or since such wonderful displays of the presence and love of God in the salvation of immortal souls. Prayer meetings were frequently held both in the town and in the country, and souls were frequently converted at those meetings, even when there was no preacher present; for the prayers and exhortations of the members were greatly owned of the Lord.

The most remarkable work of all was in Sussex, and Brunswick circuits, where the meetings would frequently continue for five or six hours together, and some times all night.

At one quarterly meeting held at Mabry's chapel in Brunswick circuit, on the 25th and 26th of July, the power of God was among the people in an extraordinary manner: some hundreds were awakened; and it was supposed that above one hundred souls were converted at that meeting which continued for two days, i. e. on Thursday and Friday. Some thousands of people attended meeting at that place on that occasion.

The next quarterly-meeting was held at *Jones's* chapel in *Sussex* county, on Saturday and Sunday the 27th and 28th of July. This meeting was favoured with more of the divine presence than any other that had been known before. The sight of the mourners was enough to penetrate the most careless heart. The divine power was felt among the people before the preachers came together. Many of the young converts from the quarterly meeting that had been held two days before at Mabry's, had come together, and uniting with other christians in singing and praying, the heavenly fire had began to kindle, and the flame of love and holy zeal was spreading among the people, which caused them to break out in loud praises to God. Some when they met would hang on each other, or embrace each other in their arms, and weep aloud, and praise the Lord with all their might. The sight of those who were thus overwhelmed with the love and presence of God, would cause sinners to weep and tremble before the Lord.

By the time the preachers came within half a mile of the chapel, they heard the people shouting and praising God. When they came up they found numbers weeping, both in the chapel and in the open air. Some were on the ground crying for mercy, and others in extacies of joy.

The preachers went among the mourners and encouraged them and prayed with them. The private christians did the same. Some were lying and struggling as if they were in the agonies of death, others lay as if they were dead. Hundreds of the believers were so overcome with the power of God that they fell down, and lay helpless on the floor, or the ground; and some of them continued in that helpless condition for a considerable time, and were happy in God beyond description. When they came to themselves, it was generally with loud praises to God, and with tears and expressions, enough to melt the hardest heart. The oldest saints had never before seen such a time of love, and such displays of the power of God.

The next day the society met early, in order to receive the Lord's supper.

While the society was collected in the house, some of the preachers went into the woods to preach, and while they were preaching the power of the Lord was felt among the people in such a manner, that they roared and screamed so loud that the preacher could not be heard, and he was compelled to stop. Many scores of both white and black people fell to the earth; and some lay in the deepest distress until the evening. Many of the wealthy people, both men and women, were seen lying in the dust, sweating and rolling on the ground, in their fine broad cloths or silks, crying for mercy.

As night drew on the mourners were collected

together, and many of them were in the most awful distress, and uttered such doleful lamentations that it was frightful to behold them, and enough to affect the most stubborn-hearted sinner. But many of these were filled with the peace and love of God in a moment, and rising up would clap their hands and praise God aloud. It was then as pleasing as it had before been awful to behold them.

Many of these people who were happily converted, left their houses and came to the meeting with great opposition to the work of God; but were struck down in an unexpected manner, and converted in a few hours. So mightily did the Lord work, that a great change was wrought in a little time.

Soon after this, some of the same preachers who had been at the quarterly-meetings mentioned above, held a meeting at Mr. F. Bonners, ten miles from *Petersburg*, where a large concourse of people were assembled; and the Lord wrought wonders among them on that day. As many as fifty persons professed to get converted at that time before the meeting closed. The cries of distressed sinners under conviction, and the shouts of happy christians were heard afar off. Some that were careless spectators in the begining of the meeting, were happily converted before the meeting ended and went home rejoicing in God, knowing that he had forgiven their sins.

They had another meeting at *Jones-Hole* church; about twelve miles from *Petersburg*, and many people assembled. They began to sing and exhort each other before the preachers came, and the Lord wrought among them, and many were crying for mercy. The preacher began to preach, but it was with difficulty that he could keep the people quiet enough to hear him at all. The old christians were all alive to God, and the young converts were so happy that they could not well hold their peace, but were ready to break out in loud praises to God. They kept in for a while; but toward the close of the sermon some of them broke out in strains of praise: the flame spread immediately thro' the whole house, and hundreds were deeply affected. Some prayed as if they were going to take the kingdom by violence: others cried for mercy as if they were dropping into eternal misery; and some praised God with all their strength, till they dropt down helpless on the floor.

The poor awakened sinners were wrestling with the Lord for mercy in every direction, some on their knees, others lying in the arms of their friends, and others stretched on the floor, not able to stand, and some were convulsed, with every limb as stiff as a stick. In the midst of this work several sleepers of the house broke down at once, which made a very loud noise; and the floor sunk down considerably; but the people paid but little or no attention to it, and many of them knew nothing of it, for no one was hurt. On that day many souls were brought into the liberty of God's children. Sinners were struck with amazement, at seeing so many of their relations and neighbours converted, and few of them were left without some good desires to be converted themselves.

The great revival of religion in 1776, which spread extensively through the south part of Virginia, exceeded any thing of the kind that had ever been known before in that part of the country. But the revival this year, far exceeded it.

It was thought, that in the course of that summer, there were as many as sixteen hundred souls converted in *Sussex* circuit; in *Brunswick* circuit about eighteen hundred; and in *Amelia* circuit about eight hundred. In these three circuits we had the greatest revival of religion; but in many other circuits there was a gracious work, and hundreds were brought to God in the course of that year. To give a full description of that remarkable outpouring of the Spirit, would exceed the bounds of this history. I have only given a short sketch of a few meetings. There were many other meetings not much inferior to those I have noticed. But the work was not confined to meetings for preaching; at prayer-meetings the work prospered and many souls were born again; and the meetings often continued all night without intermission. In class meetings the Lord frequently set the mourning souls at liberty. It was common to hear of souls being brought to God while at work in their houses, or in their fields. It was often the case that the people in their corn-fields, white people, or black, and sometimes both together would begin to sing, and being affected would begin to pray, and others would join with them, and they would continue their cries till some of them would find peace to their souls. Some account of this work was published in the news-papers at different times, and by that means spread all through the United States.

In 1788 we had seven conferences. The twenty-third conference was held in *Charleston* on the 12th of March.

The twenty fourth in *Georgia*, on the 9th of April.

The twenty-fifth at *Holstein*, on the 13th of May.

The twenty-sixth in *Petersburg* in Virginia, on the 17th of June.*

* This conference was appointed at Benjamin Crawley's, in

The twenty-seventh at Beeson Town, on the 22d of July.

The twenty-eighth at Baltimore, on the 9th of September.

The twenty-ninth in Philadelphia, on the 25th of September.

At these conferences we took in nineteen new circuits. In Georgia we took in one. The circuit that was formerly called Augusta was divided, and the lower part was now called Richmond, and the upper part *Washington.*

In South Carolina we took in *Seleuda* and *Waxsaws* circuits. In North Carolina we took in one called *Anson* ; and we took in two among the mountains, called *French Broad*, and *West New River*. In Virginia we took in below the mountains, *Buckingham*, *Gloucester*, and *Rockingham*. In Maryland, we took in *Annapolis*, *Harford* and *Cecil*. In Pennsylvania, we took in *Bristol* and *Pittsburg*. In New-York state, we took in *Dutchess*, *Shoreham*, *New City*, *Cambridge*, and *Lake Champlain.*

Some of these circuits had been taken off from the old circuits, which had been enlarged till there was room for more preachers, and then by dividing them we made two circuits out of one. But the most of them were formed where there had been none before ; and where there had been but little if any preaching by the Methodists till the present year.

We admitted on trial fifty-two young preachers. We added 11481 members to the society. By the following statement it may be seen in what part of the United States the work of God

Amelia county, but by some means he lost his reason, and the conference could not meet at his house, and were under the necessity of meeting in the town of Petersburg.

was most prosperous. The increase this year in the different states is as folows :

777 in the state of Georgia,
704 in South Carolina,
955 in North Carolina,
4761 in Virginia and Kentucky,
2475 in Maryland,
544 in Delaware and Pennsylvania,
404 in New Jersey, and
861 in New York state.

11481

This year the circuits were for the first time numbered in the minutes, and there were eighty-five. We had one hundred and sixty-five travelling preachers, which was a good supply for the circuits. We had other invitations from different parts of the country to send them preachers to labour among them ; but we were not able to answer all the demands of the people ; yet we increased and enlarged our borders greatly.

When the minutes for this year were printed, the condition of Dr. Coke's being a bishop "when in the United States," was left out, and the question was changed, and was entered thus:

Q. "*Who are the bishops of our church for the United States ?*

A. " Thomas Coke and Francis Asbury."

Two questions in the minutes were changed this year : one read thus.

Q. *Who desist from travelling with, and under the direction of our conferences?*

A. Enoch Mattson, Adam Cloud and Thomas Chew.

These three preachers were considered as being expelled from our connection, for improper conduct, though they were entered as desisting from travelling with us. Neither of these preachers came to trial to have a proper hearing. It was thought best to enter them in this manner, and let it be understood both by our preachers and people, that they were cast off from us.

The other question was altered, and stands thus:

Q. *What preachers have a partial location on account of their families, and are subject to the order of conference?*

A. Caleb Boyer, Samuel Dudley, William Cannon, Joseph Wyatt, Michael Ellis, and Ignatius Pigman.

Four preachers died this year. 1. Thomas Curtis, whose character was entered thus, "Upright in life, successful in his labours, and triumphant in his death; about seven years in the ministry."

2. "John Major, a simple hearted man, a living, loving soul, who died as he lived, full of faith, and of the holy ghost; ten years in the work, useful and blameless."

Mr. Major was from Virginia, and was one of the first missionaries that we sent to the state of Georgia. His abilities as a preacher were but small; but in exhortation he was powerful and pathetic; what he lacked in words, he generally made up in tears. Sometimes he wept from the beginning to the end of his discourse. He was often called the "Weeping Prophet." He was a useful preacher. When he left Virginia to go to Georgia, he wept much; after spending almost two years in Georgia, he closed his useful life some distance above Augusta, and not far from Savannah River.

3. "Woolman Hickson, of promising genius, and considerable preaching abilities; upright in life, but soon snatched away from the work by a consumption, and in the midst of his usefulness:

seven years in the work." His last labours were mostly in the country, a small distance from New York, and on the east side of the North River. He then returned to the city of New York, and died; and was buried in the city.

4. "Elijah Ellis, a deacon, four years in the work; steady, solid, humble, diligent and faithful; who spent himself in the work of God, in Lancaster."

From this conference in 1788, Mr. Freeborn Garrettson was appointed presiding elder of the district north of the city of New-York, including all the circuits from *New Rochelle* to *Lake Champlain*. His labours, and the labours of those preachers who travelled under his direction, were greatly prospered, and many souls were brought to the knowledge of God by their ministry.—Hundreds and thousands of people in the new circuits in that district, will have cause to be thankful for the gospel truths that were disseminated among them in the course of that year. Many were awakened, and many were converted; and old professors much revived.

The revivals of religion this year were great in many places. The revival in the south parts of Virginia in the latter part of the past year exceeded any thing of the kind that had ever been known in those parts, and indeed, it has never since been equalled. But the work this year was more extensive, though not as great in any one place. In many parts of Virginia and North Carolina, souls were coming home to God so frequently, that it was no strange thing to hear of people's being converted; and frequently many of them at the same meeting.

There was a blessed revival of religion in many circuits in Maryland, both on the Eastern and Western shores. In Baltimore town and circuit the revival was great, and about 300 joined the society.

The work of God greatly increased in Baltimore town in the course of the summer 1788, which was partly owing to a plan that was adopted, of preaching on the common, or in the Market-house on Howard's-hill, every Sunday in the afternoon, after the public service was ended in all the churches. By this means we had thousands to hear us, who did not usually attend our meeting. Many persons had been converted in town before the conference came on in September.

During the time of the conference, we were highly favoured of the Lord, and souls were awakened, and converted. On Sunday the 14th of September at 3 o'clock in the afternoon, Mr. Asbury preached in Mr. Otterbein's church; and the people were generally solemn and much affected; he then asked another preacher to pray and conclude: and whilst he was praying, an awful power was felt among the people. Some of them cried out aloud. The preachers went among them and encouraged the mourners to look to the Lord, and prayed with them; and in a little time there was such a noise among them, that many of the christian people were measurably frightened, and as there was no opportuny for them to escape at the door, many of them went out at the windows, hastening to their homes. The noise had alarmed hundreds of people who were not at the meeting, and they came running to see what was the matter, till the house was crouded, and surrounded with a wondering multitude. In a short time some of the mourners lost the use of their limbs, and lay helpless on the floor, or in the arms of their friends. It was not long before some of them were converted, and rose up with streaming eyes giving glory to God that he had taken away their sins. This meeting continued about two hours and a half, after the sermon was ended; in which time about twenty persons professed to be converted. This day of the Lord's power will never be forgotten by many who were present.

There were about 20 persons more who were converted in the course of that week, and the heavenly flame began to spread through the town pretty generally; and many of the people began to enquire the way to heaven, with their faces thitherward.

The Sunday following there was preaching in the Market house on Howard's-hill, at 5 o'clock, where some thousands of people attended. The presence and power of God was wonderfully displayed among the people, and hundreds were bathed in tears. We afterwards found out 15 persons that were awakened and brought to the knowledge of the truth by that sermon. From that time the revival of religion became more general in Baltimore.

Some of the young men in Cokesbury college were also stirred up to seek religion.

The preachers were uncommonly zealous; but none of them so much and so heartily engaged as the preachers in the South parts of the connection; where the greatest displays of the divine presence had been made manifest. Yet in every place the preachers were encouraged, and their expectations were raised, and they were looking out for greater depths of grace in themselves, and in their hearers. And the Lord gave them seals to thier ministry, and souls for their hire.

In 1789 we had eleven confeaences, which were as follows.

The thirtieth conference was held in Georgia on the 9th of March.

The thirty-first in Charleston, on the 17th of March.

The thirty-second at M'Knight's meeting house, on the Yadkin river, in North Carolina, on the 11th of April

The thirty-third in Petersburg, on the 18th of April.

The thirty-fourth at Leesburg, on the 28th of April.

The thirty-fifth in Baltimore, on the 4th of May.

The thirty-sixth at Cokesbury, on the 9th of May.

The thirty-seventh at Chestertown, on the 13th of May.

The thirty-eighth at Philadelphia, on the 18th of May.

The thirty-ninth at Trenton, New-Jersey, on the 23d of May.

The fortieth in New York, on the 28th of May.

Several of these conferences were within thirty or forty miles of each other; which was pretty generally disliked; but at that time the bishop had the right of appointing as many conferences as he thought proper, and at such times and places as he judged best; but since then, the general conference fixes the number of annual conferences to be held in each year, having appointed the bounds of each of them.

At these conferences we took in fourteen new circuits and stations. In South Carolina two, one was called *Bush River*, and the other *Little Pee Dee*. In North Carolina one called *Pamlico*. In Virginia two, *Greensville* and *Bottetourt*. In Maryland, *Baltimore Town*, which was separated from the Baltimore circuit, and for the first time had a preacher stationed in the town. In Delaware, *Wilmington*, a station, and a new circuit, called *Milford*. In New Jersey one circuit was divided, the new part was called *Burlington*. In New-York state we had four new circuits, *Newburg*, *Columbia*, *Coeman's Patent*, and *Schenectady*. We had one new circuit in Connecticut, called *Stamford*, which was the first that was ever formed in that state, or in any of the New England States. It was my lot to go to that circuit alone, and to labour by myself. Another preacher was appointed to the circuit with me, but he failed and never came, and I had to labour and suffer alone amongst a strange people.

We admitted forty five young preachers on trial this year: we had ninety-seven circuits, and added to the society 5911 members which was a great increase.

As some persons had complained of our receding from a former engagement made by some of our preachers, that "during the life of Mr. Wesley in matters belonging to Church government they would obey his commands," and as others had thought that we did not pay as much respect to Mr. Wesley as we ought; the bishops introduced a question in the annual minutes which was as follows:

Q. *Who are the persons that exercise the Episcopal office in the Methodist church in Europe and America?*

A. John Wesley, Thomas Coke and Francis Asbury, by regular order and succession.

The next question was asked differently from what it had ever been in any of the former minutes, which stands thus:

Q. *Who have been elected by the unanimous suffrages of the general conference, to superintend the Methodist connection in America?*

A. Thomas Coke, and Francis Asbury

Five of our travelling preachers died this year, namely, Henry Bingham, William Gill, John Cooper, James White, and Francis Spry.

The character given of William Gill in the minutes was, "A native of Delaware, an elder in the church, and a labourer in it for about twelve years; blameless in life, of quick and solid parts, sound in the faith, clear in his judgment, meek in his spirit, resigned and solemnly happy in his death."

From the long acquaintance I had with Mr. Gill, and knowing his public and private worth, I am led to conclude, that we had scarcely a preacher left among us to equal the deceased, either in knowledge or in goodness. Indeed, I knew of no one who had such a depth of knowledge, both of men and things, as he possessed. His company was agreeable and his conversation entertaining: his public preaching was with wisdom and animation; and he proved the goodness of his doctrine by the goodness of his life.

In the latter part of the minutes for this year, we had the following explanation of a certain rule, about which there had been some uneasiness among some of our local preachers, and private members.

"As a very few persons have in some respect, mistaken our meaning, in the 32d section of our form of discipline, on bringing to trial disorderly persons, &c.—we think it necessary to explain it.

"When a member of our society is to be tried for any offence, the officiating minister or preacher is to call together all the members, if the society be small, or a select number if it be large, to take knowledge and give advice, and bear witness to the justice of the whole process; that improper and private expulsions may be prevented for the future."

In the course of this year we had the fifth edition of our form of discipline published, and circulated throughout our connection, containing 35 sections, and 69 questions and answers. Also, the articles of religion; the scripture doctrine of predestination, election and reprobation: Serious thoughts on the *infallible, unconditional perseverance of all that have once experienced faith in Christ*, and a plain account of Christian Perfection. All these pieces were bound together in one volume.

In this edition, we had some new regulations about the trial of private members for improper conduct. The substance of which is as follows:

"If the accused person be found guilty, and the crime be such as is expressly forbidden by the word of God, sufficient to exclude a person from the kingdom of grace and glory, and to make him a subject of wrath and hell, let him be expelled. If he evade a trial by absenting himself after sufficient notice given him, and the circumstances of the accusation be strong and presumptive, let him be esteemed as guilty, and accordingly excluded."

"But in cases of neglect of duties of any kind, imprudent conduct, indulging sinful tempers or words, disobedience to the order and discipline of the church: First, let private reproof be given by a leader or preacher; if there be an acknowledgementof the fault and proper humiliation, the person may remain on trial, &c. If there be a murmur or complaint that justice is not done, the person shall be allowed an appeal to the quarterly meeting, and have his case reconsidered before the preachers, stewards and leaders who are present. After such forms of trial and expulsion, such persons as are thus excommunicated, shall have no privilege of society and sacrament in our church."

This rule for trying private members has been altered since in a few points; but the most of these regulations have continued, and been in force from that day till the present.

We had also this N. B. "From this time forward no person shall be owned as a member of onr church, without six months trial."

This rule continues in force still, and all our members are considered on trial for six months; during which time, if they wish to leave us, they may do it without any form of trial; and if we are dissatisfied with their conduct, we may cast them off without calling them to trial.

At the conference this year, the bishops proposed a new plan for directing our letters to each other, which was to this effect, that we should leave out the word reverend, and say "To A. B. Bi, shop, Elder, Deacon or Preacher." Many of the preachers adopted the plan; but others who did not favour the alteration, directed as they pleased or as they had formerly done.

In the course of this year religion was pretty lively and prosperous in our societies, and in some places it was very remarkable. In Baltimore town it exceeded any thing that had ever been known in that place. I will just mention a particular time of refreshing from the presence of the Lord. At a quarterly meeting held in Baltimore on the 8th and 9th of August, 1789, and during the following week, the kingdom of Satan suffered great loss. The first day of the quarterly meeting was profitable to numbers: many cried and wept bitterly for mercy, and some souls were born of God. Sunday, the second day, was most awful and glorious. In the love feast at eight in the morning, the society enjoyed a little Penteeost, and dwelt as it were in the suburbs of heaven. The presence of God was awfully felt, while the people one after another feelingly declared *what God had done for their souls.*

In public preaching, the word was so accompanied by the energy of the holy Ghost, that there were few but felt it's mighty power. Some of the greatest revilers of the work were constrained to tremble and weep. The congregation broke up on Sunday night very late, after many had been converted. Some were two, three or four hours on their knees, others were prostrate on the floor, most earnestly agonizing for mercy, till they could rejoice in God their Saviour. What power! What awe rested on the people!

Some, after they went home, could not sleep, but wept and prayed all night. The next day was such a time as cannot be sufficiently described.

Early in the morning, a preacher was sent for to visit a young woman, who was under conviction. He exhorted her to believe in the Lord Jesus, and then sung and prayed with her.

A considerable number of the members of society were collected to supplicate the throne of grace in her behalf. At last the Lord suddenly shed abroad his love in her heart, so that she lifted up her voice with others in loud praises to God.

This was only a small part of that day's work. About ten in the morning, a company of mourners assembled together at a private house, where the work of conversion began. First one, and then another, entered into the liberty of the children of God. The news spread; the people collected till the house and street were filled with a croud of believers, and a wondering multitude: and this continued without intermission till night. They then repaired to the church which was presently filled, and they continued there until two o'clock the next morning before they broke up.

Some, who came there quite careless, and indeed making derision of the whole, were converted before they returned. Many hard-hearted opposers were conquered at last, and earnestly sought salvation.

At the same time the country circuits throughout *Maryland*, seemed to flame with holy love. On the Eastern Shore there was a powerful work; hundreds in different parts were turning to God.

As this year was the beginning of Methodism in the New England states, and as the first circuit was now formed, it will be necessary to speak a little of that part of the work.

I myself began the new circuit at Norwalk, in Connecticut, on the 17th of June 1789, which was the first Methodist sermon that was ever preached in that place. No house could be procured to preach in; every person was afraid to give liberty. I then went into the street, and began to sing, and then prayed and preached, to a decent congregation. On the 21st of June I preached for the first time in the city of New-Haven, to as many people as could croud into the court-house.

This new circuit took in Norwalk, Fairfield, Stratford, Milford, New-Haven, Derbey, New-town, Reading, Danbury, and Canaan; with several other places within the same bounds. Many people flocked to hear the word, and sometimes they felt it. But men and women were so fond of disputation about peculiar sentiments, that they seldom left the place after preaching, without having some dispute with the preacher.

The first society that was formed in that circuit, was in Stratfield, on the 26th day of September, and there were only three women that joined; and they remained alone for some months before any one else united with them. The next class that was formed, was in Reading, on the 28th day of December. There were only two, one man, and one woman, that joined at first. It was some months after before any other person joined with them. At length the society increased, and religion revived. Aaron Sanford, the first man that joined, became a preacher; his brother also, and a lawyer, (Samuel S. Smith) joined with them and became preachers; and then another of the society began to preach. Though they were few and feeble in the beginning, they at last became a flourishing society, and four preachers were raised up among themselves.

This circuit was first called Stamford, since then it is called *Reading*.

The first Methodist meeting house that was ever built in New England, was in this circuit, near the upper edge of Stratfield, and is now called *Lee's Chapel*.

On the 27th day of February 1790, three preachers came to my help from Maryland, namely, Jacob Brush, an *Elder*, George Roberts, and Daniel Smith, young preachers. They met me at a quarterly meeting at a place called *Dantown*, on the state line between New-York and Connecticut. Their presence was reviving to the brethren, and to me in particular. On Sunday preaching was in a new unfinished dwelling house. In the time of preaching the Lord visited the people in mercy; and a great cry was raised among them, such as was not common in that part of the world. The people were alarmed; some ran out of the house, others that were above in the loft, ran to the end of the house and jumped out on the ground. In the midst of all the confusion, the christians were exceedingly happy.

At these conferences in 1789, a plan was laid for the holding a *Council*. The Bishops said, they had made it a matter of prayer; and they believed the present plan was the best that they could think of.

After some opposition had been made to the plan, and there had been some debating about it, a majority of the preachers agreed to the following plan; which was published in the annual minutes.

Q. "*Whereas the holding of general conferences on this extensive Continent would be attended with a variety of difficulties, and many inconveniencies to the work of God; and whereas we judge it expedient that a council should be formed of chosen men out of the several districts as representatives of the whole connection, to meet at stated times; in what manner is this council to be formed, what shall be it's powers, and what further regulations shall be made concerning it?*"

A. 1st. "Our bishops and presiding elders shall be the members of this council; provided, that the members who form the council be never fewer than nine. And if any unavoidable circumstance prevent the attendance of a presiding elder at the council, he shall have authority to send another elder out of his own district to represent him; but the elder so sent by the absenting presiding elder, shall have no seat in the council without the approbation of the bishop or bishops, and presiding elders present. And if, after the above mentioned provisions are complied with, any unavoidable circumstance, or any contingencies reduce the number to less than nine, the bishop shall immediately summon such elders as do not preside, to complete the number.

2dly. " These shall have authority to mature every thing they shall judge expedient. 1. To preserve the general union: 2. To render and preserve the external form of worship similar in all our societies through the continent: 3. To preserve the essentials of the Methodist doctrines and discipline pure and uncorrupted: 4. To correct all abuses and disorders: And, lastly, they are authorized to mature every thing they may see necessary for the good of the church, and for the promoting and improving our colleges and plan of education.

3dly. " Provided nevertheless, that nothing shall be received as the resolution of the council, unless it be assented to unanimously by the council; and nothing so assented to by the council, shall be binding in any district, till it has been agreed upon by a majority of the conference which is held for that district.

4thly. " The bishops shall have authority to summon the council to meet at such times and places as they shall judge expedient.

5thly. " The first council shall be held at *Cokesbury*, on the first day of next December."

This plan for having a council, was entirely new, and exceedingly dangerous. A majority of the preachers voted in favour of it, but they were soon sensible, that the plan would not answer the purpose for which it was intended. The council was to be composed of the bishops, and the presiding elders: the presiding elders were appointed, changed, and put out of office by the bishop, and just when he pleased; of course, the whole of the council were to consist of the bishops, and a few other men of their own choice or appointing.

One dangerous clause in the plan was this: "Nothing unanimously assented to by the Council, shall be binding in any district, till it has been agreed upon by a majority of the conference, which is held for that district." If then, one district should agree to any important point, and another district should reject it; the union between the two districts would be broken: and in process of time our *United Societies* would be thrown into disorder and confusion. This I saw clearly, when the plan was first proposed; and to which I then objected.

In the latter part of this year, the council met according to appointment; but not at the place where they were to meet. The annual minutes said they should meet at *Cokesbury*. But they met in *Baltimore*.

I will here transcribe the whole of the minutes of the council.

"The *Proceedings* of the *Bishop* and *Presiding Elders* of the *Methodist Episcopal Church*, in *Council assembled*, at *Baltimore*, on the first day of December, 1789."

The following members which formed the Council were present.

FRANCIS ASBURY, *Bishop*.

Elders.

Richard Ivey,	Nelson Reed,
Reuben Ellis,	Joseph Everitt,
Edward Morris,	John Dickins,
James O'Kelly,	James O. Cromwell,
Philip Bruce,	Freeborn Garrettson.
Lemuel Green,	

After having spent one hour in prayer to ALMIGHTY GOD, for his direction and blessing, they then unanimously agreed, that a general conference of the bishop, ministers and preachers of the Methodist Episcopal church, on the continent of *America*, would be attended with a variety of difficulties, with great expence and loss of time, as well as many inconveniences to the work of God. And, as it is almost the unanimous judgment of the ministers and preachers that it is highly expedient there should be a general council formed of the most experienced elders in the connection; who, for the future, being elected by ballot in every conference, at the request of the bishop, shall be able to represent the several conferences and districts in the United States of *America*: they therefore concluded that such a council should be so appointed and convened.

The council then proceeded to form the following constitution, to wit:

The aforesaid council, when assembled at the time and place appointed by the Bishop, shall have power to mature and resolve on all things relative to the spiritual and temporal interests of the church, viz.

1. To render the time and form of public worship, as similar as possible through all their congregations.

2. To preserve the general union of the ministers, preachers and people in the Methodist doctrine and discipline.

3. To direct and manage all the printing which may be done, from time to time, for the use and benefit of the Methodist church in *America*.

4. To conduct the plan of education, and manage all matters, which may, from time to time, pertain to any college or houses built, or about to be built, as the property of the Methodist connection.

5. To remove, or receive and appoint the salary of, any tutors, from time to time employed in any seminary of learning belonging to the said connection.

6. In the intervals of the council, the bishop shall have power to act in all contingent occurrences relative to the printing business, or the education and economy of the college.

7. Nine members, and no less, shall be competent to form a council which may proceed to business.

8. No resolution shall be formed in such a council, without the consent of the bishop and two thirds of the members present.

After the council had finished the constitution as above, they then proceeded, with perfect unanimity, to form the following resolutions.

1. *Every* resolution of the first council shall be put to vote in each conference, and shall not be adopted unless it obtains a majority of the different conferences. But every resolution which is received by a majority of the several conferences, shall be received by every member of each conference.

2. *Public* worship shall commence at 10 o'clock on the Lord's day, in all places where we have societies and regular preaching, if it be practicable, and if it be not, at 11 o'clock.

3. The exercise of public worship on the Lord's day, shall be singing, prayer, and reading the Holy Scriptures, with exhortation or reading a sermon, in the absence of a preacher; and the officiating person shall be appointed by the elder, deacon, or travelling preacher, for the time being.

4. *For the future* no more houses shall be built for public worship, without the consent and direction of the conference and presiding elder of

the district; unless a house should be built under the direction of the presiding elder and the travelling preachers in the circuit, and finished without the least debt remaining on it.

5. It is required, that all the parents and guardians of independent scholars in *Cokesbury* college, may punctually pay for the students' tuition and board, on or before the first day of *December*, in every year; as none will be continued there more than one year, on credit, but will be immediately sent home, in case of non-payment. And for the future, at least one fourth of the price of twelve months board and tuition must be sent with every scholar, who comes from the adjacent states; and half the said price with every scholar who comes from any distant state.

6. *Every* minister, preacher, and private member shall be permitted, and is hereby earnestly requested to devise some means, and either bring or send his proposals to the next council, for the purpose of laying some scheme for relieving our dear brethren, who labour in the extremities of the work, and do not receive more than six, eight, ten, twelve, or fifteen pounds per annum.

7. *Every* deacon shall be three years in a state of probation before he can be elected to the eldership.

8. *Considering* the weight of the connection, the concerns of the college, and the printing business, it is resolved, that another council shall be convened at *Baltimore*, on the first day of December, 1790."

I have thought proper to insert the minutes of the first council at full length, that the plan, and the whole business thereof may be understood in future; and that the reason may be known why it was opposed, and why it was so soon given up, and rejected both by the Methodist preachers and people.

When the council was first proposed, the preachers in each district were to have the power to reject, or retain the measures which had been adopted by the council. But when the proceedings of the council came out, they had changed the plan, and determined that if a majority of the preachers in the different districts should approve of the proceedings of the council, it should then be binding on every preacher in each district.

The number of conferences were increased, so that but a small number of preachers could collect at one place. There were fourteen conferences appointed for the next year.

In the latter part of the year 1790, the second and last council met, and their minutes began as follows:

" *Minutes* ; taken at a *Council* of the *Bishop* and delegated *Elders* of the *Methodist Episcopal Church*, held at *Baltimore*, in the state of *Maryland*, December 1st, 1790."

Q. " What members are present ?

A. " *Francis Asbury*, bishop ; *Freeborn Garrettson*, *Francis Poythress*, *Nelson Reed*, *John Dickins*, *Philip Bruce*, Isaac Smith, Thomas Bowen, *James O. Cromwell*, *Joseph Everitt*, and Charles Connaway.*

Q. " What power do this council consider themselves *invested* with by their electors ?

A. " First, they *unanimously* consider themselves invested with *full* power to act *decisively* in all temporal matters. And secondly, to *recommend* to the several conferences any new canons, or alterations to be made in any old ones.

* The names in Italic were members of the first council.

Q. "What can be done to promote the book-business?

Q. "Who are appointed as travelling book-stewards, by the order of the council?

Q. "How shall such stewards be appointed for the future?

Q. "What can be done to procure religious experiences and letters for the *Arminian Magazine?*

Q. "Who shall form such a committee? i. e. to examine letters and written experiences for the *Magazine.*

Q. "What books shall be published in the course of the two following years?

Q. "Shall we publish Mr. *Wesley's* four volumes of sermons, before the sitting of the next council?

Q. "What shall be done to support the credit and finish the building of *Cokesbury College?*

Q. "Can *any thing more* be done for *Cokesbury College?*

Q. "What is the *expence* of the charity boys for the present year in *Cokesbury College?*

Q. "Shall the bishop have power to draw any money out of the book profits, for the *partial* supply of any church or preacher that may be in pressing need?

A. "By the recommendation of the elder of a district, the bishop may draw as far as *three pounds* per month; but no farther.

Q. "Who are the present teachers in *Cokesbury College?*

A. "*Jacob Hall,* A. M. *Patrick M'Closkey,* and *Charles Tite.*

Q. "Can any thing be done to prevent the students of Cokesbury College from *trafficking,* or *exchanging* their property with each other?

Q. " As many of our churches are unfinished and in debt, and our grave-yards unfenced, what can be done for *their* relief?

Q. " As the presiding elders have only a *partial* supply at quarterly meetings, to *whom* shall they present their annual accounts?

Q. " As the bishop is not supplied from the circuits, to *whom* shall he render his account?

A. " To the council.

Q. " What shall be done, if an opening should be made, to settle a teacher, or preacher, among any of the *Indian nations?*

Q. " What advice shall we give our brethren who desire to erect district schools?

Q. " What can be done toward the *relief* of our preachers, who cannot obtain the salaries allowed by our canons?

Q. " Who shall be appointed to superintend the economy of the college, in the recess of the council and the absence of the bishop?

A. " *Nelson Reed, John Dickins,* and *Joseph Everitt.*

Q. " Who shall be appointed as factors, to supply the college with whatever necessaries may be wanted?

A. " William Wood, and John Brevitt.

Q. " Who shall be appointed to inspect the factors' bills, and make their payments?

A. " *Philip Rogers, Jesse Hollingsworth, Samuel Owings,* and *Emanuel Kent.*

Q. " As we think it primitive, prudent, and *decent,* that men and women should sit apart in public congregations, what can be done to promote it amongst our people?

Q. " What money is *now* in hand, belonging to the preachers' fund?

A. " One hundred and sixty-eight pounds, one shilling and four pence.

Q. "What can be done to secure money, that may be collected for this purpose, in *future?*

Q. "How shall money be drawn, from time to time, out of the fund, for the relief of distressed preachers?

Q. "As the bishop complains, that some preachers look to him for a supply of their deficiencies, what is the judgment of the council in this case?

Q. "As *some* of the members of council complain of long and expensive journies, what can be done for their assistance in future?

Q. When and where shall the next council be held?

A. "At *Cokesbury College*, or *Baltimore*, on the first day of December, 1792."

There were thirty-one questions in these minutes, which I have stated in the same form, and order in which they stood in the minutes of the council. I have also given a few of the answers. But the answers being of little or no consequence to the people in general, I have omitted the greater part of them; and only inserted such as might perhaps be satisfactory to the reader. I have thought proper to publish all the questions, that it may be seen in future, in what manner the council proceeded.

This council determined to have another meeting two years from that time. But their proceedings gave such dissatisfaction to our connection in general, and to some of the travelling preachers in particular, that they were forced to abandon the plan. And there has never since been a meeting of the kind.

When the first council met, I wrote them a letter, in which I stated my objections to their plan, and pointed out the difficulties that it would produce, and contended for a general conference; which plan was disapproved of by all the council.

The most violent opposer of the council among the travelling preachers was at first one of that body, namely, James O'Kelly. While he was at the first council, he appeared to be united to the plan, and to the members; but after he returned to *Virginia*, he exclaimed bitterly against the proceedings and against what he himself had done in the business. He refused to have any thing at all to do with the second council.

The supposition respecting this sudden change in the old man, and his hasty conduct in condemning what he had just before sanctioned, was, that he went to the first council with some expectation of being promoted in the church; but finding himself disappointed, he returned home greatly mortified.

We have sufficient reason to believe that the establishment of the council was very injurious to the Methodist connection. The plan produced such difficulties in the minds of the preachers and the people, and brought on such opposition, that it was hard to reconcile them one to another. Nothing would or could give satisfaction to the preachers but the calling together all the travelling preachers in a general conference; to which after some time the bishop consented.

In 1790 we had fourteen conferences, at the following times and places:

The forty-first conference was held in Charleston, on the 15th of February.

The forty-second in Georgia, on the 3d of March.

The forty-third in Kentucky, on the 26th of April.

The forty-fourth at Holstein, on the 17th of May.

The forty-fifth in North-Carolina, on the 24th of May.

The forty-sixth at Lane's chapel, on the 14th of June.

The forty-seventh at Union Town, on the 29th of July.

The forty-eighth at Leesburg, on the 26th of August.

The forty-ninth in Baltimore, on the 6th of September.

The fiftieth at Cokesbury, on the 11th of September.

The fifty-first at Duck-Creek, on the 16th of September.

The fifty-second in Philadelphia, on the 22d of September.

The fifty-third in Burlington, on the 28th of September.

The fifty-fourth in New-York on the 4th of October.

At these conferences we took in 20 new circuits and stations. Three of them were in the south, *Savannah*, *Savannah Town* and *Catauba*. There were six more in the west, namely, *Lexington*, *Limestone*, *Madison*, *Russel*, *Green* and *Lincoln*. The others were *Contentney*, low down in North Carolina; and *Surry* low down in Virginia, and *Stafford* in the north part of the state; and *Canauway* in the upper part of the state. *South River* in Maryland, and *Bethel* in New-Jersey, and *Randolph* high up the country. In Connecticut we took in three, *Newhaven*, *Hartford* and *Litchfield*. And one in Massachusetts called *Boston*.

We admitted on trial this year sixty eight young preachers, and added to the society 14356 members. There were more added to the society this year, than ever had been before in the course of one year. And with all we had 116 circuits on the minutes this year.

The form of the minutes was now altered, and the first question was, "*Who are admitted on trial?*" This mode of beginning the minutes has ever since been pursued. The second question is, "*Who remain on trial?*" and thus proceed up in gradation to the bishops. Formerly the first question was, "*Who are the bishops?*" and then proceed downwards to the lowest order.

Several preachers located this year; and some of them were of long standing in the travelling connection. *Henry Willis*, had travelled twelve years. *Edward Morris* nine years. *Jeremiah Mastin* five years. *Matthew Greentree* seven years. *Levin Ross* five years, and the others had travelled a shorter time.

Three preachers died this year, and the characters given them in the minutes were as follows: "*Cornelius Cook*, he was a faithful labourer and patient sufferer, while he was employed in the church for three years; and departed in peace and confidence in the month of August 1789." His complaint was singular; it was a profuse discharge of blood through the kidneys. One night after a discharge of perhaps five or six quarts of blood and water, which ran from him in a constant stream, he thought himself to be in the agonics of death; and calling up the family and other friends he bid them farewell, and said he was dying, and exhorted them all to prepare and meet him at the right hand of God. He told them he had been preaching the gospel among them, and said "I am now a dying witness of the truths which I have preached."—While the friends wept around him, and waited to see him expire, he began to revive; and after a few days he got so well as to be about again, and lived about three months longer, and then bid the world farewell.

"*James Connor*, a native of Buckingham county in the state of Virginia; two years and a half in the work; a pious, solid, understanding man; his gifts were improveable, and promised usefulness to the church. In the midst of a blameless life, he was suddenly taken away from labour and suffering, and blessed with confidence in his last moments.

"*John Tunnil*, who died of a consumption at the Sweet Springs, in July 1790. He was about thirteen years in the work of the ministry; a man of solid piety, great simplicity and godly sincerity; well known and much esteemed both by ministers and people. He had travelled extensively through the states, and declined in sweet peace."

Mr. Tunnil was elected to the office of an elder at the Christmas conference, when we were first formed into a church. His gifts as a preacher were great; and his conduct as a pious man, was worthy of imitation. He was greatly beloved in his life, and much lamented in his death. He died about a mile to the west of the Sweet Springs. His friends took his remains over the mountain to a meeting house about five miles east of the Sweet Springs, where they buried him."

There was a new rule introduced into the annual minutes this year concerning Sunday schools; which is as follows:

"Q. What can be done in order to instruct poor children (white and black) to read?

A. "Let us labour, as the heart and soul of one man, to establish Sunday schools, in or near the place of public worship. Let persons be appointed by the bishops, elders, deacons or preachers to teach (gratis) all that will attend and have a capacity to learn; from six o'clock in the morning till ten; and from two o'clock in the afternoon till six; where it does not interfere with public worship. The council shall compile a proper school book, to teach them learning and piety."

After this, Sunday schools were established in several places, and the teachers took nothing for their services. The greater part of the scholars were black children, whose parents were backward about sending them; and but few of them were regular in attending, and in a short time the masters were discouraged, and having no pay, and but little prospect of doing good, they soon gave it up, and it has not been attended to for many years.

Religion prospered this year in an uncommon manner. The great increase of members, however, was partly owing to the difference in the time of taking the account of them. Last year it was closed in May. This year in October, which extends the time to one year and five months. Had the numbers been taken in May as they were the last year, the increase would not have been so large. But there was a most blessed work of God in different parts of the country. In New England we met with great encouragement, and some souls were savingly brought to the knowledge of the truth. On the 19th of May we joined the first class in Stratford, composed of a few loving persons, who were much despised in town on the account of their religion, and their attachment to the Methodists.

In March, *New-Haven* circuit was formed, which extended along the post road from Milford to Hartford. The first sermon preached by the Methodists in the city of Harford was on the 9th of December 1789, and on the 8th of November this year a class was formed in that city; but after a while some of the members moved away, and all the others were scattered.

About the beginning of this spring, *Litchfield* circuit was formed, which took in the north west part of Connecticut state. And in the latter part of the spring we formed *Hartford* circuit, which took in both sides of Connecticut river. The first time the Methodists preached in the neighbouring towns in that circuit were as follows: On the 2d day of April 1790, in Tolland; the third day in East-Windsor; on the 7th in Windsor; on the 9th in Suffield; on the 11th in Granby; on the 22d in Infield; on the 29th in Wintonberry; and on the 3d day of May, in Wilbraham, in Massachusetts. The first sermon preached by the Methodists in the city of Middletown, was on the 7th day of December 1789.

I have given this account of the time when the Methodists first began to preach in certain towns, that the people in those parts may know when they were first visited by us. No doubt, it will be satisfactory to many, even of the rising generation.

I was appointed this year to the town of Boston, in order if possible to establish the Methodist doctrine and discipline, and to raise up a people for the Lord. I took my station on the 14th day of November. In the course of the preceding summer, Mr. Freeborn Garrettson had visited that town and preached. I made them a visit in July. On one occasion, I went out on the common, and standing on a table began to sing with only a few persons present. But having prayed and begun to preach, the number encreased so that there were two or three thousand attentive hearers. The number was still greatly encreased the next Sabbath day, at the same place, at six o'clock in the afternoon.

This may be considered the beginning of Methodism in Boston, and in all those parts of the country. Methodist preaching was a strange thing in that part of the world. On the 12th day of July the first Methodist sermon was preached in Salem; on the 15th in Newburyport; on the 16th in Danvers; on the 17th in Marblehead; on the 20th in Charlestown; and on the 14th of December in Lynn. In Boston it was hard to procure a place to preach in, and the word took but little hold on the minds of the hearers; but as soon as we began to preach in Lynn, the word had a powerful effect on the hearers who flocked to hear by hundreds. It soon appeared, that Lynn was the place that should be attended to, in preference to any other. On the 20th day of February 1791, the first class was formed in Lynn, consisting of eight persons, and that day week twenty one persons more joined with the former number, and some of them were truly engaged with the Lord, and much devoted to his service; and others were sincere seekers of salvation.

There were abundance of people in that town who were fond of hearing the Methodists, and wished to attend their meetings constantly; and on the 9th day of May, upwards of seventy men who paid tax, came together and took certificates shewing that they attended public worship with the Methodists, and paid to the support of their minister. This was done to keep them, as far as possible from being compelled by law to pay to the support of their settled congregational minister, whom they did not like.

The society in Lynn then determined on building a Methodist meeting house; which they began accordingly on the 14th of June, raised on the 21st, and dedicated it on the 26th, 1791. This was the first regular permanent society that was formed in the state of Massachusetts; and the first meeting house that was ever built for the Methodists in the state. From that time religion continued to prosper in Lynn for many months without any declension.

In the course of 1791, there was a considerable awakening among the people in different places not far from Lynn. The Methodists preached the first time in Manchester on the 11th day of January, and on the 12th in Beverly, and in Cape Ann, or Gloucester, on the 15th of February; in Weston on the 9th day of September; in Natick on the 10th; and in Needham on the 13th of the same month. Before that time they had never had a Methodist preacher among them.

We preached a long time in Boston, before we formed a society, but on the 13th day of July, 1792, we joined a few in society, and after a short time they began to increase in numbers. We met with uncommon difficulties here from the beginning, for the want of a convenient house to preach in. We began in private houses, and could seldom keep possession of them long. At last we obtained liberty to hold meetings in a school house; but that too was soon denied us. We then rented a chamber in the north end of the town, where we continued to meet a considerable time regularly. The society then undertook to get them a meeting house, but being poor, and but few in number, they could do but little. We begged money for them in Baltimore, on the Eastern Shore of Maryland, and in Delaware state, in Philadelphia, and in New-York, and by these exertions we were able to proceed, and began the building. On the 28th day of August, 1795, the *Corner Stone* was laid of the first Methodist meeting house in Boston, which was fixed at the north end and was built of wood 46 feet by 36, with galleries in front, and in both sides of the house.

After we began to preach in the new meeting house, we had large congregations to hear us, when we preached at night; but it was some time before we had the house filled with steady hearers on the Sabbath day. Most of the people that were fond of hearing us, did not like to leave their own meeting houses when their minister preached.

In 1791 we had thirteen conferences, as follows:

The fifty-fifth conference was held in Charleston, on the 22d of February.

The fifty-sixth in Georgia, on the 16th of February.

The fifty-seventh at M'Knight's, North-Carolina, on the 2d of April.

The fifty-eighth at Petersburg, on the 20th of April.

The fifty-ninth in Hanover, on the 26th of April.

The sixtieth in Alexandria, on the 2d of May.

The sixty-first in Baltimore, on the 6th of May.

The sixty-second at Duck Creek, on the 13th of May.

The sixty-third in Philadelphia, on the 18th of May.

The sixty-fourth in New-York, on the 26th of May.

The sixty-fifth in Connecticut, on the 23d of July.

The sixty-sixth at Union Town, on the 28th of July.

The sixty-seventh in Albany district, on the 23d of August.

We took in ten new circuits this year: one in South-Carolina, called *Edisto Island*, and another which extended into a part of North-Carolina, called *Union*. The others were *Queen Anns*, on the Eastern Shore of Maryland, *Northumberland*, in Pennsylvania, *Otsego* and *Saratoga*, in New-York, *Stockbridge*, in Massachusetts; the station called Boston, was changed to *Lynn* in the minutes, and another circuit formed called *Kingston*.

Several circuits were entered on our minutes this year, which are in Nova-Scotia and the West-Indies; places where we sent missionaries from our conference.

We admitted upwards of fifty young preachers on trial, and had an addition to the society of 6257 members; we also had one hundred and twenty-nine circuits this year.

Several preachers located; among them was James Haw, the first missionary to Kentucky, who had been travelling ten years.

Four preachers died this year, "*Wyatt Andrews*, who died full of faith and the Holy Ghost. As long as he could ride, he travelled, and while he had breath he praised God. *Lemuel Andrews*, four years a labourer in the vineyard of the Lord, who maintained a steady, upright walk, attentive to the work; his last days were the best to himself, and the people he preached to. He died without any expressions of the fear of death.

"*Aaron Hutchinson*, a man of clear understanding, gospel simplicity, and godly sincerity; blameless in his life, acceptable as a preacher; faithful in his labours, which ended in the short space of four years. He was patient, resigned, and confident in his last moments."

"*Eliphalet Reed*, a true Israelite, and not without his usefulness. His feeble system failed after three years labour; a man of a sweet spirit, and humble walk with God."

In the close of the annual minutes for this year, we have the following note; "Mark well! Our brethren and friends, are desired to be more cautious how they receive strange preachers, especially to preach; unless their names are on the minutes, or they can shew a parchment or a certificate from the presiding elder, or some elder in the district they may say they came from."

This note was introduced at a seasonable time. Our connexion was growing large, and some preachers were fond of going to and fro where they pleased, without any recommendation; and some of them without any qualification for the work of the ministry. Some impostors had also been travelling through the country, who belonged to no denomination; and were not so much as moral men in their conduct.

We had a pleasing revival of religion in many places during this year; and a door was opened for the spreading of Methodism in the New-England states; where many people were inviting us, and sending for us to come and preach among them. Some of them also cast in their lots with us, and joined our society. Notwithstanding there was great opposition to the Methodists in that part of the world, they continued to increase, and were more respected than they had formerly been.

The people had always been used to hear two sermons preached every Sabbath day, so that it was hard for them to be reconciled to our preaching in some places only on a week day. The common cry was, "If you would take a parish and settle among us, we should be glad to have you, and we would then hear you, and pay you well." However, we formed societies in several places, and they encreased and prospered, and souls were converted to God.

On the second day of March, this year (1791,) Mr. John Wesley died in London, at his own house in City Road. As he had been the founder, and the father of the Methodists in Europe and America, his death was felt by the Methodists in the United States. In him we lost one of the greatest ministers in the world. He was not quite eighty-eight years old when he died. The writers of his life say, "When he was upwards of fourscore years old, he persevered in his daily labours. He rose at 4 o'clock in the morning, travelled from thirty to sixty or seventy miles a day; and preached daily two, three, or four, yea, sometimes five sermons, besides reading, writing, visiting the sick, conversing with his friends, and superintending the societies wherever he went; and in all this labour and care, he was a stranger to weariness either of body or mind."

On his birth day, June 28th, 1788, he observes, "I this day enter on my eighty-sixth year. And what cause have I to praise God, as well for a thousand spiritual blessings, as for bodily blessings also! How little have I suffered yet, by "the rush of numerous years!" It is true, I am not so *agile* as I was in times past; I do not run or walk so fast as I did. My *sight* is a little decayed. My left eye is grown dim, and hardly serves me to read. I have daily some pain in the ball of my right eye, as also in my right temple (occasioned by a blow received some months since) and in my right shoulder and arm, which I impute partly to a sprain, and partly to the rheumatism. I find likewise some decay in my memory, with regard to names, and things lately past; but not at all with regard to what I have read or heard, twenty, forty, or sixty years ago. Neither do I find any decay in my hearing, smell, taste, or appetite, (though I want but a third part of the food I did once), nor do I feel any such thing as weariness, either in travelling or preaching. And I am not conscious of any decay in writing sermons, which I do as readily, and I believe, as correctly as ever.

To what cause can I impute this, that I am as I am? First, doubtless to the power of God, fitting me for the work to which I am called, as long as he pleases to continue me therein; and next, subordinate to this, to the prayers of his children.

May we not impute it, as inferior means:

1. To my constant exercise and change of air?

2. To my never having lost a night's sleep, sick or well, at land or at sea, since I was born?

3. To my having sleep at command, so that whenever I feel myself almost worn out, I call it, and it comes, day or night?

4. To my having constantly, for above sixty years, risen at four in the morning?

5. To my constant preaching at five in the morning, for above fifty years?

6. To my having had so little pain in my life, and so little sorrow, or anxious care?

Even now, though I find pain daily, in my eye, or temple, or arm, yet it is never violent, and seldom lasts many minutes at a time.

Whether or not this is sent to give me warning, that I am shortly to quit this tabernacle, I do not know, but be it one way or the other, I have only to say,

"My remnant of days
I spend to his praise,
Who died the whole to redeem;
Be they many or few,
My days are his due,
And they all are devoted him!"

The next year when he was in *Dublin* he made the following remarks on his birth-day: "This day I enter on my eighty-seventh year. I now find I grow old. 1. My *sight* is decayed, so that I cannot read a small print, except in a strong light. 2. My *strength* is decayed, so that I walk much slower than I did some years since. 3. My *memory* of names, whether of persons or places, is decayed; I am obliged to stop a little to recollect them. What I should be afraid of is, if I took thought for the morrow, that my body should weigh down my mind, and create either *stubbornness* by the decrease of my understanding, or *pevishness* by the increase of bodily infirmities. But thou shalt answer for me, O Lord my God."

On the first day of the following year, (1790) he remarks, "I am now an old man, decayed from head to foot. My eyes are dim: my right hand shakes much; my mouth is hot and dry every morning. I have a lingering fever almost every day. My motion is weak and slow. However, blessed be God, I do not slack my labour. I can preach and write still."

Mr. Wesley preached his last sermon from Isaiah 55, 6. "*Seek ye the Lord while he may be found; call ye upon him while he is near.*" This sermon was preached just a week before he died. He had his perfect senses to the last; and just before he died, he cried out with all the remaining strength he had: "*The best of all is, God is with us.*"

On Wednesday morning, the 2d day of March, after one of the preachers had prayed with him, he said, "Farewell;" which were the last words that he was heard to utter; and a few minutes before ten, while several of his friends were kneeling around his bed, without a lingering groan, this beloved pastor of thousands, entered into the joy of his Lord.

Notwithstanding the Methodists in the United States felt the loss of Mr. Wesley; yet we had been so long accustomed to do our own business, and make our own regulations, that we were under no necessity of altering any of our plans, or modes of church government on that account.

CHAPTER VII.

From the beginning of the year 1792, *in which the first regular General Conference was held, to the end of the year* 1793.

In 1792 we had eighteen conferences, according to the account published in the annual minutes. But the line of the conferences was now changed, and they were began in *Virginia*, and went forward to the south, and then turned and ended in the north. The two first conferences were held in the latter part of the preceding year: of course some things which were transacted at the conferences held in December last, will be considered as done this year; because they are published in the minutes of the present year.

The sixty-eighth conference was held at Dickenson's, in Caroline county in Virginia, on the 15th of December 1791.

The sixty-ninth at Lane's Chapel, on the 23d of December 1791.

The seventieth at Green Hill's, (N. C.) on the 21st of January 1792.

The seventy-first in Charleston, on the 14th of February.

The seventy-second in Georgia, on the 1st of March.

The seventy-third in Kentucky, on the 1st of May.

The seventy-fourth on Holstein, on the 15th of May.

The seventy-fifth at Green-Brier, on the 22d of May.

The seventy-sixth at Union Town, on the 2d of June,

The seventy-seventh at New Town, on the 15th of June.

The seventy-eighth in Baltimore, on the 22d of June.

The seventy-ninth at Duck-Creek, on the 1st of July.

The eightieth in Philadelphia, on the 7th of July.

The eighty-first at the New-Mills, on the 12th of July.

The eighty-second in New York, on the 19th of July.

The eighty-third in Lynn, on the 1st of August.

The eighty-fourth in Albany, on the 15th of August.

The eighty-fifth was a general conference, which was held in Baltimore on the 1st of November.

It was just eight months from the time the bishop began to hold these annual conferences, until he finished them. He began them on the 15th of December, and the last was on the 15th day of August.

At these conferences we took in eleven new circuits, which are as follows:

In North-Carolina two, *Scopealong* and *Trent.* And one in the south called *Highco.* In Georgia two, *Oconee*, and *Elbert.* Two in New-York, *Staten Island*, and *Tioga.* One in Massachusetts, called *Needham*; one in Rhode-Island called *Providence*; and two in Canada, *Cataroqua* and *Oswegochee.*

We admitted on trial upwards of fifty young preachers, and added to the society 2314 members this year. But several of the preachers located, viz.

Benjamin Brown, William Heath, John Easter, Sihon Smith, Michael Burdge, John Andrew, Wheeler Grissom, Charles Hardy, Thomas Williamson, John Paup, Lewis Chasteen, Michael Lard, and William Phoebus.

Two preachers were expelled from the connection, Beverly Allen, and Andrew Harpending.

Three preachers died this year, namely, Thomas Weatherford, aged 56: upwards of four years a labourer in the vineyard of the Lord: of slender system. But what was best of all, he lived the gospel, and died triumphant in the Lord.

Peter Massey, under the profession of religion for some years. He laboured faithfully in the ministry for upwards of three years, and was confirmed and established in the grace of God. An afflicted man, who desired and obtained a sudden death, by falling from his seat; he expired on the 19th of December 1791, about nine o'clock in the morning, at Cumberland, on the western waters.

George Browning, two years and a half in the ministry, a serious and devoted man, who died in peace, and rested from his afflictions, in hope of eternal glory, which God has promised to faithful souls.

At this time, 1792, we had about one hundred members in society, in the states of Connecticut and Massachusetts; the only states in New England where we had any societies formed. But we now for the first time formed a circuit in the state of Rhode-Island.

On the first day of November, 1792, the first regular general conference began in Baltimore. Our preachers who had been received into full connection, came together from all parts of the United States where we had any circuits formed, with an expectation that something of great importance would take place in the connection in consequence of that conference. The preachers generally thought that in all probability there would never be another conference of that kind, at which all the preachers in connection might attend. The work was spreading through all the United States, and the different territories, and was likely to increase more and more, so that it was generally thought that this conference would adopt some permanent regulations, which would prevent the preachers in future from coming together in a general conference. This persuasion brought out more of the preachers than otherwise would have attended.

By this time the plan of the former *council* had become exceedingly disagreeable to the greater part of our brethren, both preachers and people; and it was expected that some of the preachers would try, in that conference, to revive and establish it. But we were agreeably disappointed. For soon after we met together, the *bishops* and the preachers in general, shewed a disposition to drop the *council*, and all things belonging thereunto. And the bishop requested that the name of the *council* might not be mentioned in the conference again. No one attempted to bring forward that business afterwards.

The conference proceeded in the first place to form some rules and regulations for conducting the business which lay before them. To that end there was a committee appointed of the oldest preachers, and a few chosen from those that were younger in the work. This committee was to consider matters among themselves, and when a majority of them agreed to make any alteration in our form of discipline they were to make report to the conference. One of the rules for the regulation of the conference was this; "It shall take two thirds of all the members of the conference, to make a new rule, or abolish an old one: but a majority may alter or amend any rule."

The committee was afterwards increased, by adding more preachers to it: but after all, it was found to be of no real use; for if a few of the committee were opposed to any thing that was adopted by a majority of their brethren, when the business was brought before the whole of the conference, those that were dissatisfied before, would take an active part in the debates: and all the arguments that had been brought forward in the committee would be taken up again; which did not answer the end intended. It had been thought that a committee would arrange matters so as to expedite the business; but after trying it, we found that it had the contrary effect. The committee was then given up, and any preacher was at liberty to bring forward any motion; and the conference proceeded to establish or reject it, according to the above regulation either by the voice of a majority, or two thirds, as the case might require.

One amendment to our former plan, and to the *form of discipline*, was offered by Mr. J. O'Kelly, which was this: "After the bishop appoints the preachers at conference to their several circuits, if any one think himself injured by the appointment, he shall have liberty to appeal to the conference and state his objections; and if the conference approve his objections, the bishop shall appoint him to another circuit."

This motion brought on a long debate, the arguments for and against the proposal were weighty, and handled in a masterly manner. There never had been a subject before us that so fully called forth all the strength of the preachers. A large majority of them appeared at first to be in favour of the motion. But at last Mr. John Dickins moved to divide the question thus, 1st. Shall the bishop appoint the preachers to the circuits? 2d. Shall a preacher be allowed an appeal? After some debate the dividing the question was carried. The first question being put, it was carried without a dissenting voice. But when we came to the second question, "Shall a preacher be allowed an appeal?" there was a difficulty started, whether this was to be considered a new rule, or only an amendment of an old one. If it was a new rule, it would take two thirds of the votes to carry it. After a considerable debate it was agreed by vote that it was only an amendment of an old rule. Of course after all those lengthy debates we were just where we began; and had to take up the question as it was proposed at first.

One rule for our debates was, "That each person if he choose shall have liberty to speak three times on each motion." By dividing the question, and then coming back to where we were at first, we were kept on that subject called the *Appeal*, for two or three days. On Monday we began the debate afresh, and continued it through the day; and at night we went to Mr. Otterbein's church, and again continued it till near bed time, when the vote was taken, and the motion was lost by a large majority.

The next morning, when the conference had assembled, we received a letter from Mr. O'Kelly, and a few other preachers, directed to the conference, informing us, that they could no longer sit among us, because the appeal was not allowed. The conference then pitched upon a few preachers to wait upon the disaffected persons, and persuade them to resume their seats in the conference. But all their persuasions were of little weight: for they would not come. After a day or two Mr. O'Kelly had an interview with Dr. Coke, and raised many objections against the Dr. and against the conference. Waiting in town a day or two longer, he and the preachers that were particularly influenced by him, set off for Virginia, taking their saddle-bags, great coats, and other bundles on their shoulders or arms, walking on foot to the place where they left their horses, which was about twelve miles from town.

I stood and looked after them as they went off, and observed to one of the preachers, that I was sorry to see the old man go off in that way, for I was persuaded he would not be quiet long; but he would try to be head of some party. The preacher then informed me, that Mr. O'Kelly denied the doctrine of the Trinity, and preached against it, by saying, that Father, Son and Holy Ghost were characters, and not persons: and that these characters all belonged to Jesus Christ. That Jesus Christ was the Father, the Son and the Holy Ghost. The preacher further said, that it was his intention to have had O'Kelly tried at that conference for the false doctrines which he had been preaching; and he believed that his leaving the conference was more out of fear of being brought to trial, than on account of the appeal. But so it was, Mr. James O'Kelly never more united with the Methodists.

At that general conference we revised the form of discipline, and made several alterations. The proceedings of that conference were not published in separate minutes, but the alterations were entered at their proper places, and published in the next edition of the form of discipline, which was the eighth edition.

The title page of that edition was as follows : "The Doctrine and Discipline of the Methodist Episcopal Church in America, revised and approved at the general conference held at Baltimore in the State of Maryland, in November 1792: in which Thomas Coke and Francis Asbury presided."

In the bishops' address to the members of the Methodist socities in the United States, they say, "We have made some little alteration in the present edition, yet such as affect not in any degree the essentials of our doctrine and discipline. We think ourselves obliged frequently to view, and review, the whole order of our church, always aiming at perfection.

We determined at this conference to have another general conference at the end of four years, to be held in Baltimore on the first of November 1796. We also agreed that all the travelling preachers who should be in full connection at the time of holding the next general conference, should be intitled to a seat.

It was likewise determined, that the districts should be formed according to the judgment of the bishops ; yet so as not to include more than twelve, nor less than three circuits in a district.

Moreover it was also said, " The bishop shall appoint the time of holding the district conferences."

In the 16th page of the Form of Discipline we gave an explanatory note of the character of a supernumerary preacher. " A supernumerary preacher is one so worn out in the itinerant service, as to be rendered incapable of preaching constantly ; but at the same time is willing to do any work in the ministry, which the conference may direct, and his strength will enable him to perform."

We had also this N. B. "In case there be no bishop to travel through the districts, and exercise the Episcopal office, on the account of death, the districts shall be regulated in every respect by the district conferences and the presiding elders, till the ensuing general conference, (ordination only excepted.")

In the 4th section it is asked, Q. 1. "How is a bishop to be constituted in future?

A. "By the election of the general conference, and the laying on of the hands of three bishops, or at least of one bishop and two elders.

Q. 2. "If by death, expulsion, or otherwise, there be no bishop remaining in our church, what shall we do?

A. "The general conference shall elect a bishop; the elders, or any three of them, that shall be appointed by the general conference for that purpose, shall ordain him according to our office of ordination.

Q. 4. "To whom is the bishop amenable for his conduct?

A. "To the general conference, who have power to expel him for improper conduct, if they see it necessary."

At this conference we introduced a new rule for the trial of a bishop, which stands thus, Q. "What provision shall be made for the trial of an immoral bishop, in the intervals of the general conference?

A. "If the bishop be guilty of immorality, three travelling elders shall call upon him, and examine him on the subject: and if the three elders verily believe that the bishop is guilty of the crime, they shall call to their aid two presiding elders from two districts in the neighbourhood of that where the crime was committed, each of which presiding elder shall bring with him two elders, or an elder and a deacon. The above mentioned nine persons shall form a conference, to examine into the charge brought against the bishop: and if two thirds of them verily believe him to be guilty of the crime laid to his charge, they shall have authority to suspend the bishop till the ensuing general conference."

The fifth section had respect to the presiding elders. Such an order of elders had never been regularly established before. They had been appointed by the bishop for several years; but it was a doubt in the minds of the preachers, whether such power belonged to him. The general conference now determined that there should be presiding elders; and that they should be chosen, stationed and changed by the bishop. However, a new rule was formed respecting them as follows: "The bishop shall not allow an elder to preside in the same district, more than four years successively."

The duty of a presiding elder was to travel through his district, to take charge of all the preachers, travelling or located in the district; and to change, receive, or suspend the travelling preachers in the absence of a bishop: to be present as far as practicable at all the quarterly meetings; and to preside in the conference of his district, in the absence of a bishop. The presiding elder was to be supported by the surplus money in each circuit; but if there was no surplus, then he was to share in proportion with the preachers of the circuits.

In the eighth section we formed a rule, whereby the bishop, or a presiding elder, might receive a preacher to travel in the intervals of conference, until the sitting of the next district conference. But all preachers must be received by the conference, before their names can be printed in the minutes. A preacher received in the intervals of conference, must have a written license from the bishop or presiding elder. But no preacher shall be received by the conference to travel, unless he first procure a recommendation from the quarterly meeting of his circuit. After travelling two years on probation, being approved by the disrict conference, and examined by the president thereof, he may be received into full connection.

At the close of the section we have the following N. B. " If any preacher absent himself from his circuit without the leave of the presiding elder, the presiding elder as far as possible shall fill his place with another preacher, who shall be paid for his labours out of the quarterage of the absent preacher according to the usual allowance."

In the ninth section, we fixed the salaries of all the travelling preachers at the former sum of sixty-four dollars, with the casual addition of their travelling expenses. Their travelling expenses were to include ferriages, horse-shoeing and provisions for themselves and horses on the road, when they necessarily rode a distance.

Q. " What shall be annually allowed the wives of the travelling preachers ?

A. " Sixty-four dollars if they be in want of it."

It was then understood that the wives of the travelling preachers had not an equal claim with the preachers themselves. The preachers had a claim, however favorable their circumstance in life ; but the quarterly meeting was to judge of the condition of their wives, and if they were not in want, they were to have no claim for money. This rule was afterwards changed, and ever since the preacher and his wife have an equal claim.

Prior to this conference we had not allowed our preachers to take any thing for performing the marriage ceremony; but at this time a rule was made allowing any of our preachers to receive money if offered to them, (but not to charge) for performing the marriage ceremonies.

Q. "What plan shall we pursue in appropriating the money received by our travelling ministers for marriage fees?

A. "In all the circuits where the preachers do not receive their full quarterage, let all such money be given into the hands of the stewards, and be equally divided between the travelling preachers of the circuit. In all other cases the money shall be disposed of at the discretion of the district conferences."

In the close of the section, we had the following N. B. "No minister or preacher shall receive any money for deficiencies, or on any other account out of any of our funds or collections, without first giving an exact account of all the money, clothes, and other presents of every kind, which he has received the preceding year."

This rule was intended to keep all the preachers as nearly on an equal footing as possible, in their money matters. That there might be no jealousies or envyings among us. But that we, like brethren of the same family, might all labour together in the gospel of Jesus Christ.

In order that we might not be imposed upon by improper persons, coming from a distance under the character of Methodists, we gave this advice to him who should have the charge of the circuit, "To warn all from time to time, that none are to remove from one circuit to another, without a note of recommendation from a preacher of the circuit in these words: '*A. B. the bearer, has been an acceptable member in C.*' and to inform them, that without such a certificate, they will not be received into other societies."

This regulation we found to be of great service; for previous to this direction, persons who had been expelled for improper conduct, could easily get into our society, when they removed into places where they were not well known.

In the tenth section we formed a rule for settling disputes among our members, concerning debts. "On any dispute between two or more of the members of our society, concerning the payment of debts or otherwise, which cannot be settled by the parties concerned, the preacher who has the charge of the circuit, shall enquire into the circumstances of the case; and having consulted the stewards and leaders, shall, if agreeable to their advice, recommend to the contending parties a reference consisting of one arbiter chosen by the plaintiff, and another chosen by the defendant; which two arbiters so chosen shall nominate a third, (the three arbiters being members of our society;) and the decision of any two of them shall be final. But if either of the parties refuse to abide by such decision, he shall be immediately expelled.

"And if any member of our society shall refuse in cases of debt, or other disputes, to refer the matter to arbitration, when recommended by him who has the charge of the circuit, with the approbation of the stewards and leaders, or shall enter into a law suit with another member before these measures are taken, he shall be expelled."

This mode of settling disputes in our society, has been of great service to many of our members, both in saving of expense, and in the preservation of peace among contending brethren.

This rule for settling disputes has been altered, and it is so framed by the last general conference in 1808, that the preacher having the charge of the circuit, is to recommend to the contending parties an arbitration, when he thinks proper; and the preacher is not obliged to consult the stewards and leaders, as directed in the former rule. There is an addition made to the rule, also which is this: "But if one of the parties be dissatisfied with the judgment given, such party may apply to the ensuing quarterly meeting of the circuit, for to have a *second* arbitration appointed; and if the quarterly meeting see sufficient reason, they shall grant it, in which case, each party shall choose two arbiters, and the four arbiters shall choose a fifth, the judgment of the majority of whom shall be final; and any person refusing to abide by such judgment, shall be excluded the society."

It had been a custom for several years, to have a fast day in each circuit on the Friday after each quarterly meeting; but we now changed the time, and gave direction to the preacher having charge of the circuit, to "Take care that a fast be held in every society in the circuit, on the Friday preceding every quarterly meeting, and that a memorandum of it be written on all the class papers."

In the 19th section we formed a rule for trying of travelling preachers, who might be accused of improper conduct.

Q. "What shall be done when an elder, deacon, or preacher is under the report of being guilty of *some crime*, expressly forbidden in the word of God, as an unchristian practice sufficient to exclude a person from the kingdom of grace and glory?

A. "Let the presiding elder, in the absence of a bishop, call as many ministers as he shall think fit, at least three; and if possible bring the accused and accuser face to face. If the person be clearly convicted, he shall be suspended from all official services in the church, till the ensuing yearly conference; at which his case shall be fully considered and determined. But if the accused be a *presiding* elder, the preachers must call in the presiding elder of the neighbouring district, who is requested to attend, and preside at the trial.

" If the accused and accuser cannot be brought face to face, but the supposed delinquent flees from trial, it shall be received as a presumptive proof of guilt; and out of the mouth of two or three witnesses he shall be condemned. Nevertheless, even in that case the yearly conference shall re-consider and determine the whole matter.

Q. 2. " What shall be done in cases of improper tempers, words, or actions?

A. " The person so offending shall be reprehended by his senior in office. Should a second transgression take place, one, two, or three ministers or preachers are to be taken as witnesses. If he be not then cured, he shall be tried at the next yearly conference, and, if found guilty and impenitent, shall be expelled from the connection, and his name so returned in the minutes of the conference.

Q. 3. " What shall be done with those ministers or preachers, who hold and preach doctrines which are contrary to our articles of religion?

A. " Let the same process be observed as in cases of gross immorality; but if the minister or preacher, so offending do solemnly engage, neither to preach nor defend such erroneous doctrines in public or in private, he shall be borne with, till his case be laid before the next yearly conference, which shall determine the matter.

"Provided nevertheless, that in all the above mentioned cases of trial and conviction, an appeal to the ensuing general conference shall be allowed."

The last question and answer, above, was introduced in order to prevent the spreading of the erroneous doctrines, which had been imbibed and propagated in public and in private by Mr. J. O'K—; who, previous to that time, had taken much pains to draw off some of our preachers into his way of thinking; and had so far succeeded in his endeavours, as to get some of the preachers confused and bewildered in their minds about the doctrine of the Trinity. But in a short time those preachers who remained with us were happily delivered from the mist of darkness into which they had been drawn.

In the 21st section we have the following N.B. "We will on no account whatever receive a present for administering baptism, or for burying the dead."

This last resolve has been a standing rule among the Methodists from that day to this.

In the 22d section, the following directions were given concerning public worship on the Lord's day: "Let the morning service consist of singing, prayer, the reading of a chapter out of the Old Testament, and another out of the New, and preaching.

"Let the afternoon service consist of singing, prayer, the reading one chapter out of the Bible, and preaching.

"Let the evening service consist of singing, prayer, and preaching.

"But on the days of administering the Lord's supper, the two chapters in the morning service may be omitted."

This rule was never attended to by our preachers, except in a few places, in large towns or cities. In some cases our preachers read one chapter in public on Sabbath days, either before or after the first prayer, and always before preaching.

In the 24th section we had this request made by the conference, which carries with it the nature of a command, "The preachers are desired not to encourage the singing of fuge tunes in our congregations.

"We do not think that fuge tunes are sinful, or improper to be used in private companies, but we do not approve of their being used in our public congregations, because public singing is a part of divine worship, in which all the congregation ought to join."

We have also this direction: "Let it be recommended to our people, not to attend the singing schools, which are not under our direction."

Before these rules respecting singing were formed, many of our preachers, especially in the Northern States, had made too common a practice of singing fuge tunes in the public congregations; and by that means they had prevented many of the old saints from singing at all; and singing in public worship was likely to be wholly confined to a few; and they mostly the young people, who were particularly acquainted with the notes, and the rules of singing.

It was always a custom among the Methodists, for all the people in the congregation to sing if they could. Singing being a part of divine worship, we encouraged all to worship God; and of course we advised all to sing.

At this conference there was some alteration made in the "*Directions given to the Band Societies:*" and after the direction "To use no needless self-indulgence:" the words "*Such as taking Snuff or Tobacco,*" were left out.

The use of tobacco has been more common among the travelling preachers since, than it had been before that time. *Some of them say it is an advantage to their teeth, and others that it is good for their health.*

At this conference we made the following rule in addition to the former one respecting the trial of private members, "If a member of our church shall be clearly convicted of endeavouring to sow dissentions in any of our societies, by inveighing against either our doctrine or discipline, such person so offending shall be first reproved by the senior preacher of his circuit; and, if he afterwards persist in such pernicious practices he shall be expelled the society."

The conference saw clearly that a divisive spirit was prevailing in some parts of our connection, and that it had been kindled by some of the disaffected travelling preachers; they therefore determined to try and check it as soon as possible; being fully satisfied that some persons would do us more harm by remaining among us, if they continued to ridicule our discipline and doctrine in the manner they had done for some time, than they could do if they were separated from us.

At this conference we again employed John Dickins to superintend our printing business in Philadelphia, for which he was to be allowed a house and book room, and six hundred and sixty-six dollars and thirty-three cents per year; which was to be paid out of the profits arising from the printing business.

The conference also agreed that there should be allowed to *Cokesbury College* out of the profits arising from the printing of books among us, $4000 in the course of four years to come: $800 to be allowed the first year, and the rest to be divided equally for the remaining three years.

But the college being burnt down, before the expiration of the four years, the whole sum was not applied to the intended purpose.

We then had the two following questions:

Q. "What sum of money shall be allowed to distressed preachers out of the book fund, till the next general conference?

A. "Six hundred and sixty-six dollars and sixty-seven cents per annum.

Q. "What shall be allowed the bishop out of the book fund, for the benefit of the district schools, till the next general conference?

A. "Sixty four dollars per annum."

According to the regulations above stated, it was supposed that the profits arising from our book business would at least amount to $2500 a year.

I have taken notice of many of the rules and regulations that were adopted at this general conference, in order that it may be the better understood by such preachers and members of our connection, as were not acquainted with our proceedings at that time.

Notwithstanding we had some close debates, and some distressing hours during that conference; and with all, some of our preachers were so offended as to leave the conference before the business was half finished; yet it was a comfortable time to most of us, and we were highly favoured of the Lord with his presence and love in the last of our sitting. Our hearts were closely united together, and we parted in great union, love and fellowship.

It was eight years from the Christmas conference, where we became a regular church, to this general conference. In which time our form of discipline had been changed, and altered in so many particulars; and the business of the council had thrown the connection into such confusion, that we thought proper at this conference to take under consideration the greater part of the form of discipline, and either abolish, establish, or change the rules, so that we might all approve of, or be reconciled to, whatever might be found in the discipline.

The proceedings of this general conference gave great satisfaction to our preachers and people; and the divisive spirit which had been prevailing in different parts of our connection, was considerably checked. And nothing that was done gave more satisfaction, than the plan that was laid for having another general conference at the expiration of four years from that time; to which, all the preachers in full connection were at liberty to come.

Some of the preachers who came to the conference this year, were quite dissatisfied; but at the close of the meeting they were perfectly reconciled, and returned to their circuits fully determined to spend and be spent in the work of the ministry, and in the fellowship of the church.

However, the seeds of discord had been sown in some places, and especially in the south parts of Virginia, and had taken such root that it was impossible for us to eradicate them. The preachers who separated from us at that time, returned to Virginia, and by their endeavours the spark of contention was soon blown up into a flame. But, by the goodness and mercy of God, the preachers in general kept "*The unity of the spirit in the bonds of peace.*"

In 1793, we had 19 conferences; four of which were held in the latter part of the preceding year, after the close of the general conference.

The eighty-sixth conference was held at Alexandria on the 19th of November, 1792.

The eighty-seventh at Manchester, on the 25th of November 1792.

The eighty-eighth in North Carolina, on the 12th of December 1792.

The eighty-ninth at Charleston, on the 24th of December 1792.

The ninetieth in Georgia, on the 10th of January, 1793.

The ninety-first at John's River, on the 24th of March.

The ninety-second in the New Territory, at Nelson's, on the 3d of April.

The ninety-third at Nashville in Tennessee, on the 15th of April.

The ninety-fourth in Kentucky, on the 6th of May.

The ninety-fifth at Green Brier, on the 27th of May.

The ninety-sixth, at Union Town on the 9th of June.

The ninety-seventh at Old Town, on the 18th of June.

The ninety-eighth at Albany, on the 15th of July.

The ninety-ninth in Lynn, on the 1st of August.

The hundredth in Connecticut, on the 12th of August.

The hundred and first in New-York, on the 25th of August.

The hundred and second in Philadelphia, on the 5th of September.

The hundred and third, at Duck Creek, on the 12th of September.

The hundred and fourth at Cokesbury, on the 22d of October.

It was upwards of eleven months from the time of holding the first of these conferences, until the close of the last: of course there was no opportunity of getting the annual minutes printed and circulated before the conferences began for the following year, and many of the preachers had taken their stations for the next year; by which means, a correspondence with the old preachers was greatly obstructed. For we could not tell where the preachers were stationed until we saw the minutes; and by that time the stations or appointments were altered. There was a pretty general complaint on the account of having such a number of conferences, and because of their continuing throughout the whole year: and a reform in this point was desirable; but the bishop had the right of appointing the number of conferences, and the time of holding them in each year: and we could not arrange the business so as to have but few conferences in each year, until the general conference was held in 1796. We then fixed on a smaller number; and have never since had more than seven annual conferences in a year.

At the conferences held this year, (1793) we took in 12 new circuits, which were as follows: *Swanino* (which lay among the mountains) and *Haw River*, in North Carolina. *Hingston*, in the Western country: and *Washington*, to the west of Baltimore. *Freehold*, in New-Jersey. *Harkemer* and *Seneca-Lake*, in the north parts of New-York state: *Tolland* and *New-London*, in Connecticut: Providence, in Rhode-Island, was now called Warren. *Province of Maine*, called so after the name of the country, as no circuit had been formed in that part of New-England. *Prince George's* in Maryland; and *Savannah*, in Georgia.

A preacher was kept part of the year, in Savannah, and then it was given up without forming any society; and no preacher was sent to that city again for a long time.

We admitted on trial upwards of forty young preachers this year; and added to the society 1451 members. Eighteen preachers located, and some of them had been travelling many years. Joseph Cromwell, had travelled sixteen years; and others had been travelling from ten to thirteen years.

Four preachers were entered, withdrawn from our connection; two of them, James O'Kelly, and Rice Haggard, continued to travel and preach through the country where they pleased, and they spared no pains in trying to draw off disciples after them. The other two, John Robinson, and John Allen settled themselves. Mr. Allen went into the practice of physic, and soon gave up preaching. He has been living since that time in the district of Maine.

One preacher (James Bell,) was disowned for improper conduct; and two preachers died, namely, Benjamin Carter and John Sproul. Mr. Carter had been a professor of religion about eight years, and had been near six years in the ministry. He was a pointed, zealous preacher, and a strict disciplinarian. He was a happy man, and one that appeared to fear the face of no man. He had received a wound in the late war, which greatly injured him in his labours. He was blessed with great consolation in his last hours. He died in August 1792, in Washington county in Georgia, and was buried at Harris's meeting house.

John Sproul was a simple honest man, who gave himself wholly to God and his work. He travelled and preached for near three years; and was then taken from toil to rest. Though he was weak in body, he was fervent in spirit, serving the Lord. And we hope, that he went in peace to his eternal home.

In the close of the annual minutes for this year, we had the following CAUTION. " The brethern are requested to be on their guard against impostors. One of those characters had lately made his way through North and South Carolina, collected money, purchased a horse by falsehood, and disappeared. If a preacher is on the travelling plan, he will be sent out from the conferences ; if he is a local preacher, he can be recommended from his quarterly meeting. If doubts arise respecting any person who may appear under the character of a Methodist preacher, refer him to the preacher who has the charge of the circuit, for examination, before he is permitted to preach."

After the foregoing *caution*, we had a plan for district schools, recommended to the members of the Methodist-Episcopal church in America, by Mr. Asbury. This address was drawn up by Mr. Asbury, and not by the conferences. There were published at the end of the address, " General rules recommended for district schools." There were 13 rules for the direction of the trustees, and 18 for the regulation of the schools."

After a while some such institutions were set on foot ; one in Brunswick county, in Virginia ; one on the Yadkin in North-Carolina ; one in South-Carolina ; one in Georgia ; and one in Kentucky. But most of them fell through in a few years ; and at present they are hardly worth noticing in this history. However, there is a good school kept at present at Ebenezer, in Brunswick county in Virginia. But it is not under the direction of the Methodists. In the first place there are but few trustees remaining, some being dead, and others removed. Some of the remaining trustees are not of our society. And secondly, the present teacher has the entire government of the school: holding the house and plantation free of expense, and taking in scholars, and governing them as he pleases.

There was a good revival of religion this year, in many of the new circuits, and the way was open for us to extend our borders in various directions; but we had a great declension in many of the old circuits. When the numbers in society were taken, we found that we had gained fewer than we had for seven years before.

New London circuit in Connecticut was formed in the beginning of this year, and a preacher continued to travel in it from that time until the conference; at which time it was taken on the minutes. It then had fifty members. There had been preaching by the Methodists in most of the places that were now taken into this circuit, some time before the circuit was formed. The first sermon preached by the Methodists in the city of New-London, was on the second day of September 1789, which was upwards of three years before the circuit was formed. The first Methodist sermon that was preached was in Windham, on the 24th of June, and the first in the city of Norwich on the 25th of June 1790.

It was upwards of five years from the time of the societies being formed in New London, until they built a meeting house to assemble in. Their meeting-house was raised on the 20th day of July 1798, and the dedication sermon was preached in it two days after the frame was raised, i. e. on on Sunday the 22d of July, in the afternoon.

Warren circuit in Rhode-Island, took in Bristol, Newport, Providence, Cranston, and several places in Massachusetts. It will, no doubt, be satisfactory to many of the inhabitants of Rhode-Island, to know the time when the Methodists first came to that state. The first Methodist sermon was preached in Charles-Town Rhode-Island, on the 3d day of September 1789. The first in Newport was, on the 30th of June 1790. The first in Bristol was on the 2d of July: and the first in Providence was on the fourth of July, 1790. The first Methodist sermon preached in Cranston, was on the 11th day of November 1791.

The first meeting house that was built for the Methodists in the state of Rhode-Island was that in Warren, which was dedicated, or first preached in, on the 24th day of September 1794.

It is almost twenty years since we first began to preach in Rhode-Island, and at present we have only four or five hundred members in that state. We have had as little success in that place, as in any of the states where we have been; yet we have not as much opposition there, as we have commonly had in most places; neither are the people as much prejudiced against us and our plan, as they are in the rest of the New-England States. In this state they have no ministers settled by law: they neither have any law to tax the people for the support of ministers. The people hear such preachers as they like, and pay toward their support just as much as they please In a word, they enjoy religious liberty: and are the happiest people in this respect of any that dwell in New England. Yet, they are not more religious than the people of the neighbouring states. We have a few societies there, that are well engaged in religion, and much attached to our plan, and to our discipline.

In 1795, we took in Province-Town, twhich at first included only the one town on Cape Cod.

In the beginning of the revival of religion in that town, there was no one to guide or direct the people, till a few of them were converted; they then began to hold meetings among themselves, and to sing and pray, and sometimes read a part of the Bible, or some religious book, and sometimes talk about religion, and about their experiences. In this way they were comforted, and so continued their meetings for a season, being much opposed and despised, and remaining like sheep without a shepherd. At length one of our preachers, on his passage from New-York to St. John's, in the Province of New-Brunswick, in the British dominions, meeting with contrary winds, was obliged to put into the harbour, and come to an anchor. He went on shore, and was soon found out by the young converts and invited to preach: and after preaching among them a few times, and directing them where they might find more of our preachers, he left them. Soon after some of them came up to Boston and begged us to go down and preach among them. We consented to do so as soon as we could conveniently.

When we went to Province-Town to preach, we were gladly received by those who had lately embraced religion; and a great many of the other people attended our ministry, and were highly gratified with our manner of preaching. In a short time we formed a society; and from that time the work began to encrease much more than it had done before, and several souls were converted to God. This society was formed in the beginning of the summer 1795. After the society began to encrease considerably, the brethren concluded to build themselves a meeting-house. The plan was laid, and the timber procured at a distance, and brought to town by water, and then hauled together in order to begin to frame the house. By this time persecution began to spread through the town, and many things were said against the building. And on the 25th of August, 1795, in the night time, the mob collected privately, and took the greater part of the timbers, and carrying it over a large hill into a bottom, they cut it to pieces and built a large pen of it. Then getting a sailor's old hat, coat, and trowsers, and stuffing them so as to make them resemble a man, they fastened the image on the top of the pen, and tarred and feathered it.

This conduct was the most violent opposition that we had met with in that part of New-England. But the brethren were not discouraged by this opposition. They laid their plan, and procured more timber, and built themselves a comfortable meeting house in the latter part of that same year; and it was ready for use by the next January.

The first time that the Methodists preached in New-Bedford was on the 30th day of January, 1795. And it was a good many years afterwards, before we had a society formed in that place.

The first of our going on to Martha's Vineyard to preach, was on the 5th day of February, 1795. Some of our preachers had preached on that Island before, having put in there as they were passing and repassing from New-York to Nova-Scotia. But this was the first time that a Methodist preacher ever went to the Island with express intention to preach to the inhabitants. Some time after we had a preacher stationed there, a small society was raised, and things went on well for a season. But at last there was an unfavourable change, and we gave up the Island, and have not sent them a preacher since.

It was on the 6th day of April, 1797, that the Methodists preached the first sermon on the Island o' Nantucket. Some of the inhabitants had heard our preachers in other places, but they were never visited on the Island until that time. At the first visit I staid on the Island eighteen days, and preached sixteen sermons. Some of the people were much awakened at that time, and many were very desirous that some of our preachers should be sent among them.

In 1799, we took Nantucket on our minutes, and gave the people a stationed preacher; and have continued to do so ever since. A society was formed, and a large meeting house was built. At present they have a large congregation, and 166 members in society on the Island. The male inhabitants pretty generally follow the sea for a living; and many of them are engaged in the whale fishery; and of course they have not so good an opportunity of being religious as many other people.

Having taken a short view of the spread of our societies, and the progress of religion among us in Connecticut, Rhode-Island, and Massachusetts states, we will in the next place take a view of the difficulties and divisions that took place among our societies in the south.

I have already observed, that at the general conference held in the latter part of the year 1792, Mr. O'Kelly, and several other preachers with him, left the conference and returned to Virginia. One of them, however, came to the Manchester conference, and agreed to take his circuit as usual. Another shortly after met the bishop, and agreed to take his circuit also. We soon found that there would be but a few of the travelling preachers that would leave us to follow the disaffected party. Rice Haggard was the only travelling preacher that went off with O'Kelly, and continued to travel. Some of the local preachers became warmly attached to the old man, and fell in with him, and with his plan. They then held conference after conference, and other meetings, in order to make arrangements and consult measures for establishing some plan that might insure them success in their undertakings; and to establish themselves on a better plan, (as they expressed it) than that adopted by the Methodists. They formed many rules for governing the church; but when they were compared with our regulations, they were found to be defective. At last they renounced all rules of church government, and took, (as they said) the New Testament for their *rule* and government. They then agreed that all the rules and plans which they had formed at their conference, should not be binding, but merely advisary.

At that time there were great struggles and contentions about politics. In Virginia republican principles prevailed, and it was considered advantageous to a man to be a republican. The divisive party, with O'Kelly at the head, therefore called themselves *Republican Methodists.*

In the latter part of this year (1793) they began to form some societies, and to establish them on a kind of a leveling plan. All were to be on an equal footing. One preacher was not to be above another; nor higher in office or in power, than the other preacher. No superiority, or subordination, was to be known among them. They promised to the lay members of the church, greater liberties than they had formerly enjoyed among us. And prevailed with a good many of our people to leave us and join with them. In some places they took off from us whole societies together, and in many places they drew off a part. Others they threw into confusion; and in some places they scattered the flock and separated the people one from the other, without securing them to their own party. They took a few meeting-houses from us, and preached in them themselves. And some houses we left and would not preach in them, in order to avoid contentions.

The disaffected party then began to pour out a flood of abuse against us, to ridicule us, and to say all manner of evil against us; and with all, they took unjustifiable steps in order to set our members against the preachers. The bishop was more despised by them, than any other man. The name of bishop they abhorred. They acknowledged that the word *Bishop*, and the word *Elder* in the scriptures meant the same thing; yet they shewed great indignation against the word bishop, and were well pleased with the word elder. In this case they shewed their weakness, or their wickednèss, in condemning a word, which in substance they approved of.

The divisive spirit prevailed more in the south parts of Virginia, than in any other place. At that time O'Kelly lived in the south edge of the state, near to the country line dividing between that state and North-Carolina. There were some of our societies in the north-east part of North-Carolina, who felt the painful effects of that division, and were considerably scattered, and greatly injured. Several of our local preachers, and many of our private members were drawn off from us, and turned against us. The societies were brought into such troubles and difficulties that they knew not what to do. Many that were drawn off from us, would not join with the other party. Brother was turned against brother, and one christian friend against another. The main contention was about the government of the church; who should govern it, or in what manner it ought to be governed.

In this mist of darkness and confusion, many religious people, who had been warm advocates for the life and power of religion, began to contend about church government, and neglect the duties of religion, till they were turned back to the world, and gave up religion altogether. It was enough to make the Saints of God weep between the porch and the altar, and that both day and night, to see how "The Lord's flock was carried away captive," by that division.

These preachers who turned aside from the truth, did abundance of mischief among the people that were not religious: many of whom became so deeply prejudiced against religion and religious professors, that they would hardly attend on preaching at all. It might well be said, "Without were fightings, and within were fears."

After this O'Kelly began to ordain such preachers as would consent to be ordained by him. He condemned the Methodist ordination, and called it a "*spurious Episcopacy;*" Yet he received his ordination from the Methodists, and proceeded from that ordination, to ordain other ministers. The separate party appeared to prosper in making proselites for two or three years; and then they began to decline, and to divide from each other. In most places religion declined where they increased. In some places it was supposed that they did some good.

About the year 1801, O'Kelly published a pamphlet, in which he stiled himself and his party, "*The Christian Church.*" From that time they began to disown their former name, and refused to call themselves "Republican Methodists," any longer. Most of the societies belonging to that party, soon after the publication of that pamphlet, began to call themselves "The Christian church." A difficulty was then raised among themselves respecting the name of their party. They reasoned thus: "If we are *the Christian church*, it will imply there are no Christians but our party." Some of their party protested against the name of the denomination; and four of their preachers broke off from the new plan, and united together on a plan of their own in Charlotte county in Virginia.

They have been divided and subdivided, till at present it is hard to find two of them that are of one opinion. There are now but few of them in that part of Virginia where they were formerly the most numerous; and in most places they are declining.

It will be proper to mention here another division of less magnitude which took place in Charleston, South-Carolina, which was brought about by Mr. William Hammit, who was an Irishman by birth. Mr. Hammit had been a Methodist preacher in the West-Indies, previous to his coming to the United States. When he left his station in the West-Indies, he came to Charleston, and shewed some inclination to tarry among us. The bishop consented to his staying in Charleston; but at the same time fixed another preacher in the city. This was in the beginning of the year 1791. In the month of May following, Mr. Hammit travelled to the North as far as the city of New York, and preached there a few times. He then returned as far as Baltimore, and there preached a considerable length of time. While he was there, it was discovered that he had a wish to settle himself, if he could do it to advantage. Some uneasiness took place in the society on his account, and leaving Baltimore, he returned to Charleston in South Carolina.

Mr. Hammit had not been long in Charleston, before he began to lay his plan for a separation, and to use his influence to divide the Methodist society.

In the close of the year 1791, Mr. Hammit left the Methodists, and on Christmas day he preached in the market house in that city, for the first time after leaving us. From that time he continued to preach in the market house or in other places, where it was convenient, but never after preached among us as a Methodist preacher.

In the course of the next year, 1792, *he* drew off a great part of our society in that city. He proceeded as he had formerly done, to preach, meet the classes, and the like; but made some alterations in the government of the church, and pretended to be on a better plan than the Methodists had established. He got Mr. P. Matthews, a Methodist preacher to unite with him. Some time after that a few more preachers joined him. But none of our travelling preachers joined him.

Mr. Hammit called his party the "Primitive Methodists." He tried to make the people believe that he was on the plan that the Methodists set out on at the beginning. He procured some lots of ground in the city, and built a large church, and a dwelling house for the preacher to live in. After that they built a small meeting-house in the suburbs of the city. They built another meeting-house in George Town; and one of their preachers built a small meeting-house in Savannah in Georgia; another of their preachers went to Wilmington in North Carolina, and collected to gether a large number of black people, and built a meeting-house there.

Mr. Hammit wrote against the Methodists, and Mr. Thomas Morrill and Dr. Coke in reply. Several pamphlets were published on each side.— After some years Mr. Hammit differed with the preachers in connection with him, and the disagreement was so great that he disowned some of them, and others of them could not fellowship him; and so they divided and came almost to nothing.

Mr. Hammit died on the 14th day of May 1803, after a very short illness; which was a little more than eleven years after he left the Methodists. His name was never entered on our annual minutes in the United States; but he had been in the travelling connection with the British conference for several years.

After the death of Mr. Hammit, his society in Charleston was greatly scattered. The meeting-house which he had built in George Town was given up to the Methodists; and the meeting-house in Savannah was seldom used for public worship.

Mr. William Meredith, who had been in connection with Mr. Hammitt, went to Wilmington in North Carolina, and built a meeting-house, and collected a large society of black people, and brought them into good order; and many of them appeared to be deeply pious. Some difficulties arose between him and Mr. Hammit, and they parted some years before either of them died.

Some time in 1798, Mr. Meredith's meeting house in Wilmington was burnt down, together with the dwelling house adjoining to it, in which he lived. Not long afterwards he built another meeting house, which was much larger than the first. He then wished to be united with us, and requested of us in case he should die, that we would take charge of his society. In the latter part of the year 1799, Mr. Meredith died in peace, and left his meeting house, dwelling house and his society to us. Since then we have kept a stationed preacher in that town.

This may be considered as the beginning and end of the division which was made by Mr. William Hammit.

The first class of white people that was formed in Wilmington in North Carolina, was joined together on the 24th of December 1797. There were at that time, a few pious persons among the white people in that town, and one man that joined with us was a young preacher. But the blacks were much more attentive to religion than the whites.

CHAPTER VIII.

From the beginning of the year 1794, to the end of 1795.

In 1794 we had fourteen Conferences; three of which were held in the latter part of the preceding year

The 105th Conference was held in Baltimore, on the 20th of October, 1793.

The 106th in Petersburg, on the 15th of November, 1793.

The 107th in North-Carolina, on the 9th of December, 1793.

The 108th in South-Carolina, on the first of January, 1794.

The 109th in the New Territory, on the 2d of April.

The 110th in Kentucky, on the 14th of April.

The 111th at Mitchill's, in Bottetourt, on the 26th of May.

The 112th in Rockingham, on the 3d of June.

The 113th at Union-Town, on the twelfth of June.

The 114th in Albany, on the tenth of July.

The 115th in Lynn, on the 25th of July.

The 116th in Connecticut, on the 4th of September.

The 117th in New-York, on the 22d of September.

The 118th in Philadelphia, on the 5th of October.

These Conferences, from the beginning to the close of them, included upwards of eleven months and a half; in which time we took in several new circuits, which were as follows:—*Federal*, in Maryland; *Carlisle*, in Pennsylvania; *Lees-*

burg and *Pendleton*, in Virginia ; *Black Swamp*, in South Carolina ; *New Hampshire*, in the state of New-Hampshire ; *Marblehead*, *Orange*, and *Fitchburg*, in Massachusetts ; and *Vermont*, in the state of Vermont. The circuit in Upper Canada was divided—one part was called Upper Circuit, and the other Lower Circuit.

We admitted on trial forty young preachers. But we lost in the number of our members 2135. This was the first time that our number had decreased for fourteen years.

We lost nearly as many preachers out of the travelling connection this year as were admitted into it. According to the Minutes of the Conference, we had 29 located ; two left the Methodists, Jeremiah Cosden and Jethro Johnson ; four were dismissed for improper conduct, Simon Carlisle, David Richardson, James Johnson, and David Valleau ; and four died, Philip Cox, Henry Birchett, James Wilson, and John Wynn.

Philip Cox was a native of Britain. He had been a travelling preacher about fourteen years, in which time he had travelled through several of the United States. He was a very small man.—He said, at one time he felt so poorly, that he thought he must quit travelling ; but when he had himself weighed, he found that he weighed a hundred pounds. He then said, " It shall never be said that I have quit travelling while I weigh an hundred weight." He was a man of great spirit, quick apprehension, sound judgment, and a lover of union. He often prayed and preached to the admiration of many, and with considerable success. He married when he was upwards of fifty years old ; but continued to travel until he died. In the time of his sickness, he observed on Sunday the first of September 1793, that it was such a day of peace and comfort to his soul, as he had seldom felt. The next Sunday he departed in peace.

Henry Birchett was from Brunswick county, in Virginia; he had been travelling between five and six years, and was a gracious, happy, useful man. He freely offered himself for four years, on the dangerous stations of Kentucky and Cumberland. At the conference in 1793, he had a pain in his breast, and a discharge of blood from the lungs; yet, after asking the consent of the bishop and conference, he ventured to take his station, where he was exposed to danger from the Indians, and the small pox, which was prevailing at that time. It was said that he departed this life in much peace at Cumberland, on the western waters, in February 1794.

He was one among the worthies who freely left safety, ease and prosperity, to seek after and suffer for souls. His meekness, love, labours, prayers, tears, sermons and exhortations will not soon be forgotten.

James Wilson, was a native of the Eastern Shore of Maryland. He had been a professor of religion about fifteen years, and had been a travelling preacher near six years. His piety, prayers, and exhortations were very great. He told several of his friends a little before his death, that he found great consolation in his own soul. He departed this life at Church Hill, on the Eastern Shore of Maryland, in October 1793. We have reason to hope he died in peace.

John Wynn, was a native of Sussex county, Virginia; he had travelled near four years. He was a man of address and natural elocution. He was a son of affliction; but was upright in life, and willing to labour to the last. When he was unable to travel at large, he had a station in Winchester, and was well received, and much approved of by the people. After about seven days illness, he slept in peace on the 27th of April, 1794.

At the close of the Annual Minutes, there was published, a recommendation for a Fast-day, to be held on the last Friday in February, 1795, by all our united societies.

It was also recommended, that a day of Thanksgiving should be held on the last Thursday in October, 1795. It was requested, that all worldly concerns should be laid aside on those days, that they might be kept with all the solemnity of a Sabbath.

This was a year of great trouble and distress among the Methodists in the southern states, partly owing to the divisions that had taken place, as mentioned in the foregoing chapter, and partly to an uneasy and restless spirit that prevailed in many places, both among our local preachers and private members. Some of them contended that the local preachers ought to have a seat and a vote in all our conferences; and others said, there ought to be a delegation of lay members.

We supposed, that where there was a taxation, there ought to be a representation; but we did not tax any one. We only regulated our own business, and fixed on certain plans for governing the church, and for taking care of those persons who had put themselves under our care, and were still willing to be governed by us.

Notwithstanding the difficulties and troubles that our society met with in many of the old circuits, where there was a declension among them, we were greatly favoured of the Lord in different parts of the New England states; and many souls were awakened and brought to God by our ministry. The way was also opened for us to preach in many places where we had not been before.

The two new circuits which we took in above Boston this year, called Orange and Fitchburg, were places where there was very little stir of religion among any denomination. The people were willing to hear us, and in general we had large congregations. After we had been preaching among them a few months, we began to see some fruit of our labours, and souls were happily converted to God.

It will be necessary here to take notice of the introduction of Methodism into the Province of Maine, and of our success in that unimproved part of the country: for our greatest success at first was in places where the people were but thinly settled, and could but seldom hear a sermon of any kind. Where there were ministers regularly settled, the people were not so fond of hearing us as they were in other places; but at that time there were very few settled ministers in the Province of Maine, except in the old settled parts of the country near the sea-shore.

At the conference in Lynn, which was held on the first of August, 1793, I was myself appointed to the Province of Maine, to travel through that country, or form a circuit where I thought best.—As there had never been any Methodist preaching there, we had no one to give us a particular account of the place or people; but it was commonly understood that they were in want of preaching, and that our manner of travelling and preaching would be very suitable for that part of the country.

I set out from Lynn in September 1793, for a strange part of the world, and was the first Methodist preacher that ever went to that province to preach. The first Methodist sermon that was preached in the Province of Maine, was on the 10th of September, at a little village called *Saco*.

That place has never been very famous for religion, either before or since that time.

I travelled through the greater part of that country, from September to the end of the year. I went as far as Castine, at the mouth of Penobscot river, then up the river to the upper settlements, which then was just below the Indian settlements called Old-Town; from thence returned by the way of the twenty-five mile pond, to Kennebec river, thence up to Sandy river, and back to Hallowell, and thence through to Portland.

Although I was a perfect stranger to the people, and had to make my own appointments, I preached almost every day, and had crowded assemblies to hear. After viewing the country, I thought the most proper place to form a circuit would be on the west side of Kennebec river.—The circuit was accordingly formed, and called *Readfield.* This was the name of the first circuit that was formed by the Methodists in that part of the country, which was about 200 miles beyond any other circuit that we had in New-England. It extended from Hallowell to Sandy River.

It will, no doubt, afford some satisfaction to the people to know the exact time when the Methodists first preached among them in that circuit, and in the neighbouring towns; I will therefore state the time when we first began to preach in each town. On the 13th day of October, 1793, the first Methodist sermon was preached in Hallowell; on the 15th, in Farmington, on Sandy River; on the 17th, in New Sharon; on the 18th, in Mount Vernon; on the 19th, in Readfield; on the 21st, in Winthrop; and on the 22d, in Monmouth. These were all the towns in that circuit that we preached in, till the beginning of the ensuing year.

On the 29th of January, 1794, we preached for the first time in Sydney; on the 11th day of February in Fayette; on the 12th in Livermore; on the 14th in Wayne; on the 21st in Chesterville; on the 26th in Jay; on the 5th of March in Vassalborough; on the 7th in Harlem; on the 9th in Winslow: on the 11th in Norridgwock; on the 12th in Canaan, and on the 12th in Clinton; on the 13th in Fairfield; on the 6th day of April in Green; on the 2d day of June, in the New Vineyard; on the 16th in Strong, and on the 17th in Avon; on the 3d of July in Leeds; on the 14th in Lewis-Town. On the third day of December we first preached in Starks, and on the 4th in Anson.

We had not preached long in this circuit before religion revived, and the people began to inquire what they should do to be saved. After several persons had been converted by the instrumentality of the Methodists, and many of the old professors had been greatly stirred up in their minds, we thought it necessary to form some societies among them. The first class that we joined together, (and it was the first that ever was formed in the Province of Maine), was in Monmouth, about the first of November, 1794. The second class that was joined together, was in Readfield, a short time after that in Monmouth. After that, there were several societies formed in different parts of the circuit.

The first meeting house which was built in the Province of Maine for the Methodists, was that in Readfield, which was begun in the fall of the year 1794, and was nearly covered in by the first of December. The second was that in Monmouth, which was begun in 1795.

The first time that we ever administered the Lord's Supper in that part of the country, was in

Readfield, on the 14th day of December, 1794. The second time was in Monmouth, on the 25th day of the same month, which was on Christmas-day.

The meeting-house in Readfield was dedicated on the 21st day of June, 1795. But the meeting-house in Monmouth was not dedicated until the last day of May, 1796.

The first quarterly meeting that was ever held in the Province of Maine, was in Monmouth, which began on the 23d day of June, 1795.

The first conference that was ever held in the Province of Maine, was in Readfield, which began on the 29th day of August, 1798. We had ten travelling preachers at it, and about 200 communicants. It was not five years from the time the people there, first heard a Methodist ; yet after they began to unite with us, they flourished and increased so fast, that now we could collect at one meeting about 200 members of our society. When we made a return of the number in society in 1795, which was about eight months from the time we joined the first members together, we had 268 in society.

The second circuit in the Province of Maine, was called Portland ; we had preached in it occasionally for some time, and had the circuit regularly formed in the beginning of 1795 ; but it was not taken on the annual minutes until the conference which was held in July. The Methodists began to preach in some of the towns in that circuit for the first time as follows :

The first time we preached in Portland was on the 12th day of September, 1793, and on the 13th in Freeport. On the 9th day of January, 1794, in Buxton ; on the 10th in Gorham ; on the 7th day of April, in Perjepscot, and on the 7th also in

New-Gloucester; on the 2d of July, in Turner; on the 16th, in Gray; on the 27th of December in Falmouth; and on the 11th of December, 1795, in Scarborough.

The first class was formed in the town of Portland about the first of October 1795. The first quarterly meeting for that circuit was held in Poland, on the 4th day of December 1795. We here administered the Lord's Supper, for the first time in that circuit.

The first meeting-house that was built for the Methodists in that circuit, was that in Falmouth, which was dedicated on the 19th day of June 1797.

The third circuit formed in the Province of Maine, was called Penobscot, which took in both sides of the Penobscot river. Mr. Joshua Hall was the first preacher that went to that circuit, after it was formed. He was sent there from the New-London conference in 1795.

The first time that the Methodists preached in the towns belonging to that circuit were as follows: on the 29th of September, 1793, in Penobscot; on the 1st of October, in Buckstown; on the 5th in Orrington; on the 6th in Hampden; and on the 7th in Frankfort; on the 9th at the twenty-five mile pond, and on the 18th of April 1795, in Bangor; on the 4th of June, at Union River; on the 5th in Blue hill; on the 8th in Prospect; on the 9th in Belfast; on the 11th of July, 1797, in Castine; on the 14th in Vinalhaven. The first class formed in Vinalhaven, on Fox-Island, was on the 14th of July 1797.

There was a great revival of religion in the Penobscot circuit in the course of the last mentioned year; it began about the first of the summer, and it spread through several towns: many professed to be awakened and converted, and some of the Christians professed to be sanctified. I suppose there never was such a gracious out-pouring of the Spirit on saints and sinners in that place before, since the first settlements were made in those parts. Many stout-hearted sinners were conquered, and brought into the liberty of God's children. One thing in this revival was new and strange to most of the people in that part of the country. Some of the people when struck under conviction, would fall helpless on the floor; and some Christians, when very happy, would lose the use of their limbs, and lie helpless for some time. But the work was generally acknowledged to be of God.

In 1796, we took in another new circuit called *Bath*, near the mouth of Kennebec river. The preacher was to spend most of his time in the town of Bath; but was to travel as far as the town of Union. The first time that the Methodists preached in Bath, was on the 15th day of September 1793. And the first time in the town of Union, was on the 22d of September 1793. We were not as successful in our labours in Bath, as we were in many other places: the disputes about the settled minister ran high; and the contention was too severe on both sides. In Union there was a good work began, and souls were awakened and brought to God: and religion has been prospering more or less in that place ever since.

The first time the Methodists preached in Thomas-town was on the 11th day of June 1795. Since that time we have raised a society there, and some souls have been brought to the knowledge of God. The prospect of religion in that part of the country was very small when we first went among them; and the people who enjoyed religion were pretty generally opposed to us, and were afraid that our plan would hurt the cause of religion; yet we had not laboured among them long, before the Lord gave us seals to our ministry, and worked by us, in the conversion of many souls.

This same year, 1796, we formed a circuit in the upper towns on Kennebec river, and called the circuit Kennebec; but it is now called Norridgwock. We had some good times in that part of the country; and many souls to this day have cause to bless God that ever we preached the gospel among them; and that ever they cast in their lots among us.

In 1797, we took in a new circuit low down in the Province of Maine, and called it Pleasant River, after the name of the river where the centre of the circuit was to be. The first Methodist preaching in that country was on the 26th of April 1795, at Pleasant river; on the 27th of April at Mechias. On the first day of May the Methodists preached on Moose-Island. On the 28th at Chandler's river; and on the 31st in Steuben. On the first day of June, at Eastern Bay and on the second day of June in Goldsborough. And in 1796, we preached for the first time in Sullivan, on Frenchman's Bay, on the 6th day of May; on the 7th day of May in Trenton; and on the 10th in Eden, on Mount Desert; and on the 13th in Sedgewick. This was the beginning of Methodism in that part of the world. However, the circuit was after a short time withdrawn from Pleasant river, and fixed at Union river, and for many years past our preachers have not gone as far down the country as Pleasant river, but have continued the lowest circuit at Union river.

In 1800, we took in another circuit in the Province of Maine, called Bethel, which lay pretty high up the Androscoggin river; and took in most of the new settled towns, and settlements in that part of the country. When we first went into that unimproved part of the country, we found but few persons who had a clear sense of the favour of God. We laboured under many hardships and difficulties; and had many things to discourage us. But the Lord stood by us, and cleared the way before us, and gave us favour in the eyes of the people. And it was not long before we saw some fruit of our labours in that place also.

I have taken a particular view of the beginning of Methodism in the Province of Maine, and have been particular in giving an account of it's spreading through various parts thereof for a few years after we first began to preach in that part of the country. And we must acknowledge the work is the Lord's.

In 1809, we had eighteen circuits in the Province of Maine, and 2848 members in society.—And the prospect was pleasing. A considerable number of preachers have been raised up in those parts, and others are coming up to the help of the Lord against the mighty.

We will now take a view of Methodism in New-Hampshire state; which was the last state in the union, where we formed societies The first circuit was called Chesterfield, which lay in the south west corner of the state, near to Connecticut river, which divides New-Hampshire from Vermont. The first society formed in the state was in Chesterfield, some time in the latter part of the year 1795. At which time, there were but a few that felt freedom to unite with us; yet after some time a few more cast in their lots; and other societies were soon formed in other places. The circuit was not entered on the annual minutes until the year 1796.

Some time after this there was a circuit formed higher up the state called Landaff; and in that place religion prospered very much, and many souls were soon brought into the liberty of God's children; and the work of the Lord spread greatly among the people.

The first sermon that the Methodists preached in the state, was in Portsmouth, on the 15th of July, 1790. We used to preach occasionally in that town from that time; but we never made any parcular stand till last year, 1808, which was eighteen years from the time of our first beginning there. In the course of the last year, one of our preachers took his station in the town, and purchased an old meeting-house that was formerly occupied by another denomination; and he had a good congregation to hear him. We may consider the year 1808, as the beginning of Methodism in the town of Portsmouth.

For some years past, we have had a society in Poplin. The first time that the Methodists preached in that town was on the 17th of October, 1795, and on the next day they first preached in Brintwood. We continued to preach in Poplin occasionally, till at last the people united and built a meeting house for the use of the Methodists: before that time they had no house for public worship.

We have prospered considerably in that state within a few years past, and have now (1809) as many as nine or ten circuits there, and between one and two thousand members in society.—The way appears to be open at present for us to do more good in that state than we have ever done before. One advantage in our favour is the change that has taken place in the laws of the state, which compelled the people to pay, or support the settled minister of the town or parish.—But the people are now at liberty to pay or not to pay, and we have found many more places open for us to preach, than there were formerly.

The first circuit that we formed in the state of Vermont, was called Virshire. This circuit was taken on the minutes in 1796. We had been preaching in that town, and in many of the neighbouring towns some time before that, but had no societies formed. We had some societies in the state which belonged to circuits in other states. But Virshire was the first circuit that was formed within the state; and it reached from the towns near Connecticut river to Mountpelier, to the north of Onion river, which runs into Lake Champlain. Many of the places where we preached in that circuit, were quite new settlements: the houses were very small, and but scattering through the country. The preachers had to encounter many difficulties, and to endure many hardships. But one thing which made up for all the difficulties was this, the people were fond of attending meeting by day or night, and were very kind to the preachers. And the best of all was, sinners we. e soon awakened, and in a little time some of them became the happy subjects of the favour of God, and were zealously engaged in trying to help forward the work of the Lord as far as they could. Since then we have prospered considerably in this new part of the country.

I have given a brief account in the preceding pages of this chapter, of the beginning and spread of Methodism in the Province of Maine, New-Hampshire, and Vermont states; but it is only a sketch. To give a full account of all the revivals of religion, of all the societies that were fromed, of all the young preachers that were raised up, and of all the oppositions and persecutions we met with, would fill a volume. This being intended for a short history, I have given the reader an account of the most material things that took place in the beginning. But no one can form a proper idea of what the Lord has wrought in those parts, except they have been eye and ear witnesses of it. One thing is evident, and cannot be denied, that hundreds of people who were formerly notoriously wicked, are now civil, sober, and religious. I have thought proper, for the satisfaction of the people who live in that country to mention the time when we first preached in particular towns, and when we first formed societies.

I shall now pursue the history of the whole body of Methodists according to my general plan.

In 1795, we had only seven conferences; two of which were held in the latter part of the preceding year.

The 119th conference was held in Baltimore, on the 20th of October 1794.

The 120th in Petersburg, on the 25th of November 1794.

The 121st in Charleston, on the 1st of January 1795.

The 122d in Kentucky, on the 1st of May.

The 123d in New-London, Connecticut, on the 15th of July.

The 124th in New-York, on the 22d of September.

The 125th in Philadelphia, on the 5th of October.

From the beginning of these conferences to the end was twelve months within a few days.—This year we took in the following circuits, which had not been entered on our annual minutes before. Two in the Province of Maine, *Penobscot* and *Portland.* In Massachusetts, *Province-Town.* In Connecticut, *Pomfret.* In New-York *Otsego*: and one in Canada, called *Niagara.*

The circuits were not numbered in the minutes this year, which was contrary to our custom for several years past.

We took in 45 young preachers upon trial, which was very encouraging to us; but on the other hand, we lost out of the travelling connection forty preachers and some of them had travelled many years. Considering the standing of those we lost, we were not as strong a body this year as we were the last; notwithstanding we had more preachers to travel and labour, 32 preachers located, three left us, and five died. Those who died were Hardy Herbert, John Ahair, Thomas Boyd, Emory Prior, and Simon Miller. Part of their characters were as follows:

1st. Hardy Herbert, was a native of North-Carolina, but was brought up in South-Carolina, near the banks of Broad river. He professed faith in Christ when he was 16 years old. He began to travel when he was young, and laboured in the work of God about six years; in which time he travelled in several circuits in South-Carolina and Georgia, and in the north parts of Virginia. He was a youth of genius, and was a pleasing speaker. He was an elder in the church of God. Finding his constitution weak, he wished to decline travelling at large; and went to Norfolk, where he married. Soon after that he was taken sick, and after a short illness he died; and as was generally believed, in the fear and favour of God, on the 20th of November 1794, and in the 25th year of his age.

2d. John Ahair, was a native of North-Carolina; he was of a meek spirit, and was a zealous man. He was weak in body, but was strong in faith and in love. He travelled about three years, and then departed this life in November 1794. He was about 26 years of age.

3d. "Thomas Boyd was a deacon in the church. He was born in Europe, and died in Bedford county in Pennsylvania, in September 1794, and in the fourth year of his public labours. He was a man of a tender spirit, and was much afflicted before his death. After giving strong proof of his piety, by an innocent life and conversation, he went to his long home in peace.

4th. "Emory Prior, was an elder in the church. He was a native of the Eastern Shore of Maryland, and died May 1795, having been travelling about six years. He was a man of a very slender constitution, and was much afflicted for four years last past. He was a man of an excellent spirit, and of a sound judgment. Being worn out with affliction, he closed his feeble life on earth, with a death answerable to his life, in sweet peace and consolation. He was about forty-five years old.

5th. "Simon Miller, was a native of Pennsylvania, born in Lancaster county, a German by descent. He laboured faithfully for four years, through Pennsylvania, Maryland, and Delaware states. He was a man of deep experience and useful gifts. He could speak both in German and English. He departed this life at Milford, in the state of Delaware, in September 1795, and was much lamented."

We found our number of members was less this year by 6217, than it was last year. Such a loss of members we had never known since we were a people. There was a restless spirit in most parts of our connection and many were scattered by the division in the south of Virginia.

This year we had an alteration in the form of our minutes. The numbers in society were put down before the stations of the preachers. Which method has been generally pursued ever since.

In the close of the minutes there was direction given for a public fast, to be held by all our societies throughout the United States, on the last Friday in March 1796—And for a day of thanksgiving to be held on the last Thursday in October following.

In the latter part of this year 1795, we formed the first society in New-Hampshire state, and then for the first time, although we had laboured about 26 years—we could say that we had societies in all the United States.

CHAPTER IX.

From the beginning of the year 1796, *including the second General Conference, to the end of* 1799.

In 1796, we had eight conferences; seven annual conferences, and a general conference. Two of these conferences were held in the close of the preceding year.

The 126th conference was held in Baltimore, on the 20th of October 1795.

The 127th at Salem Chapel in Mecklenburg, Virginia, on the 24th of November.

The 128th in Charleston, on the 1st of January 1796.

The 129th in the New Territory on the 20th of April.

The 130th in Thompson, in Connecticut, on the 20th of September.

The 131st in New-York on the 30th of September.

The 132d in Philadelphia on the 10th of October.

The 133d, being a general conference, was held in Baltimore, on the 20th of October.

We took in several new circuits this year: in the bounds of the Western conference, *Shelby* and *Logan*; and in the Province of Maine, *Bath* and *Kennebec*; and in New Jersey, *Cape May*. The circuit in New-Hampshire we called *Chesterfield*, and that in Vermont, *Vershire*.

This year we admitted on trial upwards of thirty young preachers; and lost out of the travelling connection forty; twenty-eight of them located; nine died; two withdrew, and one was expelled.

Those who died were Jacob Brush, Stephen Davis, William Jessop, Reuben Ellis, Richard Ivey, Francis Acuff, John Jarrell, Zadock Priest, and Benjamin Abbott. We never before lost so many old preachers by death in one year.

1st. Jacob Brush, was a native of Long-Island. He had been a travelling preacher about ten years. He was an active zealous man of God, and a great friend to order and union. He exerted himself much in preaching and in praying. But being for a long time subject to an inflammatory sore throat, he could not labour as constantly as he would otherwise have done. He was greatly beloved and esteemed by the brethren wherever he travelled. He died in New York of the Epidemical fever, in the month of September, 1795, being about thirty-three years of age. Those who knew him have no doubt but he died in the Lord, and now rests from his labours.

2d. Stephen Davis was a native of Gloucester county in Virginia. He died in Norfolk of the yellow fever, in August 1795. He was about 30 years of age. He had been a travelling preacher about seven years. He was a pious man, and possessed a very strong memory. He was persuaded to take part with those who made a division among us in the south of Virginia, but he was soon convinced of his error, and became a faithful and successful defender of the order and government of our connection, and greatly assisted in promoting the union of our body. He laboured frequently with his own hands, when he had it in his power; and when he died, he left his clothes and money to be divided among the travelling preachers belonging to the Virginia conference. We have sufficient reason to believe that he died in the fear and favour of God.

3d. William Jessop, was a native of Sussex

county in Delaware state. He had travelled and preached about eleven years, and was a man of great simplicity and godly sincerity. He laboured beyond his bodily strength; and had travelled and preached in Virginia, Maryland, Delaware, Pennsylvania, New-Jersey and New-York states. He had also spent some years in preaching the gospel in the British provinces of Nova-Scotia, and New-Brunswick. He was a tender-hearted preacher, and spake with great animation. He said some time before he died, that he had not heard a sermon from any Methodist preacher for some years without weeping under it more or less; and yet, during that time he did not remember that he had ever wept, while he himself was preaching. He died in Lancaster county, Pennsylvania, in the latter end of the year 1795. He appeared to be remarkably happy in the close of his life, and after taking something to moisten his mouth, he turned over and said, "It is enough. Glory, glory, glory;" and died in peace.

4th. Reuben Ellis, had been travelling and preaching about 19 years, in which time he had preached in North-Carolina, South-Carolina, and Georgia; in Virginia, Maryland, and Pennsylvania. His preaching was weighty and powerful; he was a faithful friend, who sought not his own ease, but the glory of God, and the salvation of men. He married in the last year of his life, but continued to labour in the word and doctrine. He was a native of North-Carolina, where he began his ministerial labours. He was a large man, but of a slender constitution. His last station was in Baltimore, where he ended his warfare in February 1796.

5th. Richard Ivey, was a native of Sussex county in Virginia; he had travelled and preached about 17 years. He had travelled pretty extensively, from New Jersey to the south parts of Georgia, and was a man of quick and solid parts, and preached with a good degree of animation. A little before his death, he returned home to his native place, and was making some preparation to settle himself, when he was taken sick, and died in the latter part of the year 1795.

6th. Francis Acuff, was born in Culpepper county in Virginia, and was brought up in Sullivan county in Tennessee. He died in August 1795, in Kentucky, in the 25th year of his age. He had travelled upwards of two years; and was a man of improvable parts, was much beloved, and greatly lamented by his family and christian friends.

7th. John Jarrell was an honest hearted man, faithful in his ministerial labours, and considering the charge of his family, his bodily weakness and affliction, he served the church of God in an unexpected manner. He travelled all the circuits in Delaware, and the Eastern Shore of Maryland. He preserved his character as a minister and a christian, and was a plain and lively preacher; a friend to discipline, order and union. He travelled and preached about ten years. His last illness was short; and he died in Wilmington, Delaware state, in June 1796.

8th. Zadock Priest, was a native of Connecticut, and had been travelling and preaching upwards of two years; but was taken with a discharge of blood from the lungs, which prevented him from travelling the circuit where he was appointed. He then returned home to his friends. But his disorder soon terminated in a consumption. He returned to Norton in Massachusetts, where he was confined about three weeks, in which time he expressed a strong confidence of the favour of God, and had no doubt of future salvation. He died in peace on the 22d of June 1796, in the 27th year of his age.

9th. Benjamin Abbott, was an aged man when he became a travelling preacher, and he travelled about seven years before he died. He had been a local preacher for many years, and had often travelled a few weeks at a time, either on his own appointments, or in the place of another preacher. He travelled considerably through New Jersey, New-York, Connecticut, Pennsylvania, Delaware, and Maryland states. He was of a child-like simplicity: possessed great faith, and an unshaken confidence in God. As a speaker, he was properly a great blunderer, and his language incorrect; more so than was common; yet he spake with power, and with the demonstration of the Spirit. He was owned of God in the conviction, conversion, and sanctification of many souls. He was one of the wonders of America, no man's copy, but an uncommon zealot for the blessed work of sanctification, and preached it on all occasions, and in all congregations. He was an innocent, holy man, his whole soul was often overwhelmed with the power of God. His last labours were upon the eastern shore, where his strength failed. He then returned home to his friends in New-Jersey, where he lay sick for a short time, and shouted, and praised God as long as he was able; and then died in August 1796. Some time after his death, the account of his life and gospel labours was published, and the book is called Abbott's Life.

This year we took an account of the number of the members in our society in each state separately, which was as follows:

	Members.		*Members.*
Province of Maine	357	Massachusetts	824
New-Hampshire	68	Rhode-Island	220

Connecticut	1050	North-Carolina	8713
New-York	4044	South-Carolina	3659
New-Jersey	2351	Georgia	1174
Pennsylvania	3011	Tennessee	546
Delaware	2228	Kentucky	1750
Maryland	12416	Upper Canada	474
Virginia	13779		
		In all—	56,664

We lost in number this year 2627 members. We have been going back, and our numbers decreasing for three years past, in which time we have lost 10979 members in number. The declension was mostly in the middle states, and especially where the divisive spirit most prevailed.

As the general conference was to be held in Baltimore this year, the preachers belonging to the annual conference which used to meet at Baltimore were called to attend the annual conference at Philadelphia, and of course took their stations from that place, and were twice entered on the annual minutes for that year: once as they were appointed from Baltimore conference, and then as they were appointed from Philadelphia.

Our general conference was held this year in Baltimore, which began on the 20th of October 1796, at which we had 120 travelling preachers who were members of that conference. After we had finished the business of the conference, we had the minutes published before the preachers left town, that they might take them to their several circuits.

There were several alterations made at that time, in our form of discipline, and several new regulations were formed.

It was agreed that the annual conferences which had been called district conferences, should in future be called yearly conferences; and our whole connection was divided into six yearly conferences.

The first was called the New-England conference.

The second, the Philadelphia conference.

The third, the Baltimore conference.

The fourth, the Virginia conference.

The fifth, the South-Carolina conference.

The sixth, the Western conference; and the bounds of each conference was fixed: But the bishop was allowed, if he saw proper, to have another conference in the Province of Maine. Before this regulation was established, the bishop had the power of appointing the number of conferences at his own discretion.

We also made a rule for all the preachers remaining on trial, to continue in their circuit during the time of the sitting of the yearly conference, and for none to attend at such times, but those who were in full connection, or to be received into full connection.

We also for the first time, drew up, and published in our general minutes a deed, for the better securing of all our meeting-houses; and it was determined as far as it was consistent with the laws of the different states, it should be carried into effect. We concluded to have nine, seven, or five trustees to each house.

The deed began as follows: This indenture, made this day of in the year of our Lord, &c. The deed may be seen at full length, in the Form of Discipline, page 197.

We made the following rule, that every travelling deacon shall exercise that office for two years, before he be eligible to the office of an elder; except in cases of missions, when the yearly conferences shall have authority to elect for the elders' office sooner, if they judge it expedient.

We agreed also to change the name of our Armenian Magazine, and call it the Methodist Magazine. This was done and the work was continued for two years, and then it stopped; and has never been revived since.

At this conference we first set on foot our chartered fund in Philadelphia, which still continues, and is profitable to our connection. It is as follows:

Q. "What further provision shall be made for the distressed travelling preachers, for the families of travelling preachers, and for superannuated and worn out preachers, and the widows and orphans of preachers?

A. "There shall be a chartered fund, to be supported by the voluntary contributions of our friends; the principle stock of which shall be funded under the direction of trustees, and the interest applied under the direction of the general conference, according to the following regulations, viz.

1st. "That no sum exceeding sixty-four dollars, shall in any one year be applied to the use of an itinerant, superannuated, or worn-out, *single* preacher.

2d. "That no sum exceeding one hundred and twenty eight dollars in any one year, shall be applied to the use of any itinerant, superannuated, or worn out *married* preacher.

3d. "That no sum exceeding sixty-four dollars in any one year, shall be applied for the use of each widow of any itinerant, superannuated, or worn-out preacher.

4th. "That no sum exceeding sixteen dollars shall be applied in any one year, for the use of each child or orphan of an itinerant, superannuated, or worn-out preacher.

5th. "That the elders, and those that have the

oversight of circuits, shall be the collectors and receivers of subscriptions, &c. for this fund.

6th. "The money shall, if possible, be conveyed by bills of exchange, through the means of the post, to our general book steward, in Philadelphia, who shall pay it in to the trustees of the fund: otherwise it shall be brought to the ensuing yearly conference.

7th. "There shall be no money drawn out of the fund till the first day of August, 1798.

8th. "The interest shall then be divided into six parts, and each of the yearly conferences shall have authority to draw that sixth part out of the fund, according to the regulations before prescribed. And if in one or more conferences, a part less than one sixth be drawn out of the fund in any given year, then, in such case or cases, the other yearly conferences held in the same year, shall have authority, if they judge it necessary, to draw out of the fund, according to the above regulations, such surplus of the interest, which has not been applied by the former conferences: and the bishops shall bring the necessary information of the interest of the fund, respecting the year in question; from conference to conference.

9th. "The present stock of the preacher's fund, shall be thrown into the chartered fund.

10th. The produce of the sale of our books, after the book debts are paid, and a sufficient capital is provided for carrying on the business, shall be regularly paid into the chartered fund.

11th. "But the annual subscriptions of the travelling preachers, to the preacher's fund, shall be reserved for extraordinary cases, which the chartered fund may not reach.

N. B. We need not be urgent on our benevolent friends to promote this great charity. Their own feelings, we well know, will sufficiently prevail, when proper light is given them on the subject. Our brethren who have laboured on the mountains, on the western waters, and in the poorer circuits in general, have suffered unspeakable hardships, merely from the want of some established fund, in which the competent members of our society might safely lodge what their benevolent hearts would rejoice to give, for the spread of the gospel. On the same account, many of our worn-out preachers, some of whom quickly consumed their strength by their great exertions for the salvation of souls, have been brought into deep distress; and the widows and orphans of our preachers have been sometimes reduced to extreme necessity, who might have lived in comfort, if not in affluence, enjoying the sweets of domestic life, if the preachers who were the husbands on one hand, and the fathers on the other, had not loved their Redeemer better than wife or children, or life itself. And it is to be lamented, if possible, with tears of blood, that we have lost scores of our most able married ministers—men who like good householders, could, upon all occasions, bring things new and old out of their treasury, but were obliged to retire from the general work, because they saw nothing before them for their wives and children, if they continued itinerants, but misery and ruin. But the present institution will, we trust, under the blessing of God, greatly relieve us in, if not entirely deliver us from, these mighty evils. For we have full confidence, that the hearts of our friends will be engaged, and their hands stretched forth on this important occasion; and a provision will be made, sufficient to preserve such objects of charity from want, *which is all that is aimed at or desired.*"

The conference then chose nine trustees for the chartered fund, viz.

John Dickins,
Thomas Haskins,
Jacob Baker,
Henry Manly,
Burton Wallace,
Josiah Lusby,
Hugh Smith,
Caleb North,
Cornelius Comegys,

all of Philadelphia. The Articles of Association are as follows.

ARTICLES OF ASSOCIATION,

Of the trustees of the fund for the relief and support of the itinerant, superannuated, and worn-out ministers and preachers of the Methodist Episcopal Church in the United States of America, their wives and children, widows and orphans.

ARTICLE I.

It is provided and declared, that the name, stile, and title of this corporation shall be, "The "Trustees of the fund for the relief and support "of the itinerant, superannuated, and worn-out "Ministers and Preachers of the Methodist Epis- "copal Church (in the United States of America) "their Wives and Children, Widows and Or- "phans." And that the said trustees shall consist of John Dickins, Thomas Haskins, Jacob Baker, Henry Manly, Burton Wallace, Josiah Lusby, Hugh Smith, Caleb North, and Cornelius Comegys, and their successors, qualified and appointed as is herein after mentioned. And they are hereby vested with full powers for carrying into effect the benevolent and charitable purposes, in this instrument mentioned and declared.

ARTICLE II.

It is provided and declared, that the said trustees, and their successors, by the name, stile, and title aforesaid, shall be able and capable in law, to take, receive, have, hold, possess, and enjoy, all and all manner of lands, tenements, rents, annuities, franchises, and hereditaments, and any sum or sums of money, and any manner and portion of goods and chattels, given, granted, or devised unto them or their successors, by any person or persons, bodies politic or corporate, agreeable to the intention of the donors respectively, and according to the objects, articles, and conditions, in this instrument mentioned and declared. And by the name, stile, and title aforesaid, shall be able and capable, in law, to sue and be sued, plead and be impleaded, in any court or courts, before any judge or judges, justice or justices, in all manner of suits, complaints, pleas, causes, matters, and demands whatsoever, and all and every matter and thing therein to do, in as full and effectual a manner as any other person or persons, bodies politic and corporate, within this commonwealth, may or can do.

ARTICLE III.

It is provided and declared, that in case of the death, resignation, or expulsion from membership (according to the rules and discipline from time to time adopted by the itinerant ministers and preachers of the said church, in their general conference assembled) of any one or more of the members of the said corporation, or their successors, then and in such case it shall be the duty of the remaining trustees to nominate double the number of those whose seats may have been vacated as aforesaid, and to make a representation thereof, in writing, to the itinerant ministers and preachers of the said church, in their next general canference assembled; whose duty it shall be then and there to proceed to choose, and, by a majority of votes, appoint one or more persons (as the case may be) out of the whole number of those nominated by the trustees, as aforesaid, to fill such vacancy or vacancies, in order to keep up the number of *nine* trustees for ever: and upon every such choice and appointment, a certificate shall issue from the said general conference, signed by their president and countersigned by their secretary, and directed to the trustees of the said corporation, containing the name or names of the person or persons so chosen and appointed, which said certificate shall be registered in the books of the said corporation; and the person or persons thus chosen and appointed shall be vested with all the powers and immunities of a member of the said corporation—provided, nevertheless, that no person or persons shall be eligible as a trustee or trustees of the said corporation, who has not been a member of the said church (according to the rules and discipline thereof, as aforesaid) at least five years next preceding his or their election and appointment as aforesaid, and who shall not be, at least, twenty-five years of age.

ARTICLE IV.

It is provided and declared, that the said corporation shall meet at least once in every year (for the dispatch of their necessary business) at such time and place as a majority of them may judge most convenient and proper: And when so met they shall have power to make such by-laws, rules, and regulations for their government, in the management of their affairs, as a majority of them may judge necessary; and also at every such annual meeting, they shall proceed to choose, and, by a majority of votes, appoint two of their own number, to act, the one as president, and the other as secretary to the said corporation, who may continue then in office from year to year, as a majority of the said corporation may think proper.

ARTICLE V.

It is provided and declared, that if, at any time hereafter, a majority of the trustees should deem it expedient, by deed or otherwise, to grant, bargain sell, convey, or otherwise dispose of any part or parcel of the estate, real or personal, of, and belonging to, the said corporation, or charge or encumber the same, then, and in such case, it shall be their duty to make a representation thereof in writing to the itinerant ministers and preachers of the said church, in their next general conference assembled, who shall then and there judge of the necessity or expediency of such proposed sale; and if two thirds of the ministers and preachers, assembled as aforesaid, shall consent and agree thereto, a certificate shall issue from the said general conference, signed by their president and countersigned by their secretary, declaring such approbation and consent, and specifying the kind and amount of the property to be sold or otherwise disposed of; which certificate shall be transmitted to the said trustees, who shall cause the same to be recorded in the books of the said corporation —provided, always, that the monies arising from such licensed sale shall be vested, by the said trustees (as soon as conveniently may be) in such other securities and property, as, in the judgment of a majority of them, will be most productive and safe. And provided further, that the annual interest and income, arising from the money so vested, shall be exclusively applied in the manner and for the uses and purposes in this instrument mentioned and declared.

ARTICLE VI.

It is provided and declared, that the annual rents, interest, and income of the estate real and personal, which now does, or at any time hereafter may belong to the said corporation and their successors, shall by them be held subject to the exclusive order and control of the itinerant ministers and preachers of the Methodist Episcopal Church in the United States of America, in their general conference (from time to time) assembled: And the said ministers and preachers, thus assembled, are hereby vested with full powers to appropriate and point out the mode of applying the same, to the objects, under the limitations, and for the uses and purposes herein mentioned and expressly declared.

ARTICLE VII.

It is provided and declared, that the object and design of the fund hereby intended to be established, is expressly for the purposes of relieving the distresses, and supplying the deficiencies of the itinerant and superannuated, or worn-out ministers and preachers of the Methodist Episcopal Church in the United States of America, who *remain in connection with, and continue subject to the order and controul* of, the general conference; as also for the relief of the wives and children, widows and orphans, of *such* ministers and preachers, and for no other use, intent, or purpose whatever.

ARTICLE VIII.

It is provided and declared, that no sum exceeding sixty-four dollars shall in any one year be appropriated and applied to the use of an itinerant, superannuated, or worn-out *single* minister or preacher; also that no sum exceeding one hundred and twenty-eight dollars, in any one year, shall be applied to the use of an itinerant, superannuated, or worn-out *married* minister or preacher; and that no sum exceeding sixty-four dollars, in any one year, shall be applied to the use of each widow of such ministers and preachers as are herein before mentioned and described; and also that no sum exceeding sixteen dollars shall be applied, in any one year, to the use of each child or orphan, of such ministers and preachers as are herein before particularly mentioned and described.

ARTICLE IX.

It is provided and declared, that no sum or sums of money, under any pretence whatever, shall be drawn from the fund hereby intended to be established, other than for the uses and purposes, and under the limitations and restrictions, herein before expressly mentioned and declared—provided, nevertheless, that the trustees of the said corporation and their successors, shall have power to draw and apply, from time to time, as much money, belonging to the said fund, as in the judgment of a majority of them, may be wanting to defray all the necessary expenses of conducting the business of the said corporation.

ARTICLE X.

It is provided and declared, that it shall be the duty of the trustees, to cause regular and fair accounts to be kept (in books to be provided for that purpose) of the funds of the said corporation, as well as it respects the kind and amount of the capital stock, and of the annual interest and income thereof, as of all and every sum or sums of money, which shall from time to time be drawn therefrom, for the objects, under the limitations, and for the uses and purposes herein before particularly mentioned and declared—And further, it shall be the duty of the said trustees and their successors, at every general conference of the ministers and preachers as aforesaid, to prepare and lay before them a statement of the affairs of the said fund, for their inspection and examination : which said statement shall be signed by the president and countersigned by the secretary of the said corporation, certifying that the same is fair and correct.

Some of the first trustees have resigned or died: the present trustees are

Jacob Baker, president,
Thomas Haskins, treasurer,
Caleb North,
Hugh Smith,
Joseph L. Inglis, secretary.
Henry Foxall,
William Lowber,
Samuel Harvey,
Lemuel Green.

If any person has a wish to make a donation by *Will* to this fund, it will be proper to express it in the following manner:

"I give and bequeath to the President and Trustees of the Charter of the Methodist Episcopal Church at Philadelphia in the state of Pennsylvania, the sum of dollars, and the annual interest and income thereof to be by them applied in the manner, and to the objects, mentioned, and prescribed in the articles under which they are associated."

Many of our friends willingly subscribed to this valuable institution, and several thousand dollars were collected in a short time. Some valuable legacies were also left by will to the trustees of this fund. The value of the chartered fund has been increasing from year to year. At present (1809) it affords relief to many of our preachers who are in straitened circumstances.

We now formed several rules respecting local preachers:

1. "No local preacher shall receive a license to preach till he has been examined and approved at the Quarterly Meeting of his circuit; which license shall be drawn up in the following words, viz. 'N. M. has applied to us for liberty to preach as a local preacher in our circuit; and after due enquiry concerning his gifts, grace and usefulness, we judge he is a proper person to be licens-

ed for this puspose; and we accordingly authorise him to preach.

2. "Before any person shall be licensed as a local preacher by a quarterly-meeting he shall bring a recommendation from the society of which he is a member.

3. "A local preacher shall be eligible to the office of a deacon, after he has preached four years from the time he received a regular license, and has obtained the testimonial which is directed in the fourth section of the first chapter of the form of discipline. The testimonial must be signed by three elders, three deacons, and three preachers.

"Signed in behalf of the Quarterly Meeting, N. M. President of the Meeting."

At the General Conference in 1808, there was an alteration made on this subject; and it now stands thus, "A local preacher shall be eligible to the office of a Deacon, after he has preached four years from the time he received a regular license, and has obtained a testimonial from the quarterly meeting of the circuit to which he belongs, after proper examination, signed by the president, and countersigned by the secretary, and his character has passed in examination before, and he has obtained the approbation of the yearly conference."

In 1796, for the first time we fixed a rule to make some allowance to local preachers in given cases.—1. "Whenever a local preacher fills the place of a travelling preacher, he shall be paid for his time, a sum proportionable to the allowance of a travelling preacher; which sum shall be paid by the circuit at the next quarterly meeting, if the travelling preacher, whose place he filled up, were either sick or necessarily absent; or, in other cases, out of the allowance of the travelling preacher.

2· "If a local preacher be distressed in his temporal circumstances, on account of his service in the circuit, he may apply to the quarterly meeting, who may give him what relief they judge proper, after the allowance of the travelling preachers, and of their wives, and all other regular allowances, are discharged."

At the same time we formed a rule for the trial of local preachers, which is as follows: "If a charge be brought against a local preacher, or local deacon, or elder, the preacher who has the oversight of the circuit, shall summon three or more local preachers of the neighbourhood, or for want of local preachers, so many leaders or exhorters. And if they, or the majority of them, on due examination, judge that the local preacher, deacon, or elder aforesaid, has been guilty of such a crime, or has preached such false doctrines, as require his suspension from all public offices in our church, the preacher who has the oversight of the circuit, shall accordingly suspend him from all public offices, till the ensuing quarterly meeting.

"And in such case, and in every case where a meeting, assembled as above described, shall deem the said local preacher, deacon, or elder, culpable, the next quarterly-meeting shall proceed upon his trial, and shall have authority to clear, censure, suspend, or expel him, according to their judgment. And the presiding elder, or the preacher who has the oversight of the circuit, shall, at the commencement of the trial, appoint a secretary, who shall take down regular minutes of the evidence and proceedings of the trial; which minutes, when read and approved, shall be signed by the said presiding elder or preacher, and also by the members of the said quarterly-meeting, or by the majority of them.

"And in case of condemnation, the local preacher, deacon, or elder, condemned. shall be allowed an appeal to the next yearly conference, provided that he signify to the said quarterly-meeting his determination to appeal; in which case the said presiding elder, or preacher who has the oversight of the circuit, shall lay the minutes of the trial above mentioned, before the said yearly conference, at which the local preacher, deacon, or elder, so appealing, may appear; and the said yearly conference shall judge and finally determine from the minutes of the said trial, so laid before them."

Previous to the forming of the above rule, the local preachers had been brought to trial when accused, before the society of which they were members, and were tried as if they were mere private members.

We also formed the following rule respecting the sale and use of *Spiritous Liquors*, &c.

"If any member of our society retail or give spiritous liquors, and any thing disorderly be transacted under his roof on this account, the preacher who has the oversight of the circuit shall proceed against him as in the case of other immoralities; and the person accused shall be cleared, censured, suspended, or excluded, according to his conduct, as on other charges of immorality."

At that time it was thought proper to have another bishop elected and ordained, and the conference voted that it should be done during the sitting of that conference. After the vote was taken, a difficulty arose about the manner of choosing, or electing a man to be ordained a bishop; and before the point was settled, Dr. Coke begged that the business might be laid over until the afternoon, which was done. When we met in the afternoon the Dr. offered himself to us, if we saw cause to take him ; and promised to serve us in the best manner he could, and to be entirely at the disposal of his American brethren, and to live or die among them. The conference at length agreed to the Dr's proposal, and concluded that if the Dr. tarried with us we could do with two bishops, without ordaining a third, and the former vote for choosing another bishop was dropped.—The Dr. then gave us the following instrument of writing :

"I offer myself to my American brethren entirely to their service, all I am and have, with my talents and labours in every respect ; without any mental reservation whatsoever, to labour among them, and to assist bishop Asbury ; not to station the preachers at any time when he is present ; but to exercise all the episcopal duties, when I hold a conference in his absence, and by his consent, and to visit the West Indies and France when there is an opening, and I can be spared."

[Signed,] THOMAS COKE.

Conference-Room,
Baltimore, October 27, 1796.

On Sunday the fourth day of December, while the congregation was assembled in the afternoon for divine service, in our church in Light-Street in the city of Baltimore, and the preacher was preaching to them, there was a cry of fire heard from without, which had broke out near the church ; the flames soon spread to the church, and in a very short time the House of God was burnt down ; and the Preacher's house that stood near it, was much damaged. The Academy, or School-Room was also laid in ashes. This destruction of property by fire, was just twelve months to a day from the time that Cokesbury College was burned.

In 1797 we had seven conferences: There were but six appointed on the annual minutes, but it was thought best to take in the conference in Virginia, which was held in 1796, and that also which was held in this year, which would make seven in all, and by that means the conferences would be changed about, so as to begin them in future in the south, and finish them in the north. By the regulations made at the late General conference, we could not have more than seven conferences in one year, unless there were new circuits enough formed to compose a conference.

The 134th Conference was held at Mabry's Chapel in Virginia, on the 15th of November, 1796.

The 135th in Charleston, on the 5th of January, 1797.

The 136th at Bethel School, in Kentucky, on the 1st of May.

The 137th at Wilbraham, Massachusetts, on the 19th of September.

The 138th at Duck Creek on the 10th of October.

The 139th in Baltimore, on the 21st of October.

The 140th at Laine's Chapel, on the 25th of November

At these conferences we took in the following circuits; *Pleasant River* in the province of Maine, and *Sandwich* and *Martha's Vineyard* in Massachusetts.

We had for three years together been declining in numbers; but this year we began again to increase, and we had an addition of 1999 members.

We admitted on trial about 40 young preachers, and we lost out of the travelling connection 47; 43 of them located; two were expelled; and two died, namely, *John Ragan* and *Albert Van Nostrand.*

1. John Ragan, a native of Ireland. He was a travelling preacher about seven years, in which time he travelled in Maryland, New-York, and New-Jersey, and in Nova-Scotia also. He was an elder in the church, and a conscientious man, both as a christian and a minister. He was a useful minister, and was remarkably fond of reading. On a visit to Philadelphia in August last, he took the yellow fever, of which he died in the beginning of September, soon after his return to Bethel circuit in New-Jersey.

2. Albert Van Nostrand, a native of Long-Island, in the state of New-York, about 40 years of age. Soon after he became a travelling preacher, he left the work, and was not admitted into full connection; a few years afterwards he began to travel again, and at last died in the work; and he had a good character given him in the annual minutes.

We had so many preachers located this year, that we could not well supply the circuits, or enlarge our borders in new places, as we wished to have done.

On the 19th day of October the new meeting-house in Light-street, in the city of Baltimore, was dedicated. It was built on a lot adjoining to that on which the former house was burnt ten months before.

About this time the yellow fever prevailed much in many large towns, so that we could not conveniently hold our conferences in them in the fall season of the year. Our conference that was appointed in Philadelphia this year, could not therefore be held with safety. Notice being given in time, it was held in Duck Creek. It was then judged best by the bishop and preachers in general, to change the time of holding the annual conferences from the fall to the spring of the year.

In order to bring about this alteration, the Virginia conference was added to the minutes for the present year; and of course the stations of the preachers for that conference, are entered twice on the same minutes.

In the course of this summer, Mr. Asbury's strength failed through severe affliction, and many of his friends despaired of his life. He was confined for some time to the house; and when he found himself able to travel, he went only from the house of one friend to that of another. He thus pursued his rout to the north a little beyond New York, where his strength failed, and he consented to stop and go no farther; and gave up all thoughts of getting to the New-England conference, which was to begin on the 19th of September. He wrote me a mournful letter respecting the sufferings of his body, and the anxiety of his mind on account of the preachers and the work of God in New-England; and withal, requested me to come to him after the close of the conference, and to travel with him, or go on his appointments to the south, in case he should not be able to go himself. He said he had made it a matter of prayer, and there was no one that would do to travel with him, or to take his appointments, but myself.

The conference at Wilbraham made choice of me to preside in that meeting, and to station the preachers. The business was conducted to the satisfaction of the preachers, and peace and love dwelt among us. At the close of the conference the preachers gave me a certificate, signifying their approbation of the proposed plan, "for me to travel with the bishop, and to fill up his appointments when he could not be present."—Having obtained a satisfactory recommendation from the conference, I took leave of the preachers in the north, and set out to the south, and met with Mr. Asbury, and went in company with him to the conferences in Duck-Creek, Baltimore, and at Laine's Chapel in Virginia. I did the principal part of the business of the bishop, except that of stationing the preachers. The conferences in general approved of my travelling with the bishop, and of my assisting him in the business of the conference, taking the minutes, &c.

The conference in Virginia requested Mr. Asbury to stop travelling for a season, which he at last consented to do. But he only intended to stop for a few weeks, and then to meet me again. After stopping he found himself growing worse, and concluded to go no farther. He then wrote, directing me to go on without him, and do the best I could; for he was obliged to decline going to the south.

In 1798 we had seven Conferences. As the plan had been laid in the preceding year, we now began the conferences in the south, that we might attend those that were appointed in the large towns in the spring of the year, before the sickly season came on.

The 141st Conference was held in Charleston, on the second of January 1798.

The 142d at Salem meeting-house, in Virginia, on the ninth of April.

The 143d at Holstein, on the first of May.

The 144th in Baltimore, on the second of May.

The 145th in Philadelphia, on the fifth of June.

The 146th in Readfield, Province of Maine on the twenty-ninth of August.

The 147th in Granville, Massachusetts, on the nineteenth of September.

At these conferences we took in a few new circuits; one of them was in the back part of New-York state, called *Chenango*; and one in

Vermont state called *Vergennes.* We also sent a preacher to Providence, in Rhode-Island state.

We added 1506 members to the society this year, which was a goodly increase. We took about 25 young preachers upon trial. We lost 16 out of the travelling connection; 12 located, one left us, and three died, namely, *James King*, *Michael H. R. Wilson*, and *John Dickins*.

James King was a native of Gloucester county in Virginia. His travels and labours were principally in Georgia, and South Carolina. He had a good understanding, and great zeal, and in the two last years of his life he preached with great animation, and the work of God revived under his ministry. He died in Charleston of the yellow fever in 1797. He was about 25 years old when he died. He was greatly esteemed by the religious people, both as a christian and a minister of Jesus Christ.

Michael H. R. Wilson, was a young preacher, and was never admitted into full connection; but contrary to our common custom, an account of his death was entered on the minutes, and a short character given him. He was born on the 27th of October, 1770, and departed this life April 24th, 1798, at Strasburg in Pennsylvania. He was patient under afflictions, and enjoyed peace in his soul. And in the painful struggle with death, he rejoiced in the Lord.

John Dickins, was a native of Great Britain, born and educated in the city of London. He first joined the Methodists in Virginia in 1774, and was admitted as a travelling preacher in 1777. He travelled extensively in Virginia and North-Carolina in the time of the revolutionary war.— He located in 1781, and never travelled a circuit regularly afterwards; but two years after he located, namely, in 1783, he took a station in New-

York, where he continued for several years as a stationed preacher, and the superintendant of our Book business. In 1789 he was stationed in Philadelphia as Book Agent to superintend our printing business, where he continued till he closed his useful life by the yellow fever, on the 27th of September 1798, in the 52d year of his age. He was a man of quick and solid parts, a sound and close reasoner, and a very plain, practical, and pointed preacher. He was peculiarly attentive to his duty, and very conscientious in the discharge of the exercises of prayer, both in the family and in the closet. His skill and fidelity as editor, inspector, and corrector of the press, were exceedingly great. He conducted the whole of his business with punctuality and integrity. He closed his life with uncommon joy and peace, and had a full assurance of eternal life. His death was more sensibly felt by the Methodist connection in general, than we had ever known or felt in the death of any other preacher that had died among us.

The conference that was held in Readfield this year, was the first that we ever held in the Province of Maine. Many people came together on that account, especially on the day that some of our preachers were ordained. Several came out on that day with their carts with cakes &c. to sell; and many of them appeared as disorderly as if they were at a public vendue, or in the court-yard. No one interrupted us in the meeting house, but many were walking to and fro, and paid no attention to the meeting.

We had ten travelling preachers at that conference, much united in love, and in the work of the ministry; and we had some good accounts from different places, of a gracious revival of religion.

In the bounds of the Granville conference we had more than 1000 members added to the society; upwards of 200 of them had joined us in the state of Vermont.

In the course of this year, our society in the city of Richmond in Virginia began to build a meeting-house in that place, and after some time they finished it; but their difficulties in paying for it were very great.

This year I took an account of all our local preachers in their different circuits, as correctly as I could; I could not get a correct account from every circuit; but I found that there were about 850 local preachers in our connection; and only 269 travelling preachers. We had in all about 1119 travelling and local preachers in the United States, happily united in the same work in their different stations; endeavouring to save themselves, and them that heard them.

The number of local preachers whose names I collected, in the different states was as follows: In

Georgia	33	Connecticut	13
South-Carolina	55	Rhode-Island	3
North-Carolina	148	Massachusetts	3
Virginia	251	Province of Maine	6
Maryland	103	Supposed to be in Kentucky, Tennessee and those circuits that sent in no account to me, about	60
Delaware	21		
Pennsylvania	50		
New-Jersey	53		
New-York	51		

In all 850 local preachers, some of them are only licensed to preach, others of them are ordained deacons; and many of them were formerly in the travelling connection, and are elders in the church.

In 1799, we had only 6 conferences, and they were begun in the South.

The 148th conference was held in Charleston, on the 1st of January 1799.

The 149th, at Jones's chapel, Virginia, on the 9th of April.

The 150th, at Bethel Academy, Kentucky, on the 1st of May.

The 151st, in Baltimore, on the 1st of May.

The 152d, in Philadelphia, on the 6th of June.

The 153d, in New-York, on the 19th of June.

It was but a little more than six months from the beginning to the end of these conferences. The minutes were soon circulated among the people; at which both the preachers and people were much pleased; as they could see where the preachers were stationed; and knew who were dead or located, before the close of the year.

At these conferences we took in about forty young preachers upon trial. But we lost almost as many out of the travelling connection. 29 preachers located, and three died. Those who died, were John Norman Jones, William Wilkerson, and Hezekiah Calvin Worster.

Mr. Jones was a native of Virginia, and had been a travelling preacher upwards of eight years. He was a man of great zeal, and preached with much animation. He was a very plain man in his dress and manners. He was a man of afflictions and weakness of body, and almost worn out with his sufferings, yet he was unwilling to leave the work of God; and when unable to travel through the changing seasons of the south, he was stationed first in George-town, and then in Charleston: in which places he shewed himself to be a Christian, and a minister of Christ. In his last affliction, he appeared to have an unshaken confidence in God, through Jesus Christ. He died in the city of Charleston, in the state of South-Carolina, in 1798.

William Wilkerson, was a native of Virginia; he entered as an itinerant preacher in 1793, and closed his useful life in Gloucester county in the same state in 1798, with a short illness of a bilious fever. When he was first taken with the fever, he had a strong impression on his mind that his sickness would be unto death. Of course he manifested no desire for men or means in that case. He was from all that we could discover in his life and death, a good minister of Jesus Christ.

Hezekiah Calvin Worster was admitted as an itinerant preacher in 1793. After travelling in a few circuits in the states of Massachusetts, New-York, and New-Jersey, he offered himself a missionary for Upper Canada, where he was owned and honoured of God in a peculiar manner. He was a man of grace, and of a good understanding, and was very zealous in his ministerial labours; but he was of a slender habit of body, and could not endure all the hardships of travelling, and his great exertions in preaching. There was a great revival of the work of God where he laboured in Canada, which caused him to labour and preach more than his bodily strength could bear. When he found his strength to fail, he returned home from Canada in June, sick with the consumption, and on the 6th of November following he died, which was in 1798. He was an example of patience and resignation to the will of God, and professed much of the love of God in all his sickness. When he was almost done speaking, his father asked him if his confidence was still strong in the Lord: he answered, "Yes, strong! strong!" A short time before his death, when his bodily strength failed fast, he said, "The nearer I draw to eternity, the brighter heaven shines upon me."

This year we took in the following circuits, *Oconee* and *St. Mary's* in Georgia; *French Broad* in North-Carolina; *Kanawha* in Virginia; *Mohawk* in Cayuga, and *Plattsborough* in New-York; *Essex*, *Whitingham*, and *Windsor* in Vermont; *Nantucket* and *Merrimac* in Massachusetts; and *Miami* in the North-west Territory, now, Ohio state.

Our borders were greatly enlarged this year, and the way was opening for us to spread farther, and to send forth more labourers into the vineyard of the Lord. We had an addition to the society this year of 1182 members. Great peace and harmony prevailed throughout our connection, both among preachers and people, and the prospect of a great revival of religion was more pleasing than it had been at any one time for some years; and in some places there was a good stir of religion, and many souls were brought into the liberty of the children of God.

In January, George Clark went to St. Mary's in Georgia to preach, and if possible to form a circuit. He found the people in different places entirely destitute of preaching of every kind; and when he went to preach he had to direct the people when to stand, when to kneel down, &c. Some persons who were grown to years, said they had never heard a sermon, or a prayer before in all their lives. I suppose the two counties where he travelled principally, i. e. Glenn and Camden, were at that time less acquainted with the public worship of God, than any other part of the United States. However, before the close of the year some of the people became constant attendants on the word, were much reformed in their lives, and some of them were truly converted to God.

In the latter part of the year, namely on the 23d day of December 1799, there was a society formed in the town of Augusta in Georgia, which was the first class that was ever joined together in that town. After some time the society built a convenient meeting house; and for a few years past a preacher has been stationed in that town, to that society only.

In the course of this year Tobias Gibson went to the *Natchees*, on the Mississippi to preach the gospel in that country. He was the first of our preachers that went into that uncultivated part of the world. He was not appointed to that place when he first went; but being much afflicted and not able to travel a circuit, he had liberty to travel where he pleased for the benefit of his health. Feeling his mind drawn toward that new settled part of the country, he determined to visit it, which he did as soon as he could. He was afterwards well satisfied that the Lord had sent him to that place. The fruit of his zealous labours and fervent prayers was soon made manifest; and souls were awakened and brought to God. His conduct in going there was highly applauded by the conference which was held in the beginning of the year 1800, at which time he was regularly appointed on the minutes for the same station.

This year Ezekiel Cooper was regularly appointed by the Bishop and the Philadelphia conference, to superintend the book concern as editor, and general book-steward, in the room of John Dickins deceased.

In settling the debts of the book concern the greater part of the money in hand was paid away, and the principal part of the money belonging to the book fund was in out-standing debts, and was yet to be collected: the conference therefore determined that no more drafts should be made on the book concern until it's debts were paid, and the capital should be sufficient to carry on the business without any further embarrassment. Although the preachers were in want of some assistance from the book fund, yet we judged it best to be just before we were generous, and therefore determined first to clear the business of all it's incumbrances, before we divided any more of the profits.

CHAPTER X.

From the beginning of the year 1800, *including the third General Conference, to the end of* 1803.

In 1800, we had eight conferences; however one of them was a general conference.

The 154th conference was held in Charleston, on the 1st of January 1800.

The 155th, at Blunt's,(a) in Virginia, on the 9th of April.

The 156th, at Holstein, on the 1st Friday in April.

The 157th, at the Stone Chapel, on the 1st of May.

The 158th was a general conference in Baltimore, on the 6th of May.

The 159th, in Duck Creek, on the 2d of June.

The 160th, in New-York, on the 19th of June.

The 161st, in Lynn, on the 18th of July.

The whole of these conferences were held in less than seven months time, at which we took in several new circuits which were as follows: *Natchees* in the Mississippi territory; *Orangeburg* in South-Carolina; *Wilmington* in North-Carolina; *Sciota* in Ohio; *Chenango* west of New York; *Landaff* in New-Hampshire; *Bethel* in the Province of Maine; and *Grand River* in Canada.

We admitted upwards of forty young preachers on trial this year, which was a great help to us. But on the other hand we lost 31 out of the travelling connection; 24 located, 3 withdrew

(a) This conference which was held at Blunt's in Isle of Wight county, was appointed to be in Norfolk; but the small-pox was prevailing much in Norfolk at that time, so that we could not meet in the town with safety.

from our connection, and 4 died; viz. William Early, Thomas Haymond, Benton Riggin, and Robert Bonham.

William Early was a native of Virginia, brought up in Bedford county. He acted as a local preacher for a few years, and was then received on trial, as an itinerant, in 1796. He was a zealous man, and a powerful preacher. His labours were greatly owned of God, and rendered a blessing to many souls. It was supposed that he took the yellow fever in Newbern, North-Carolina; but he continued to travel till the fever came on him so severely that he was forced to lay down by the side of the road, where one of the neighbours found him and asked him to his house, where he went and took his bed, and after a few days died of the fever, in September 1799. In the hour of death it was said that he was happy in God. In him the church lost a faithful, laborious, and useful servant.

Thomas Haymond was admitted on trial in 1790, and quit the work, and located in 1796. After two years he entered into the travelling connection again, and after travelling a little more than a year, he died on the 13th of June 1799. He was a plain man in his manners, and appeared to possess great goodness of heart. He was a solemn upright man, and often preached, and travelled more than his feeble frame could well bear. He exercised great patience under his last affliction, which lasted about fifteen days; he then died triumphantly.

Benton Riggin was a native of Somerset county, on the Eastern Shore of Maryland. He was of a slender habit of body, and had been accustomed to a sedentary life in his youth. He was a man of considerable abilities. He was a lively, useful, and acceptable preacher. He died at

Fell's-point, in September 1799. He had been a travelling preacher upwards of 12 years.

Robert Bonham was son of Hezekiah Bonham. His father was a preacher of the gospel. He was a young man of an upright walk; was lively in his ministry, and active in his duties. He began to travel in 1793, but he was only a supernumerary for a few years before he died; he was lingering out his life in a consumption for three years before his death. At the general conference when he was almost gone, he said he was resigned to the will of God, and felt his soul happy in the love of God. He died in Baltimore in June 1800.

Notwithstanding we took more preachers into the travelling connection this year, than we lost out of it, I considered ourselves not as well supplied as we were before: for we had only taken in young preachers; and many of them that had located were old and successful labourers in the ministry, and were well qualified to guide the Lord's flock.

We added to the society this year 3543 members, which was very encouraging to those who laboured and travelled night and day for the salvation of precious souls.

That the reader may see where our societies are most numerous, and where we haye prospered most in the past year, I will insert the following account. The first row of figures against each state, shows how many there are in society in that state; and the next figures show how many each state has gained or lost in the course of the past year.

States.	*No.*	*Gained.*
Georgia	1655	121
South-Carolina	4682	25
North-Carolina	8472	552

States.	*No.*	*Gained.*
Virginia	13390	558
Tennessee	743	112
Kentucky	1741	4
Maryland	12046	399
Delaware	2493	78
Pennsylvania	3187	lost 122
New-Jersey	2030	138
New-York	6363	406
Connecticut	1571	74
Rhode Island	227	31
Massachusetts	1577	168
New-Hampshire	171	40
Province of Maine	1197	80
Vermont	1096	492
Ohio	257	257
Natchees	60	60
Upper Canada	936	70
In all	64894	3543

This year we had 156 travelling elders, and their names were printed in the annual minutes in regular rotation: the oldest travelling preacher was set down first, and the next oldest, as they were found on the minutes, was set down next, and so on till the youngest elder was set down last. But those who had been part of their time located, were all entered at the bottom of the list, with this † mark to each name, that they may be known from the rest of the elders.

There was an alteration made in the 6th question and answer, in the annual minutes this year, and it was printed thus:

Q. 6. "*Who are the Bishops?*

A. "Thomas Coke, Francis Asbury, Richard Whatcoat."

This year we held our third regular general conference, which began in Baltimore on the 6th day of May, and continued until the twentieth.

We had 119 preachers present, who were regular members of that conference.

Some time previous to the meeting of the preachers in that conference, Mr. Asbury had said that when they met he would resign his office as superintendant of the Methodist connection, and would take his seat in the conference on a level with the elders. He wrote to several of the preachers in different parts of the connection, and informed them of his intention; and engaged other preachers to write to their brethren in the ministry, and to inform them of his intention to resign. Withal, he wrote his resignation with an intention to deliver it in to the conference as soon as they met, and to have it read in their first meeting. He said, he was so weak and feeble both in body and mind, that he was not able to go through the fatigues of his office.

When conference met and proceeded to business, they first took up Mr. Asbury's case thus, Q. "Whereas Mr. Asbury has signified his intention of resigning his official station in our church on account of his weakness of body, what is the sense of the conference on this occasion?

A. 1. "The general conference consider themselves under many and great obligations to Mr. Asbury for the many and great services which he has rendered to this connection.

2. "This conference do earnestly entreat Mr. Asbury for a continuation of his services as one of the general superintendants of the Methodist Episcopal Church, as far as his strength will permit."

Mr. Asbury told the conference, that he was still feeble both in body and mind, but was much better than he had been for some time before and notwithstanding he had been inclined to resign his office, he now felt willing to do any thing he could to serve the connection, and that the conference might require of him.

Dr. Coke then obtained liberty to return to Europe again, upon the condition that he should return to America as soon as his business would allow; or, at farthest, by the next general conference.

We then had the following questions and answers:—

Q. "Whereas it appears, that Mr. Asbury's weakness of body will not admit of his travelling as extensively through the United States as the situation of the connection requires, what further help will this conference afford him?

A. "Another bishop shall be elected and consecrated.

Q. "In what manner shall the votes for the election of a bishop be taken?

A. "By ballot."

There was then a lengthy debate respecting the powers the new bishop should possess. Some were of the opinion that he ought to act under the direction of the old bishop, and be governed by him; but it was finally determined that they should be on an equal footing, and be joint superintendants.

The conference then proceeded to vote for a bishop: On the first balloting, no one had a majority. They balloted a second time, and the tellers reported that there was a tie between Richard Whatcoat and Jesse Lee. They proceeded to a third ballot, when Richard Whatcoat was declared to be duly elected by a majority of four votes.

On the 18th of May 1800, Richard Whatcoat was ordained a bishop, by the laying on of hands, by Dr. Coke, Mr. Asbury, and some of the Elders.

At this conference it was agreed to raise the allowance of the travelling preachers, &c. four dollars in each quarter; which will amount to $80 per year, instead of sixty-four. We also agreed to make some allowance for the children of preachers, and for orphans. The whole of the following regulations were formed at that time:

1. "That the annual allowance of the travelling preachers shall be eighty dollars, and their travelling expences.

2. "The annual allowance of the wives of travelling preachers shall be eighty dollars.

3. "That each child of a travelling preacher shall be allowed fourteen dollars annually to the age of seven years, and twenty-four dollars annually from the age of seven to fourteen years. *Nevertheless*, this rule shall not apply to the children of preachers whose families are provided for by other means in their circuits respectively.

"The allowance of the superannuated, worn-out, and supernumerary preachers, shall be eighty dollars annually.

"The annual allowance of the wives of superannuated, worn-out, and supernumerary preachers shall be eighty dollars.

"The annual allowance of the widows of travelling, superannuated, worn-out, and supernumerary preachers, shall be eighty dollars.

"The orphans of travelling, superannuated, worn-out, and supernumerary preachers, shall be allowed by the annual conferences, if possible, by such means as they can devise, sixteen dollars annually."

There was a plan laid for raising supplies for the above allowances; part of the plan had been in use before, and part of it was entirely new. What we called *The Preachers' Fund*, or the preachers' subscriptions to the fund, which was generally two dollars a year, was to be applied to that purpose: also, the monies which were accounted for to the annual conferences for marriages. And whatever surplus of money was in the hands of the stewards, after paying their circuit preachers, all the public collections which every preacher that had the charge of a circuit was to make, were to be brought to the conference. A *public collection* was to be made at every annual conference; which, together with the profits arising from the chartered fund, &c. was to be applied for the purpose of making up the allowances of the preachers, their wives, widows and children.

The conference then gave the following directions for building or renting dwelling-houses for the use of married travelling preachers:

1. "It is recommended by the general conference, to the travelling preachers, to advise our friends in general to purchase a lot of ground in each circuit, and to build a preacher's house thereon, and to furnish it with at least heavy furniture; and to settle the same on trustees appointed by the official members of the quarterly meeting, according to the deed of settlement published in our Form of Discipline.

2. "The general conference recommend to the country circuits, in cases where they are not able to comply with the above request, to rent a house for the married preacher and his family, (when such are stationed upon their circuits respectively) and that the annual conference do assist to make up the rents of such houses as far as they can, when the circuit cannot do it."

The conference elected Lemuel Green, and Henry Foxall, trustees of the chartered fund, in the room of John Dickins, deceased, and Cornelius Comegys, resigned.

There was a small alteration made in the rule for trying our members, and the private members in future were to judge whether the accused person was guilty or not, of the crime charged upon him; and after the society had found him guilty, the officiating preacher was to pass sentence on him according to the rules laid down in the form of our discipline. But in case the preacher should differ in judgment from the society respecting the innocency or guilt of the accused person, he might refer the business to the next quarterly-meeting where it should be determined.

Until this time our preachers were to give an account of all the private gifts they received, whether it were money, cloathing, or any thing else, towards their support; and it was to go in part of their quarterage, or else it was to be applied to make up the deficiencies of the other preachers at the next conference. At this conference it was agreed, the preacher might receive any present, and not give an account thereof.

It was now determined that there should be seven annual conferences, and that of New-England should be divided. That one should be called the *New-England Conference*, and the other the *New-York Conference*: and the bounds for each was fixed. It was then said, "Let each annual conference pay it's proportionable part toward the allowances of the bishops." This was the first time that a regular plan was laid for the support of the bishops; formerly the bishop received the greater part of his support from private friends; and the deficiency was generally made up by particular societies.

Another rule was made in the words following: "A record of the proceedings of each Annual Conference, shall be kept by a secretary chosen for that purpose; and a copy of the said record shall be sent to the General Conference."

We also formed a new rule respecting the next general conference, which was in the words following: "No preacher shall have a right to sit as a member in the next general conference, unless he is in full connection, and has been a travelling preacher four years." Previous to this time all our preachers who had been admitted into full connection, were entitled to a seat in the general conference, although they might have travelled only two years.

There was a new rule formed respecting the ordination of coloured, or black people, to the office of Deacons, among us, which is in the following words: "The bishops have obtained leave by the suffrages of the general conference, to ordain local deacons of our African brethren in places where they have built a house or houses for the worship of God; provided they have a person among them qualified for that office, and he can obtain an election of two-thirds of the male members of the society to which he belongs, and a recommendation from the minister who has the charge, and from his fellow-labourers in the city or circuit." Dated May 20, 1800.

This rule is at present but little known among the Methodist preachers themselves, owing to it's having never been printed; yet it is a regular rule which has been standing for nine years.—When the rule was formed, there were many of the preachers, especially from the southern states, that were much opposed to it; but a majority of the preachers voting for it, it was carried: some that were opposed, moved that it should not be printed in our Form of Discipline, and a vote of the conference was obtained to enter it on the journals only, and most of the preachers were opposed to it's being made public. Richard Allen, of Philadelphia, was ordained a deacon on the

11th day of June, 1799, and was the first coloured man that was ever ordained by the Methodists in the United States. Several others have since been ordained in New-York and Philadelphia, and one from Lynchburg, in Virginia. As the rule has not been known in general among our preachers, I have thought it proper to give it this publication.

We appointed the next general conference to be in the city of Baltimore, on the sixth day of May, 1804.

While the general conference was sitting in Baltimore, the preachers were very useful in the beginning of a glorious revival of religion in that place. And at the close, the preachers parted in great peace and love, and sat out for their stations in different parts of the United States.

The revival of religion which took place in Baltimore during the conference, began particularly in Old Town, where the people held meeting in a private house, and some of the preachers attended them in the afternoon of each day. Several were converted. The work then began to spread, and souls were converted in the different meeting-houses, and in different private houses, both by day and by night. The old christians were wonderfully stirred up to cry to God more earnestly, and the preachers that tarried in town for a few days were all on fire of love. Such a time of refreshing from the presence of the Lord had not been felt in that town for some years. The young people were greatly alarmed, and many of them were changed from darkness to light, and from the power of Satan to God.

About two weeks after the close of the general conference, we held our annual conferenee at Duck Creek cross-roads; and a good many of the young converts, and of the old christians from

Baltimore came over to that meeting. It appeared to be a place highly favoured of the Lord, and a wonderful display of the divine power was soon seen among the people, and many souls were brought into the liberty of the children of God in a short time. The conference sat in a private room, while the local preachers, the young travelling preachers, and other people were almost continually engaged in carrying on the meeting in the meeting-house, and in private houses. At one time, the meeting in the meeting-house continued without intermission for 45 hours, which was almost two days and nights. When the preachers attended to preach, the people tried to be as quiet as possible till the sermon was ended; but some times they would break out in loud praises to God, so that the speaker could not be heard: and when they were silent till the sermon was ended, they commonly gave vent to their full hearts immediately, and in a few minutes the house would ring with the songs of praise. Thus they continued day and night. Some of the people when they were almost worn-out, would go home in the evening or at midnight, and take a little sleep, and then as soon as they awoke, they would hurry off to meeting again, at any hour of the night. Many of the saints, as well as sinners would tremble, shake, and fall helpless on the floor, and remain in that condition for a considerable time. They continued in this delightful frame during the sitting of the conference, which lasted almost a week: during which time there were but few hours together, in which there was no one converted. Many people were converted in private houses when by themselves, or when they were at prayer in the family. I believe I never saw before, for so many days together, such a glorious work of God, and so many people brought to the knowledge of God by the forgiveness of their sins. I think there were at least 150 souls converted at that place, in the course of that week. From that time and place, the heavenly flame spread through the Eastern Shore of Maryland, and the lower counties of the Delaware state, in an uncommon manner. The preachers and people carried the fire of love with them to their different circuits, and places of abode. Thousands of people will have cause to bless God for that conference.

About the same time there was a most remarkable revival of religion in the western country, both in Tennessee, and Kentucky states; such a work as had never been seen in that part of the world, since the first settling of the country.

I suppose the Methodist connection hardly ever knew such a time of a general revival of religion through the whole of their circuits, as they had about the latter part of the year 1800.

The work of the Lord which began at Duck Creek cross-roads, at the conference in June, had such an effect on the inhabitants, that 117 persons, in and about that little village, joined our society in the course of a few days; and the greater part of them had been converted within a few weeks. In all our societies in that neighbourhood, there was a considerable ingathering of precious souls; and many stubborn sinners were conquered and changed both in heart and life. The work of the Lord continued to spread and revive on the Eastern Shore throughout the summer and autumn.

Religion revived very much in Philadelphia also in the latter part of the year, and many souls were happily converted; and our societies were considerably increased.

In December, by a letter from Wilson Lee, then of Baltimore, I was informed there had been a great revival of religion in that city, and in some of the neighbouring circuits. In Frederick circuit about three hundred and thirty-two had professed to find peace with God, through our Lord Jesus Christ in the course of a few months. In Montgomery circuit three hundred and thirty had professed to be converted since the first of last May, and the work was still increasing, and going on with speed in both the above mentioned circuits. In Baltimore the work was still going on, and they had great and good times. In Hartford circuit there had been about sixty souls brought to the Lord, and the work was still lively. From this account we may see how the people were favoured of the Lord in the western parts of Maryland. Truly we may say the Lord has no respect to persons; but in every nation he that feareth him, and worketh righteousness is accepted of him.

There was also a gracious work of God in the state of Vermont, and in other parts of New-England; some of our preachers wrote that at a quarterly meeting held in Vershire, the Lord was present indeed; several found the Lord, and others, who had already believed, were overwhelmed with the power of God. About fifty members had been added in Essex circuit, which extended into, and included part of the British dominions, (Lower Canada); there were upwards of eighty members added to the society, and the greater part of them professed and evidenced a change wrought by grace.

In Plattsburg circuit, which lies on the west side of Lake Champlain, there was a singular display of God's converting and sanctifying power mong the people, and about sixty members were added to the society.

The revival reached to some parts of New-Hampshire state. There was a good prospect in Landaff circuit; there had been about sixty members added to the society, and the work was still increasing.

There was a good revival in Chesterfield circuit, and particularly in Charlton; where many people had been converted, and about forty members added to the society.

In Pittsfield circuit there was a good ingathering of precious souls to Christ, and to his church; at a quarterly meeting held in the latter part of the year, some of the wicked and the wise fell to the floor. Some were converted, and six professed sanctification. About seventy members were added to the society, and the work was enlarging, and in a flourishing way.

In Granville circuit there was a revival of religion, and especially in Westfield and Chester, and the societies were much increased.

In some parts of Connecticut, religion prospered very much; and in Tolland circuit there was a good revival: at a quarterly meeting held for that place, they had a great and good time. The meeting which began on Saturday, continued until three o'clock on Sunday morning, and the work spread in different directions. Upwards of sixty members joined the society.

The work was very prosperous in New London, and some souls were happily changed from nature to grace. Indeed, there was a greater work of the Lord in the conversion of souls in that part of New-England, than had ever been known among the Methodists in those parts of the country.

In 1801 we had seven conferences:

The 162d conference was held in Cambden, S. C. on the 1st of January 1801.

The 163d, at Drumgoole's, in Brunswick, on the 9th of April.[a]

The 164th, at Holstein, on the 1st of May.

The 165th, at Pipe Creek, (Maryland) on the 1st of May.

The 166th, in Philadelphia, on the 1st of June.

The 167th, in New-York, on the 16th of June.

The 168th, in Lynn, near Boston, on the 17th of July.

At these conferences, we took in several new circuits, *Hanover* in New-Hampshire; *Barnard* in Vermont; *Ottawa* and *Erie* in Canada.

We took on trial upwards of 50 young preachers; and lost 36 out of the travelling connection; 32 located, and 4 died. Those who died were James Tollison, Abraham Andrews, Salathiel Weeks, and Charles Burgoon.

1. James Tollison was a native of South Carolina. He travelled and preached between nine and ten years; in which time he preached from Georgia to New-York. He possessed good gifts, and was a man of an excellent understanding: He was pious, and uniform in his religious deportment. He was much beloved where he travelled, both by the preachers and people. He died in Portsmouth, Virginia, of the yellow fever, in August 1800. He manifested great resignation to the will of God in his afflictions, and appeared to have a lively sense of the love of God at the close of life. He made his will and left all he possessed to the Methodist preachers. His clothes were brought to the next conference in Virginia, and given to the travelling preachers.

(a) This conference was appointed on the 1st day of April; but the bishops said they forgot the time, and directed the preachers to make their appointments beforehand, so as to bring them to conference on the 9th of April.

2. Abraham Andrews was a native of England. He came to America in 1796, and was permitted to travel and preach among us. He died in August 1800, in the sixty-sixth year of his age.

3. Salathiel Weeks was a native of Prince George county, Virginia. He laboured faithfully in the ministry for several years, till his constitution failed, and he fell into a consumption; under which complaint he languished for a few years, and then died in November 1800, at his own house.

4. Charles Burgoon was a native of Maryland. He was of a dejected spirit, and often laboured under peculiar trials. He was much afflicted with various diseases, and for several years lingered out his life in weakness and affliction; and died in peace, in the latter part of the year 1800.

We added this year 7980 members to our society. The great revival of religion which took place last summer, and continued throughout the year, was now to be discovered in the great increase of our number. We had no return made of the number in Kentucky, Tennessee, or Rhode Island states; so that we inserted in our annual minutes this year, the same numbers that were entered for those states in the preceding year. We were sensible that a large number had been added to our society in the western states, Kentucky and Tennessee, but as the returns did not come to hand we could not do otherwise than take the old number.

During this year, 1801, the work of God spread and revived greatly in most parts of our connection; but our societies increased more in Maryland and Delaware states, than in any of the other states. However, the work was pretty general; and by letters written from different parts of the United States, we were assured the work continued to prosper throughout the year.

The work of the Lord prospered greatly in some parts of New-Hampshire and Vermont this year also: one preacher says, "Landaff circuit in New-Hampshire is all in a flame; upwards of one hundred have been converted to God, and the work goes on still in a most glorious manner. In Chesterfield circuit near one hundred have joined our society, and the prospect is brighter than it has been. In Vershire circuit, in Vermont, there is a good work: more than one hundred have joined society, and the power of the Lord is remarkably displayed; many fall down being overwhelmed with the power of the Lord. Weathersfield circuit has been gradually gaining ground the whole year, and now the times of refreshing are come from the presence of the Lord. In the town of Athens we had a most melting time: the power of the Lord was present to heal; and eighty-three joined society that day, although there was no society there before."

In the latter part of May there was a meeting, called an annual meeting, held at Dover in Delaware state, which continued for several days, and ended on the last day of the month: at which time the Lord wrought wonders in convicting and converting precious souls. On the last day of the meeting about one hundred and thirteen persons, white and black were joined in society. Many more went from that blessed meeting under deep conviction, and earnestly groaning for redemption in the blood of Jesus.

There was a good work of God in Baltimore, and through the Baltimore district, which included several circuits. It was supposed by the preachers, that upwards of one thousand souls were converted in that district in the course of a few months. In Annapolis, which is the seat of government, there was a very great display of the power and love of God, and many souls were converted, and added to the Society.

About this time CAMP MEETINGS were first introduced. But I never could learn whether they began in the upper parts of South-Carolina, in Tennessee, or in Kentucky. However, I believe they took place through necessity, and without design: and that there was no plan laid for them in the beginning. In the new parts of the country, where the people were but thinly settled, there were such crowds of people collected together, that no house could hold them, and there were not neighbours enough to entertain them. The ministers were obliged to preach in the woods, and some of the people to lodge on the ground in order to be at the meetings the next day. Sometimes they had meetings for three or four days together, and on some occasions where the work of the Lord was uncommonly powerful, and souls were under deep distress, the meeting would continue all night without intermission. In some cases persons were struck down by the power of God, and lay helpless most part of the night and could not be taken away. In such cases ministers and people felt it their duty to tarry with their friends, and to encourage and pray with such as were under distress. After awhile, the people expecting to be detained all night at some of their great meetings, began to prepare some kind of tents, made out of cloth, or bushes, and carried provisions with them, in order that they might tarry both day and night at the place of meeting, without being a burden to any one; and without being altogether exposed to the night air, or to the weather when it was wet or disagreeable. As it became more common to make such preparation for encamping, and the people saw the good effects of staying together, and keeping up the meeting through the night, where there was a particular manifestation of the divine presence, it was thought proper to advise the people to come prepared so to tarry. In some cases public notice was given, for the people to come to meeting prepared to lodge on the ground, and to bring provision both for man and beast, that they might stay together three or four days, and wait upon the Lord continually. As the people were invited to come and to encamp on the ground, they soon gave those meetings the distinguishing name of CAMP-MEETINGS. After that, when the name of a Camp-Meeting was heard of, the people knew what provision was necessary to be made for that purpose.

In our annual minutes for this year we published the number of Methodists in Europe and America; which was as follows:

In Europe, - -	109,961
In Nova-Scotia, Newfoundland, and the West-Indies,	13,667
In the United States and Canada,	72,874
Total in Europe and America	196,502

Mr. Wesley first began to form societies in 1739, which may be considered as the first regular societies of the Methodists that were established. From that time they have spread and increased in the course of sixty-two years to an unexpected number, as may be seen in the preceding statement.

The following table will shew the increase, and decrease of the Methodists in each state for five years past, viz. from 1796 to 1801.

States.	*in* 1796	*in* 1801
Georgia - -	1174	1663

States.	*in* 1796	*in* 1801
South-Carolina -	3659	4644
North-Carolina -	8713	8114
Tennessee - -	546	743
Virginia -	13779	13650
Kentucky - -	1750	1741
Maryland -	12416	15594
Delaware - -	2228	4123
Pennsylvania	3011	3828
New-Jersey - -	2351	3159
New-York -	4044	7034
Connecticut -	1050	1567
Rhode-Island -	220	227
Massachusetts -	824	1665
New Hampshire -	68	524
Province of Maine -	357	1386
Vermont		1607
North West Territory, since Ohio state		366
Natchees - -		80
Canada -	474	1159
	56,664	72,874
		56,664
Total increase in five years		16,210

In 1802 we had the established number of conferences, 7 in all. One alteration took place, which was that the western conference was held in the latter part of the preceding year.

The 169th conference was held at Ebenezer, in Tennessee, on the 1st of October 1801.

The 170th, in Cambden, S. C. on the 1st of January 1802.

The 171st, at Salem meeting-house, on the 1st of March.

The 172d, in Baltimore, on the 1st of April.

The 173d, in Philadelphia, on the 1st of May.

The 174th, in New-York, on the 1st of June.

The 175th, at Monmouth, in the Province of Maine, on the 1st of July.

From the first to the last of these conferences was 9 months, which made it more inconvenient for the preachers to get the annual minutes and circulate them among the people, than it had been for some years before.

At these conferences we took in several new circuits: *Broad River*, in Georgia; *Fredericksburg*, in Virginia; *West Wheeling*, near the Ohio river; *Broad-Kiln* and *St. Martins*, on the Eastern Shore; *Dauphin*, in Pennsylvania; *Cape-May*, in New-Jersey; *Ulster* and *Weston*, in New-York; *Adams* and *Grand Isle*, in the Pittsfield district; *Athens*, in the New-London district; *Lunenburg*, *Bridgewater*, and *Woodstock*, in Vershire district; *Poplin*, in New-Hampshire; *Hallowell* and *Falmouth*, in the Province of Maine. Our borders were greatly enlarged this year; we took in many new circuits, and divided several of the old ones: and some change was made in the names of others.

I have been under the necessity of mentioning the names of some of the new circuits as belonging to particular districts, without being able to tell what state they were in: owing to a change in the form of the annual minutes. For some years back we took the numbers in society by states, and this year for the first time they were taken by districts; of course we cannot tell how many members we have in each state.

We admitted on trial near 70 young preachers this year, which was a pretty good supply for all our circuits. We lost 8 preachers only out of the travelling connection, and each of them located. We were more favoured in this particular than we had been for a long time; so few located:

and there was not a death among all the itinerant preachers.

We added 13,860 members to our society this year. This was the most prosperous year that the Methodists had ever seen in the United States. However, there was one year, 1790, in which we added almost 500 more; but the number of young preachers this year was considerably greater; and withal, we kept so many of the old preachers in the work, that we might well say *The Lord is our helper and we will not fear.*

The work had spread through the middle states from the time of holding our general conference in 1800, and had been going on for some time in Kentucky and Tennessee states. There was scarcely any part of the country where the Methodist preachers travelled and laboured, in which there was not a revival of religion.

The accounts given in the news-papers and in private letters, both by ministers and private christians, of the number of souls converted at *Camp-Meetings*, and other meetings, far exceeded any thing of the kind that I had ever heard of before in the United States.

In the south parts of Virginia where our societies had been kept in confusion for some years, by a divisive party that separated from us; even there the Lord was pleased to pour out his Spirit upon the people, and to cause Zion to lift up her drooping head. Old Christians became closely united; and many sinners were brought into the favour and love of God. In that revival, it was remarkable to see what a number of young people who had been brought up by religious parents, were brought under serious impressions, and afterwards happily converted.

We had very pleasing accounts of the prosperity of religion from various places. A letter from

South Carolina informed us, that the sacred flame was spreading through Georgia and South-Carolina, and that hundreds of sinners had been awakened and converted in the course of half a year.

At that time, what we now call Camp-Meetings were frequently called *General-Meetings*; and in some cases the Methodist, Presbyterian, and Baptist ministers would all unite in carrying on the same meeting. The same letter says, that in June the Methodists held a general meeting at the Hanging Rock, where they had fifteen ministers, some of them were Methodists, and the others Presbyterians and Baptists; about three thousand people attended with them. The work of the Lord began on Friday night. The preachers were singing, praying, or preaching all night. Saturday evening it began again; and on Sabbath evening, at the close of the sacrament, some fell to the earth beneath the power of the Lord; the work went on, and the meeting continued all night. On Monday morning the people again came together, and began to sing and exhort, and the Lord was present. That was the greatest time of all. The people were crying for mercy on all sides. We judged that twelve or fifteen found peace with God.

About the middle of this year, there was a remarkable revival of religion in many parts of North-Carolina. High up the Yadkin River the work of the Lord was very great, and more or less people were frequently converted at public preaching. One preacher said he preached as often as his strength would admit of, and the power of God attended his meetings, and from three to four, and sometimes from seven to eight were brought into the glorious liberty of the children of God, at a meeting. He formed a society at Snow-Creek of about fifty members; and another in another neighbourhood of about the same number. One preacher admitted about fifty members in going once round the Yadkin circuit.

At a quarterly meeting in Guilford circuit in May, between forty and fifty persons professed to be converted in the course of that meeting. And at another quarterly meeting held at Hickory Mountain meeting house, in the month of June, in Haw-River circuit, they had the greatest time of the power and presence of God, that they had ever seen at that place.

The Lord wrought wonders in the state of Virginia in the course of that year. At a quarterly meeting held at Mabry's chapel in the spring of the year, we had about ten persons converted. At Merrit's chapel there were thirteen who professed to find favour with the Lord. The heavens dropped down righteousness upon the people in Greensville circuit, and at the quarterly meeting held at a meeting house, called the *Barn*, we had twelve who said they were converted. In Sussex circuit, it was supposed that one hundred were brought into the liberty of God's children in the space of six weeks. This great work began at Jones's chapel at a quarterly meeting, where sixteen souls professed to find peace with God, through our Lord Jesus Christ.

In the latter part of the year, there was a remarkable revival of religion in Norfolk and Portsmouth. This work began principally by the labours of Mr. John Chalmers, a local preacher, from Baltimore, who visited that place, and preached for a short time, and had private meetings with the people; from which time souls were awakened, and many of them happily changed both in heart and life.

There is an account given of a meeting held in Rockingham, which continued nine days; during that memorable week, business was wholly suspended, and both merchants and mechanics shut up their shops, and little else was attended to, but waiting upon the Lord; and there was a constant croud of people from the country. On Sunday, the last day of the meeting, the way was opened for the people to join society, and one hundred and seven offered themselves; most of whom lived in, or near the town. The number of those who lived at a distance, and shared in that gracious visitation, has not been ascertained; but it is probable it bore a proportion to those in the town.

At Alexandria there was a great out-pouring of the Spirit upon the inhabitants of the city. At a quarterly meeting held at Christmas, they began the siege, which lasted sixteen days, during which time, on a moderate calculation, one hundred found peace with God; and one hundred and ten joined our society. This work was principally among the young people.

There was a wonderful display of the goodness of God in the conversion of precious souls in different parts of Maryland. The preachers joined about one hundred and fifty persons in Calvert circuit, in the course of three months, and some were converted every time the preachers came round. Ten or twelve white people and about twenty blacks, found peace at a quarterly-meeting.

There was what the people called an annual meeting, held in Dover, Delaware state, which began on Friday night the fifth of June, and continued till the next Friday morning, and then broke up a little before the break of day; at which time and place many precious souls were both awakened, and happily converted to God.

The work of God spread and prevailed much in the Ohio state, and one of the preachers said that their congregations were large in general, and in places where formerly fifty persons made a respectable congregation, a thousand was then but a tolerable gathering. At a quarterly meeting held near the Miami, the Lord was with the people of a truth, and many souls were brought to the knowledge of God. We may say, this work is of God, and ye cannot overthrow it.

In 1803 we had 7 conferences, but one of them was held in October in the preceding year; but was entered on the minutes for that year.

The 176th conference was held at Cumberland, in Tennessee, on the 2d of October 1802.

The 177th, in Camden, on the 1st of January 1803.

The 178th, at Drumgoole's, Virginia, on the 1st of March.

The 179th, in Baltimore, on the 1st of April.

The 180th, at Duck-Creek cross-roads, on the 1st of May.

The 181st, in Boston, on the 2d Thursday in June.

The 182d, at Ashgrove, on the 1st of July.

There were several new circuits taken in this year.

In the Western conference, they changed the names of some of the circuits, and left out Cumberland, Green, and Russel, and entered the following ones, *Nollechucky*, *French-Broad*, *Clinch*, *Powel's Valley*, *Nashville*, *Red-River* and *Barren*.

In the South-Carolina conference *Sandy-River*.

In Baltimore conference, *Deerfield*, near the Ohio.

In Philadelphia conference, they left out Mohawk, and Oneida, and entered *Littleton*, *Otsego*, *Black-River*, *Westmoreland*, *Pompey*, and *Ontario*.

In New-York conference, they took in *Quebec*, *Montreal*, and *St. Johns*, all lying in Canada; and *Ashburnham* in New London district.

In New-England conference they took in two circuits, *Bristol* and *Bowdoinham*, both of them were in the province of Maine.

We took about 50 young preachers on trial this year; and we lost 18 out of the travelling connection: 14 located, and 4 died, namely *Lewis Hunt*, *Edmund Wayman*, *John Leach*, and *Anthony Turk*.

1. Lewis Hunt was a native of Virginia. He travelled principally in Kentucky, and the Ohio states. He was said to be a useful preacher while he travelled. A few weeks before his death, he returned to his father's in Fleming county, Kentucky, where he died of a consumption, in apparent possession of an assured peace with God, and a calm and tranquil mind, on the 8th of December 1801.

2. Edmund Wayman was born on the Western Shore of Maryland. He died in Hampshire county, Virginia, on the 21st day of April 1802. He was in the travelling connection about five years. During his last illness he said but little, but appeared to possess great tranquillity of mind, and died in peace. He was about forty years old.

3. John Leach was a native of Burlington county in New Jersey. He was an itinerant preacher about five years. He was a pious circumspect christian; and a minister of good abilities, and was acceptable and useful in his preaching. The two last years of his life he laboured under great and heavy afflictions, which he bore with great pa-

tience. He died of the dropsy in October 1802. He left the world in great peace.

4. Anthony Turk was a native of New York state, and descended from the Low-Dutch. He was a zealous indefatigable preacher; subject to great afflictions, and peculiar trials. He expressed some time before his death, and in his last illness, an increasing sweetness in communion with God. His last sickness was short and severe, but he gave great marks of patience, resignation and victory in death, to them who attended him. He departed this life March 13th, 1803, in Freehold circuit, Monmouth county, New Jersey.

We added 17,336 members to the society this year, which was a much larger number than we had ever added in any one year. Our ministers and people, throughout the connection were uncommonly devoted to God; and much engaged to promote his cause. CAMP MEETINGS were encouraged in many places; and attended by many ministers, and by thousands of people in the lower parts of Virginia and North Carolina; at which seasons the Lord was pleased to visit us in a remarkable manner, both saints and sinners, old and young people; so that the mouths of many gainsayers were stopped, and the hearts of many sinners were touched, and happily changed and renewed.

The first Camp meeting that was ever held in the lower parts of Virginia, was in Brunswick county, at a new meeting house, which was named CAMP-MEETING-HOUSE, that it might be remembered in future, the first Camp-meeting in that part of the world, was held at that place. The meeting began on the 27th day of May 1803, and broke up on the 30th. During which time there were upwards of 30 souls who professed a real change of heart.

The next camp-meeting which was held in that part of the country, was in the same county, at a meeting house called the *Barn*, which began on the 19th of August, in the same year, where we had about an hundred souls converted.

To give a full account of the spread of the gospel, and of the revival of religion among us this year, would exceed the bounds of a short history. Yet it may be profitable to mention a few particulars, that the reader may see in what places the Lord was pleased to make known his goodness, in the salvation of many souls.

In the latter part of the preceding year, in the month of October, there was a general camp-meeting at a meeting house called Rehoboth, in Warren county in Georgia. The ground was opened in an oblong form, having the meeting-house in the middle. On the second day, souls were converted to God; and the work spread through the assembly. Toward the close of the meeting it was proposed, that all who had been converted during that meeting, should rise up on their feet; when upwards of fifty stood up. It was thought that as many as one hundred souls were converted at that meeting. The Lord was pleased to favour the people in Georgia in 1803, with an uncommon prosperous time in religion and many souls were brought to God at public and at private meetings.

Another account says, "At the quarterly meetings in Broad river, and in Appalachie circuits, there were about thirty or forty converted at each place."

The quarterly meeting at Harris's chapel in Washington county was remarkably favoured with the presence of the Lord. Conversions were clear and powerful; and not many short of one hundred professed converting grace at that time.

At a camp-meeting at Stinchcomb's chapel, forty or fifty souls found the Lord in the forgiveness of their sins. And at the camp-meeting near Liberty chapel, many souls were awakened, and about fifty converted.

This account of the glorious spread of religion, and of so many souls being brought to God, must be pleasing to all who love the Lord Jesus Christ in sincerity. Indeed, Georgia has been a great place for religion, from that day to this; and old professors have generally been very lively in religion.

In South-Carolina religion gained ground, and in many places it might be said to be all in a flame. In July, there was a camp-meeting held in Sandy river circuit, which was said to be the greatest time among sinners that some of them ever saw. On Saturday the Lord began to shake Satan's kingdom in a powerful manner. On Sunday, and Sunday night, the power of darkness gave back. Many sinners were on the ground crying for mercy, and many believers crying for perfect love. About twenty persons found redemption in the blood of Jesus at that time.

In North-Carolina the work of the Lord spread greatly, and was known both among saints and sinners. A short account of the camp-meetings in the lower part of that state says, " At the first camp-meeting, I suppose there were twenty-seven persons converted. Several at the second and third, about ten at the fourth, and about sixty-seven at the last."

In Virginia, there was a very great ingathering of precious souls. There was a quarterly meeting in February in Rockingham circuit, which was held in Harrisonburg, which continued for four days and nights, with but little intermission. It was impossible to ascertain correctly the number that were converted; but it was thought there must have been thirty or upwards. It was said, that three or four hundred were taken into society there in the course of a few months.

At a quarterly-meeting held at Shepherd's Town, there were twelve or fifteen souls converted. And at Leesburg, where quarterly-meeting was held, the Lord was with the people of a truth. Some persons professed to be converted, on Saturday, and others on Sunday. On Monday and Tuesday the preachers went from house to house to talk to the distressed, and to sing and pray with them: and as soon as they would begin to sing and pray, the room would be crouded with the people. On Tuesday and Tuesday night, they were singing, praying and exhorting for sixteen hours together, in which time fifteen souls professed to get converted. It was pretty certain, that in the course of this meeting there were forty souls or upwards converted to God.

There was a quarterly meeting in Winchester circuit, which was held for four days, as a kind of camp-meeting, where the Lord was eminently present; and upon a moderate calculation, it was thought that there must have been from forty to fifty converted.

There was a gracious stir of religion in Front-royal also, and many souls were converted in that little village.

The prosperity of religion was not less in Maryland than in other states. The Lord visited the people in an extraordinary manner in several places; and particularly at a camp-meeting held in the woods about fifteen miles above Baltimore, and a little to the east of the road that leads to

Reister's-Town. This meeting was held in September, and began on Saturday and ended on Monday. The first day and night was owned of God, and several were converted by the beginning of the Sabbath morning. On Sunday the congregation was exceedingly large ; and about the middle of the day the work was visible, and pretty general. Little else was heard but the cries of the distressed for mercy, or the shouts of the christians, *Glory to God in the highest.* On Monday morning the christians felt more of the power and love of God than in any other part of the meeting. That day is still remembered by them as " The happy Monday, the blessed 26th of September 1803." It was thought that one hundred souls were the subjects of an extraordinary work, either of conviction, conversion or sanctification. Such a continual power and increase of the love of God for three days together, was seldom or never known by those who were present, as they witnessed at that time.

There was a gracious reformation, and many converted in the city of Middletown, in the state of Connecticut, in the course of the summer and fall of the year. A number of the inhabitants went from the city by water down the river to what they called a kind of field-meeting, where the work began, and several were awakened ; and some of them were converted as they returned home. From that time the work revived and a good many persons were in a short time brought to the knowledge of God by the forgiveness of sins.

In Kentucky, the work of the Lord was very great : in Limestone circuit there were about three hundred added to the society, and sinners were flocking home to God in every direction. This work was not confined to one place, but spread greatly through the state. The work was great in Tennessee, and very many were raised from a death of sin, unto spiritual life.

At that time there was great union between the Presbyterians and the Methodists; and they frequently communed together, and united in holding camp-meetings, and in preaching together. In the Western states, religion revived among other denominations as well as the Methodists.

CHAPTER XI.

From the beginning of the year 1804, *including the fourth general conference, to the end of the year* 1806.

In 1804 we had 8 conferences, one of which was a general conference.

The 183d conference was held at Mount Gerrizim, Kentucky, on the 2d of October 1803.

The 184th, at Augusta, in Georgia, on the 1st of January 1804.

The 185th, at Salem meeting house, on the 10th of April.

The 186th, in Alexandria, on the 27th of April.

The 187th was a general conference, held in Baltimore, on the 6th of May.

The 188th, at Soudersburg, on the 23d of May.

The 189th, in New-York, on the 12th of June.

The 190th, at Buxton, (Province of Maine) on the 15th of July.

We took in some new circuits, divided some, and changed the names of others this year.

In the Western conference we took in *Wilderness*, *Wayne*, *Livingston*, *Illinois*, and *Guyandott*; in Baltimore conference, *Greenfield*; in New-York conference, *Montgomery*; and in Canada, *River Le French*; and in New England conference, *Magog*, *Barre*, *Grantham*, and *Scarborough*.

At these conferences we admitted on trial upwards of 70 young preachers, which were more than were ever admitted among us in any one year. We lost 48 preachers out of the travelling connection; 2 were expelled, 42 located, and 4 died; namely, William Ormond, Nathan Jarratt, Rezin Cash, and David Brown.

1st. William Ormond was a native of North-Carolina, born in Dobbs county. He had been a travelling preacher upwards of twelve years. His constitution had been failing for some time, by reason of his constant, fervent, zealous labours in the late revivals of religion where he had been. He was a good preacher, and very useful. He travelled in all the Southern states from Maryland to Georgia. It was supposed that he took the yellow fever in Norfolk, of which he died on the 30th of October 1803, in Brunswick county, Virginia. In his last sickness he suffered with great patience, and was frequently so happy, that he would praise God with a vocal voice, and shout when left alone, "Glory, glory: victory, victory, compleat victory." The manner in which he died, afforded great satisfaction to all who were present with him.

2d. Nathan Jarratt was a native of North Carolina. He had been travelling upwards of four years. He was a man of great zeal, and had a pleasing voice. He was a good preacher, and was useful in most places where he laboured; and he was much beloved by the brethren in general. He died in the triumph of faith on the 28th of October 1803. The night before he died, he broke out in a rapture of joy, and sung a few lines of a hymn, and then in a few moments he sweetly slept in Jesus.

3d. Rezin Cash was a native of Maryland, Montgomery county. He had been a travelling preacher above nine years. He was a man of great solemnity of mind, and goodness of heart. He lingered away his life; but died in peace in 1803.

4th. David Brown was a native of Ireland. He came to this country a local preacher; he became an itinerant preacher among us in 1794, and after travelling a little more than nine years, he died on the 5th of September 1803. He was greatly beloved by the brethren while he lived, and was much lamented when he died. His piety commanded respect. His travels were not extensive; but were chiefly confined to a few circuits to the northward of New-York, and adjacent to the city. He ended his life at Ashgrove on Cambridge circuit.

This year we added 9064 members to our society; making in all 113,134 Methodists in the United states: including those which are under our care in Canada. Thus hath the Lord blessed and prospered us in our christian and ministerial labours in the course of less than 40 years.

This year we held our fourth general conference in Baltimore, which began on the sixth day of May. We had 111 preachers present, who were regular members of that conference. I will here give an account of the number of preachers from each annual conference, of which there are seven.

From the	Western conference	-	3
	South-Carolina do.	-	5
	Virginia do.	-	17
	Baltimore do.	-	30
	Philadelphia do.	-	37
	New-York do.	-	12
	New-England do.	-	4
			108
	And 3 bishops		3
	The whole was		111

From this view it may be seen, that we had not a proportionable part of preachers, from each part of the connection; the three conferences in the extremities of the work had only 12 members in the general conference. Baltimore and Philadelphia conferences furnished 67 members, which was almost two-thirds of the preachers which composed that conference; while the other five annual conferences furnished but little more than one-third of the members, being only 41 in the whole. We saw the necessity of making an alteration in that point; but after all, we let it remain as it was. All the preachers that attended this general conference, had been regularly travelling for four years. We had not as many members present as we had at the two general conferences preceding it, but we considered it of greater weight than the former ones, because of their age in the ministry. In the former general conferences we allowed all the preachers who had been travelling two years, to be members; but in this the youngest members had been travelling four years.

We had no minutes of our general conference published in a pamphlet this year, (although it had been done at the preceding general conferences) but the alterations and additions which were made to our rules, were put into the chapters, sections, and paragraphs, where they belonged in the Form of Discipline.

We had several new regulations made at this general conference; one was as follows: "The bishops shall allow the annual conferences to sit a week at least." Before this rule was established, the bishop could conclude the business as soon as he thought proper.

The following rule was also formed: "The bishop shall not allow any preacher to remain in the same station or circuit more than two years successively." In some cases, prior to that rule, the bishop had appointed a preacher or preachers to the same place for three years together. We now determined on a better plan, and formed this rule, to prevent any preacher from wishing or expecting such an appointment in future.

The following rule was formed respecting the president of the annual conference, in case the bishops should be absent. "In case there are two or more presiding elders belonging to one conference, the bishop, or bishops, may by letter or otherwise appoint the president; but if no appointment be made, the conference shall elect the president from among the presiding elders, by ballot, without debate."

It was for the first time determined, that the assembly of the official members at quarterly-meeting, should be called "The quarterly-meeting conference." The rule reads thus: "The quarterly-meeting conference shall appoint a secretary to take down the proceedings of the quarterly-meeting conference, in a book kept by one of the stewards of the circuit for that purpose."

The following new regulation was also formed: "The presiding elder shall not employ a preacher who has been rejected at the preceding annual conference, unless the conference should give him liberty under certain conditions."

There was an alteration made, also, concerning our members marrying out of society. The rule until this time was, that if any of our members married with *unawakened* persons, they should be expelled from the society; but it was now so modified that they should not be expelled, but "be put back on trial for six months."

The above rules and regulations I have taken from the first part of our Form of Discipline. At this conference we concluded to print the Form of Discipline in two parts; the first to be called the spiritual, and the second the temporal part of the discipline. It was also determined, that the first part of the discipline should be published alone, for the benefit of the black people in the south, who were members of our society, and were taught to read.

In the second, or temporal part of the discipline, we made some alterations. We determined that the Book-business should be removed from Philadelphia to New-York; and the printing and binding of our books, &c. should be done in the last mentioned city. Ezekiel Cooper was re-elected as General Book Steward; and John Wilson was afterwards chosen an Assistant Book Steward, to assist Mr. Cooper in the book business.—There were a few regulations made for circulating the books, collecting bad debts, &c.

There was a motion made at this conference to appoint another bishop, but there were only a few members in favour of it, and of course there was not much said on the subject.

The conference closed in peace, and the preachers parted in much love; but we had to lament before the Lord, that there was very little stir of religion among us during the sitting of the conference. One principal reason of our barrenness I believe was owing to an improper plan which was adopted by the conference in the beginning of their business, which was this; to admit men, women and children into the galleries of the meeting-house to hear our debates. After a few days we were obliged to close the galleries and sit in private, according to our usual plan. It was to the preachers a good conference, but there was very little visible good done among the people in general.

Religion prospered among us very much during this year also; and we had pleasing accounts from almost every part of the connection.

In June there was a camp-meeting about ten miles from Wilmington, in North Carolina, where the power of God was present, both to wound and to heal. The cries of the distressed, and the shouts of joy from those that were healed, were truly awful and pleasing. The work broke out the first day, and continued to increase until Sunday evening. The slain of the Lord were many, and it was supposed that as many as seventy souls found peace with God, through our Lord Jesus Christ. Other meetings in that part of the country were greatly favoured of the Lord; and some persons of all descriptions were the subjects of the pardoning love of God, from the hoary-headed sinner, to children of nine years old. It was thought, that in the space of four or five months time there were three hundred souls converted in and about Bladen circuit.

In various places in Virginia the work of the Lord was very great. A letter from Harrisonburg, Rockingham county, mentioned, that at a quarterly-meeting in June, at Moffit's meeting-house, there were about 27 persons converted.—Another quarterly meeting was held at Edward Mitchell's, in Bottetourt county, which continued for five days; during that time eighteen professed to be converted. The next noted meeting was on Indian Creek, at Bethel, near Cook's, which continued four days, and it was thought that 30 souls were savingly delivered from their sins at that time. There was another quarterly meeting held for Greenbrier circuit at Mount Tabor, in the Little Levels, which continued six days, and it was supposed at least one hundred souls were converted before the meeting ended.

The next meeting was in Old-Town, in Alleghany circuit, which continued three days; in which time about eighteen persons professed to find peace with God.

They then had a camp meeting in Buttetourt circuit, on Glade-Creek, which broke up on the 5th day, where about fifty souls professed justifying faith.

The preachers went from that camp-meeting into the town of Fincastle, and began meeting at 3 o'clock on Wednesday, and the meeting continued until Thursday evening, in which time about twenty souls were happily converted.

There was another camp meeting held in August on Linvill's Creek, which continued nine days, and some of the people tarried on the ground until the tenth day. They took an account of 74 that were converted at that time, and had reason to believe that a good many more were the subjects of a real change. Another camp-meeting was held immediately afterwards at Rehoboth, in Greenbrier circuit, which continued six days; and it was thought that fifty persons were brought into the liberty of God's children at that meeting. From thence the preachers went to the Big Levels, and held another camp meeting, where about 20 souls found peace with God through our Lord Jesus Christ.

At these meetings, and a few others of the same kind, in that part of the country, there were, in the course of a few months, between three and four hundred souls adopted into the family of God.

In the latter part of the summer or beginning of autumn, there was a camp meeting held low down in Virginia, near the town of Suffolk, where the power and presence of God was wonderfully displayed. The meeting began on Friday, and continued with but little intermission till Monday night, in which time it was thought that three or four hundred persons were converted to God. The accounts from that meeting appear to be incredible to those who were not present; but those who were eye and ear witnesses, think it to be too great to be sufficiently described.

During this year Mr. Stith Mead laboured among the people of Bedford, Amherst and Campbell counties, and a few other places, where the Lord greatly owned his labours in the Gospel.—He gives an account of upwards of eleven hundred who were converted principally at the meetings where he was, in the course of six months. It appeared as if the kingdoms of this world would soon become the kingdoms of the Lord, and of his Christ. These camp meetings were the first that had ever been held in that part of Virginia.

The town of Lynchburg shared largely in that revival, and many precious souls in that place were brought to the knowledge of God, and became members of our society.

Maryland was much favoured of the Lord again this year also. There was a camp-meeting held at a place called Hampton, belonging to General Ridgley, about ten miles from Baltimore, which began on September the 20th, and closed on the 24th, in which time it was thought that there were at least fifty souls converted. There were about thirty preachers present, who were closely united together in helping forward in this great work. The cries of the distressed, and the shouts of the saints made the forest ring, and echo back the praise of God. That meeting will be remembered with thankfulness by many who were present, till their dying day.

There was a gracious work of God in the Province of Maine this year. At the conference that was held there, in Buxton, in July, there was a wonderful display of the power of God, in the awakening of sinners; and it was supposed that between forty and fifty were converted at that time.

In the beginning of August, there was a quarterly meeting in Durham, which continued three days; it was thought that twenty souls experienced the pardoning grace of God; and many more went away deeply wounded. From that time the work spread and increased considerably.

In the month of September, there was what they called a field-meeting in Readfield, where there were above thirty souls who professed to be converted; and some professed a deeper work of grace. And in Bethel there was a great revival of religion, and many were brought to know the Lord: not less than about forty persons in the course of two or three months.

There was a gracious manifestation of the divine presence among the people in the Mississippi territory in the course of that year. Several white people and some blacks were brought to the knowledge of God; and there was a considerable awakening among the careless part of the people. The preachers that travelled and laboured in that part of the work, were much encouraged to hope for better days. Hitherto the Lord hath helped us.

In 1805 we had 7 conferences.

The 191st conference was held at Mount Gerrizim, Kentucky, on the 2d of October 1804.

The 192d, at Charleston, on the 1st of January 1805.

The 193d, at Edmund Taylor's, N. C. on the 1st of March.

The 194th, in Winchester, on the 1st of April.

The 195th, in Chester town, on the 1st of May.

The 196th, at Ashgrove, on the 12th of June.

The 197th, in Lynn, on the 12th of July.

We took in several new circuits this year. In the Western conference we took in *Licking*, *Roaring-River*, *Hartford*, and *Mad-river*; in Baltimore conference, *Munroe*, which lies about the Sweet-Springs in Virginia; in Philadelphia conference, *Scipio*; in New-York conference, *Haverstraw*, and *South Britain*; in New-England conference, *Loudon*, *Tufftenborough*, and *Livermore*; the last of these lies in the Province of Maine.

This year, at the several conferences, we admitted about eighty young preachers upon trial.

There was some alteration made in the annual minutes of the conference this year, and for the first time we were told into which of the conferences each of the preachers were admitted on trial, or admitted into full connection, &c. &c. as follows. Q. Who are admitted on trial? A. In the Western conference, such persons: In the South-Carolina conference, such persons, &c. which gave us a better view of the state of the connection than we could have from the former plan.

We lost 37 preachers out of the travelling connection this year: 25 of them located; 2 withdrew from us; 4 were expelled, and 6 died. Those that died, were Benjamin Jones, Tobias Gibson, Nicholas Waters, Wilson Lee, John Durbin, and Daniel Ryan.

1. Benjamin Jones was born near George-town in South Carolina. He was admitted upon trial in 1801, and died in the latter part of January 1804, having travelled just three years. He was found dead, and lying in the water, in a branch of the Brown Marsh, which runs into the Waccamaw lake. It was supposed by some people that he died in a fit, and fell from his horse into the water, where it was about two feet deep.

But others think there was reason to believe that he was murdered by some person, and thrown into the water. However, we have never been able to determine by what means he died. He was a solemn, serious, pious man; and we have no doubt but what he left his sufferings with his life.

2. Tobias Gibson was born in South Carolina, near Pee Dee, in 1771. He travelled considerably in South-Carolina, North Carolina, and Georgia, and then went to the Mississippi territory, and was the first missionary to the Natchees where he spent five or six years, and then died in peace on the 5th day of April 1804, in Claiborne county. He was very soft, affectionate, and agreeable in his conversation; his voice in preaching was very piercing, and melting. He was much devoted to God in private, and was very fond of reading, and of private prayer. He was beloved by all christians; and his labours were greatly owned of God. He laboured and preached in the circuits till his strength failed, and he could keep his station no longer. He then travelled about for the benefit of his health for a season; and wishing to be of some use to his fellow creatures, he concluded to go to the Natchees, and sat off by himself, without being sent by the conference: after he got to his destined place, his ministerial labours were so much owned of the Lord, that he was satisfied that the Lord had directed him to that part of the world. After that he was appointed by the conference to the same place, from year to year, till he died in peace.

3. Nicholas Waters was born in Maryland, and began to travel a circuit in 1776, and after travelling two or three years he located, and continued in a located state for about 20 years. He began to travel again in 1799, and after travelling

upwards of five years, he died in Charleston on the 10th of August 1804, in the 65th year of his age. He was quite resigned to death, and left the world in peace.

4. Wilson Lee was born in Sussex county, in Delaware state, in November 1761. He began to travel in 1784, and after travelling steadily for a little more than 20 years, he died October 11th 1804. He professed to be a witness of the perfect love of God, for many years before he died. He was a very animating speaker, and spared no pains in trying to bring souls to God. In private conversation, he was cheerful and solemn. He had a good turn for taking care of the church of God. When he acted as a circuit, or a stationed preacher, or as a presiding elder, he was generally approved of, and was rendered a blessing to the people to whom he preached. A few months before he died, when he was so low that he could not speak louder than his breath, he said to me with great solemnity. "I have given up the world; I have given up the church; I have given up all." He had frequently discharged blood from his lungs; and he closed his life while the blood was pouring out of his mouth. *Mark the perfect man, and behold the upright, for the end of that man is peace.* In the death of Wilson Lee the church has lost a faithful friend, and the preachers have lost a pattern of piety.

5. John Durbin was born in Frederick county, in Maryland, 1778. He began to travel in 1803, and died on the 25th of February 1805. He was only remaining on trial when he died, and was never admitted into full connection; yet he had his character given in the annual minutes.

6. Daniel Ryan was a native of Philadelphia, born in 1774. He was admitted on trial in 1800, and died on the 3d of February 1805, having tra-

velled almost five years. He was much respected where he travelled, and was looked upon as a good man, and a useful preacher. He appeared to be quite happy and resigned in his last illness.

This year we added 6811 members to our society, and the work of the Lord greatly prospered in most parts of our connection.

When we took the number of our travelling elders this year, we found that we had, according to the minutes, 212; the youngest of them had travelled four years, and several of them had travelled above twenty.

The Methodists have increased more of late years in the United States, than formerly. We have more preachers, more circuits, more members, and (I may say) more religion, than we ever had at any one time before.

The first Camp Meeting that was ever held on the Eastern-Shore, began on the 25th of July this year, in a beautiful place in the woods about three miles south of Duck-Creek Cross Roads, in Delaware state, which continued the four following days. Thousands of people attended that meeting, and I suppose two hundred persons were converted among the white people, and many of the blacks became the subjects of the same work. I think it exceeded any thing that I ever saw, for the conversion of souls and for the quickening influence of the Holy Ghost upon the hearts of believers. I took an account of sixty-eight Methodist preachers who were at that meeting. While some preached and others exhorted, the rest had their work to do in praying and in talking to the people. The work went on beautifully and powerfully. It was said, that the noise occasioned by the cries of the distressed and the shouts of the saints, was heard at the distance of three miles. Surely the Lord was in that place.

From that meeting the work of the Lord spread greatly on the Eastern-Shore, both in Maryland and Delaware states ; and hundreds were converted and added to the society in the course of a few months after that meeting.

The work of the Lord was very great in many places in the latter part of the summer, and religion prospered greatly. Our camp-meetings and quarterly meetings in different places, were greatly honoured with the presence of God, in the justification of precious souls. Many old christians were renewed in love, and many backsliders were reclaimed. It was quite common to hear of ten or twenty souls being converted at a common meeting, where the people met to hear a sermon, or to hold a prayer meeting. And it was quite common to hear of fifty or a hundred souls being converted at a quarterly-meeting or a camp-meeting. While sinners were coming home to God, Christians were advancing in the divine life, and the preachers were greatly animated and blessed in their souls and in their labours. And many young preachers were raised up to the help of the Lord against the mighty.

This revival of religion was not confined to the Methodists alone, but other denominations were highly favoured of the Lord. However, my business is to speak particularly of the Methodists, and to point out some of the many things which the Lord hath done for them.

In 1806 our conferences were as follows :

The 198th conference was held in Scott county, Kentucky, on the 2d of October 1805.

The 199th, in Camden, on the 30th of December 1805.

The 200th, in Norfolk, on the 14th of February 1806.

The 201st, in Baltimore, on the 14th of March.

The 202d, in Philadelphia, on the 14th of April.
The 203d, in New-York, on the 16th of May.
The 204th, at Canaan, in New-Hampshire state, on the 12th of June.

This year we took in the following circuits: At the Natchees, and in the Louisiana country, we took in *Wilkinson*, *Claiborne* and *Appelousa*; in South-Carolina conference, *Montgomery* and *Milledgeville*; the latter place is the metropolis of Georgia. In Baltimore conference, *Fell's point circuit*, *Monongahela*, *Lycoming*, and *Staunton*; in Philadelphia conference, *Lyons-town*; in New-England conference, *New-Bedford*, *Northfield*, and *Centre-harbour*; and in the Province of Maine, *Durham* and *Vasselborough*; and Penobscott being divided, one part was called *Orrington*, and the other *Hampden*. We also took in *St. Lawrence*, in Canada.

At these conferences we admitted upon trial upwards of 80 young preachers; and lost out of the travelling connection 52 old preachers: 48 of them located, 1 died, 2 withdrew from our connection, and one was expelled.

Benjamin Iliff died. He was a native of Bucks county, Pennsylvania. He began to travel in 1801, and died on the 29th of May, 1805. He was ordained an elder at the conference held in Chester town, in 1805, and his family being sick, he obtained liberty to leave the conference before it rose. On his way home he was taken ill, and in a few days after he came home he died. He was considered as an uniform good man, and an acceptable preacher. He was happy in his last sickness, and had a desire to depart and be with Christ; and his happiness appeared to increase with his illness. He told his friends that he had not a doubt of his acceptance with God. His last words were these, "*I have lost sight of the world ; come, Lord Jesus, come quickly.*" We rest satisfied that he ended his sufferings and sorrows with his life, and believe that the day of his death was better for him than the day of his birth.

We added 10625 members to the society this year ; which was a large number of precious souls to be brought into the fold of Christ in one year. But it is an easy thing with the Almighty to forgive sins, and to do a great work in a short time.

There was a change made in the annual minutes this year, and for the first time the usual list of elders was left out of the minutes, and only those entered who were ordained elders this year. However, in the stations the elders names were printed in italic.

This was a prosperous year among the Methodists, and the work of God was carried on in many places, in an uncommon manner, both in the conversion and sanctification of precious souls. Indeed, the work was so great, that it appeared to be almost incredible among christians themselves who had never seen any thing to equal it before.

On the Eastern Shore of Maryland and Virginia, it was said that more than 1000 persons were converted at one camp-meeting which lasted about five days and nights. The account was not merely a report, but it was given by ministers and people, who were eye and ear witnesses ; and who had taken great pains to ascertain the exact number of those who during that meeting openly professed to be delivered from the burden of their sins. The preachers appointed different men to attend in different parts of the congregation, for the express purpose of taking an account of such as got converted, and to report accordingly ; and from their report there were upwards of a thousand converted at one meeting ; and a greater number, at another meeting of the same kind.

If any one does not credit these remarkable accounts, they will feel their objections, and their objections cannot be removed by any arguments whatever. It will likely be asked, were not many of these converts deceived? Perhaps they were. We cannot tell certainly. Some of them were but little known; they were strangers in a strange place. We could only hope the best concerning them. To their own master they must stand or fall. But the christians who were acquainted with the people while they were careless about their souls, and were present with them while they were under conviction, and at the time they professed to be converted, can tell pretty well whether they were deceived or not. One thing appears to be certain, which is this, that there never was a time among the Methodists, in any part of the United States, where so many professed to be converted in a few days, as there were at the meetings just mentioned.

The Eastern Shore has been favoured at different times with very great revivals of religion, and with a large number of old steady solid christians for many years past; but the revival of religion at this time exceeded every thing of the kind that had ever been known among them before. It became quite common to begin their quarterly meetings on Friday, and continue them until Sunday night, or Monday forenoon; and for some hundreds of people to attend them in their waggons and carts, and with their tents; and to lodge in the woods by the meeting-houses, while the meeting lasted. It appeared for a long time as if nothing could stand before the work of the Lord; but the faithful, fervent prayers of the saints would bare down all before them. Ministers and people being happily united together, they strengthened each other's hands in the Lord, and each felt willing to bear the other's burden, and so fulfil the law of Christ.

The revival of religion was very great in many other places beside the Eastern Shore; and most of the United States were favoured with the awakening and converting grace of God. The people were oft times awakened and brought to the knowledge of God in the course of the same day; and some have been converted within a few hours from the time of their first awakening. Some who came to meeting in the forenoon quite careless and wicked, have gone away before night, happy in God. I have seen some fall beneath the power of God, as if they were struck dead, and then lie helpless and speechless for a short space, while their friends have prayed for them; and at last they sprang up of a sudden, and with a loud voice gave praise to God, in that he had forgiven their sins.

I cannot omit mentioning one strange circumstance which took place this year at a camp-meeting which was held at Maise's chapel, in Amelia circuit in Virginia, which began on the 17th day of October. A young woman, N. W. was under conviction, and on Sunday night she fell on the floor, and was both helpless and speechless. After some time she was taken into a tent, and her friends sat up with her all night. I went to see her next morning, and advised a friend of her's to give her a tea-spoonful of water, which was done, but without any visible effect. About 9 o'clock in the forenoon she spoke for the first time, and said, "Love, love, love: Glory, glory, glory." She then sunk away into her helpless state again. In the afternoon she was taken home by her father in a waggon; but continued speechless. After a day or two, her parents not knowing but some bodily disorder might attend her, concluded to send for a doctor, who came, and not knowing what to do for her, they called in another doctor, who was supposed to have more experience than the first; but both of them agreed that it was a supernatural power, and not a bodily disease. However, they took a little blood from her, supposing it could do no harm. One of them tarried with her two or three days. On Tuesday night following she came to herself, and spake and praised God for his goodness to her soul, and declared that the Lord had forgiven her sins. When her speech returned, she was well and happy, and able to go about, and attend to business. She was just nine days and nights in that helpless condition, and not able to speak; during which time she ate nothing, except such things as were poured into her mouth, and which she could swallow without chewing. I conversed with her a few days after she came to herself, and she told me that the Lord converted her soul the next morning after she lost her speech, at which time she spoke as before observed, and said, "Love, love, love: Glory, glory, glory." She told me further, that for some days and nights she never slept; and that she understood most of the conversation, and the circumstances that took place in her presence. But she said toward the last of her confinement, she sometimes slept, and felt herself thereby refreshed; and in a certain case when one of her young companions came to see her, she raised her hand to shake hands with her, and burst into a flood of tears. She told me that when she recovered she felt rather weak, as she supposed for the want of food; but she was quite well, and happy in God.

In the foregoing narrative, I have just stated facts as I received them; part of which I saw and heard, and all the rest I believe. Yet I cannot account for it, but am satisfied that it was the work of the Lord; and am persuaded that the young woman was, according to her profession, truly born again while she was under that strange operation

CHAPTER XII.

Containing a list of all the itinerant Methodist preachers, who have laboured in connection with the Methodist conference.

I have divided the preachers into the first, second, third, and fourth classes or divisions.

The first class of Methodist preachers, includes all who began to travel from the year 1769, to the close of 1784, at which time we received ordination among us, and became a church.

The second class of Methodist preachers, includes all who began to travel from the beginning of 1785, to the first general conference in the year 1792.

The third class of Methodist preachers, includes all that began to travel from the year 1793 to 1800, including eight years.

The fourth class of Methodist preachers, includes all that began to travel from the year 1801 to 1806.

The figures before the names denote the period when those preachers began to travel.

Those marked thus * at the end of the name, died in the work.

Those marked thus † located, or stopped travelling.

Those marked thus || left us, and withdrew from our connection.

Those marked thus ‡ were expelled, or considered as turned out from us.

Those without a mark are considered as travelling preachers still, and are entitled to a seat in our conferences. A few of them are supernumeraries, and some are superannuated or worn-out preachers.

The figures after the name, shew the year in which the preacher died, located, left us, or was expelled.

The names will be inserted alphabetically as it respects the first letter of the sirname, and no further. The first name on the list that begins with A, will be inserted; and the next preacher who began to travel, whose name begins with A, will be the second on the list, and so on in every other case.

THE

FIRST CLASS, OR DIVISION, OF METHODIST PREACHERS,

From the year 1769 *to* 1784.

John Wesley, the founder and father of the Methodists, formed the first society at Oxford, in November 1729, and sent the first itinerant preachers to America in 1769. He died * 1791.

Charles Wesley, the first to whom the appellation of *Methodist* was given at Oxford, in 1729, during his brother's absence in Lincolnshire. He died * 1788.

A

1767 Francis Asbury(*a*)
78 Philip Adams* 1782
81 David Abbott† '84
81 Beverly Allen‡ '92
83 Tho. Anderson† '93

B

63 Richard Bordman* (*b*) '82
77 Ed. Bailey* '80
80 Caleb Boyer† '88
81 Philip Bruce
82 John Baldwin† '95
1783 Samuel Breese† '93
83 Thomas Bowen† '96

C

75 John Cooper* '89
77 Jos. Cromwell† '93
77 Tho. S. Chew‡ '88
77 Le Roy Cole‡(*c*) '85
79 Philip Cox* '93
80 J. O. Cromwell† '93
81 John Coleman† '84
81 Adam Cloud‡ '83
83 Thomas Curtis* '88

(a) He came to America in 1771.
(b) He came to America in '69.
(c) He was soon after his expulsion restored to the travelling connection.

1783 Wm. Cannon† 1788
76 Thomas Coke (*d*)

D

74 Wm. Duke† '79
74 Ed. Drumgoole† '78
65 Jas. Dempster‡(*e*)'75
77 John Dickins*(*f*)'98
79 Joshua Dudley† '83
80 Micajah Debruler† '85
81 Samuel Dudley† '88
83 Wm Dameron† 88

E

77 Reuben Ellis* '96
81 Joseph Everitt*1809
81 Micajah Ellis† 1788
82 Ira Ellis† '97
82 John Easter† '92

F

76 James Foster† '79
80 Thomas Foster† '92
81 Jon. Forrest† '93
84 John Fidler† '87

G

74 Philip Gatch† '78
75 Wm. Glendenning‖ '85
76 Freeborn Garretson
77 William Gill* '89
79 Rd Garretson† '83
82 James Gibbons† '84
83 Lemuel Green† 1800
83 Matthew Greentree† 1790

H

76 Joseph Hartley† '81
1779 John Hagerty† 1794
81 James Haw† '91
82 Tho. Haskins† '86
82 Woolman Hickson* '88
83 James Hinton† '85
83 Tho. Humphries†'95

I J

78 Richard Ivey* '95
82 Henry Jones† '88
84 Thos. Jackson† '90
84 Wm. Jessop* '95

K

73 John King† '76

L

74 Robert Lindsey† (*g*) '88
77 John Littlejohn† '79
81 Jeremiah Lambert* '86
83 Jesse Lee
84 Wilson Lee* 1804

M

76 Thos. M'Cluer†1782
78 Wm. Moore† '81
78 John Major* '88
79 James Morris† '85
80 George Mair* '85
80 Jas. G. Martin† 85
80 George Moore† 1804
81 Ed. Morris† 1790
81 Henry Medcalf* '84
81 James Malory† '84
81 Enoch Matson‡ '88
82 John Magary† (*h*)

(d) He came to America in 1784.
(e) He came to America in 1775.
(f) He located in 1781, and after two years he took his station again.

(g) He was an Irishman by birth, and went to Europe in the time of the revolutionary war, and travelled and preached until 1788.
(h) He returned to Europe

1782 Peter Moriarty
83 Henry Merritt† 1796

O

78 James O Kelly‖ '93
79 Henry Ogburn† '90

P

65 Jos. Pillmore‖(*i*) '85
76 Francis Poythress† 1801
77 Caleb B. Peddicord* 1785
77 Edward Pryde† '81
80 Moses Parks† '90
80 Wm. Partridge† '89
81 Ignatius Pigman† '88
83 Wm. Phoebus† '92
84 Simon Pile† '92

R

62 Thos Rankin†(*k*)'87
74 Daniel Ruff† '81
74 Isaac Rollings‖ '81
63 Martin Rodda†(*l*)'81
79 Samuel Row† '85
79 Nelson Reed† 1800
83 Wm Ringold† 1785
84 John Robertson† '87
84 James Riggin† '90

S

68 Geo. Shadford (*m*)
74 Sam. Spraggs‖ 1778
76 John Sigman† '80
77 Samuel Strong† '79
83 Francis Spry* '89
83 Richard Swift† '93
84 Isaac Smith† '96
84 John Smith

T

76 Isham Tatum† '81
77 John Tunnil* '90
82 Wm. Thomas† '90

V

75 Thomas Vasey‖ (*n*) '86

W

70 Rich. Wright†(*o*)'77
69 Robt. Williams† '74
73 Wm. Waters†(*p*) '83
73 Abraham Whitworth‡ '74
74 John Wade† '77
76 Nicholas Waters*(*q*) 1804
78 Henry Willis*(*r*)'08

(i) He returned to England, then left the Methodists and came again to America, and was ordained a Minister of the Church of England.

(k) He came to America in 1773, and after a few years returned to Europe.

(l) He came to America in 1775, and returned to Europe after a short time.

(m) He came to America in 1773, and returned to Europe with the two preachers above-mentioned.

(n) He came to America in 1784, got ordination by the Bishop of the Church of England, and then returned to England.

(o) He came to America in 1771, and returned to Europe.

(p) He was the first travelling preacher raised up in America.

(q) He located in 1779, and remained so for near twenty years.

(r) He located in 1790, and never after had more than a nominal station.

1780 Samuel Watson† 1783
81 James White* '89
81 Joseph Wyatt† '88
84 Thomas Ware
69 Richard Whatcoat* (s) 1806

(s) He came to America in 1784, and was ordained Bishop in 1800.

Y

1773 Jos. Yarberry† 1775
79 Andw. Yergain† '81

The whole of the foregoing names being added together make 125. The whole of these preachers were admitted into full connection. Several of them came from Europe, most of whom returned again; the others were preachers raised up in the United States in the course of 15 years.

The circuits were much larger at that time than they are at present; and the preachers were generally sent much farther from their friends. It was a common practice for preachers to stop travelling as soon as they were married. Another reason why the married preachers located was, they were not allowed any support for their families. But the main reason why so many stopped was their wish to stay at home with their families.

We cannot count more than ten preachers out of the foregoing 125, who are now in the travelling connection, and only 25 have died in the work.

THE SECOND CLASS, OR DIVISION, OF METHODIST PREACHERS,

From the year 1785 *to* 1792.

A

1785 Robert Ayres‖ 1789
86 Daniel Asbury† '91
87 Lemuel Andrews* '91
1787 Jeremiah Able† 1791
88 John Allen‖ '93
89 Ben. Abbot* '96
89 John Andrew† '92
89 Josiah Askew† '98

1790 Fredus Aldridge† '97
90 Hezekiah Arnold† '97
91 John Ahair* '94
91 Samuel Ansley

B

85 Henry Bingham* '89
85 Jacob Brush* '95
88 Michael Burdge† '92
88 Ben. Barnes† '94
88 Henry Birchett* '94
88 Jn. Bloodgood† 1809
89 Anthony Banning† '91
89 Ben. Brown† '92
89 Jonathan Bird† '99
89 Stephen Brooks† '93
90 Gam'l Bailey† 1804
90 John Ball† 1795
90 Thomas Boyd* '94
90 Thomas Bell† '97
90 James Bell‡ '93
90 Geo. Browning* '92
90 Robert Bonsall† '94
90 Chs. Burgoon* 1800
90 Ben. Blanton† 1801
90 John Bonner† 1800
91 James Boyed‖ 1795
91 John Buxton
91 John Beard† '95
91 Lewis Browning† '94
91 Shadrach Bostwick† 1805
91 Wm. Bellamy† 1796
92 Richard Bird† '97
92 Secly Bunn
92 William Burk
92 William Bishop
92 David Bartine

C

85 Robert Cloud† '94
1785 Ezekiel Cooper
85 Robert Cann† 1794
87 Ben. Carter* '92
87 Cornelius Cook* '89
87 Charles Connaway† '97
87 Geo. Callehan† '91
87 James Conner* '90
87 Lewis Chasteen† '92
88 John Chalmers† '97
88 Valentine Cook† 1800
88 Grif'h Callehan 1792
88 John Cooper, jr.† (a)
88 David Candall† '94
89 John Crawford† '94
89 John Crawford† '95
89 Jeremiah Causden‖ '94
89 Jas. Campbell† 1805
90 Geo. Cannon† 1797
90 Samuel Cowles† '97
90 Simon Carlisle‡ '94
90 Joshua Cannon† '97
90 Wm Calbert
91 John Clark‖ '96
91 John Clark, jr.‖ 1800
91 James Coleman
91 James Covel† 1797
92 Coleman Carlisle† '95
92 Ephraim Chambers† 1806
92 Geo Clark† 1801

D

85 Stephen Dickins† 1787
88 Jos. Doddridge‖ '91
88 Archer Davis† '93
88 Stephen Davis* '95

(a) He went to Nova-Scotia, and after a while located.

1788 Lewis Dawson† 1794
88 Wm. Dougherty† '93
88 Dar's Dunham† 1800
90 Daniel Dean† 1796
91 Robt. Dillon† '96
92 James Dawley† '95

E

85 Elijah Ellis* '88
88 John Ellis† '94
90 Thos. Easter† '96
90 Thos. Everard† '94
91 Samuel Edney† '94
91 Wm. Early† '95

F

88 John Fore† '97
89 Dan. Fidler† 1808
89 Walter Fountain† 1794
89 Thornton Fleming
90 Jas. Fleming† '96
91 Ben. Fizler† '98
91 Sam Fowler† 1801
92 Wm. Fulwood† 1796

G

88 Robt. Green† 1800
88 Wm. Gasway† 1791
89 Wheeler Grissom† '92
90 Enoch George† '99
91 Aquila Garrettson† '97
91 Nath. Greaves† 1802
92 Tobias Gipson* 1804

H

85 Hope Hull† 1795
85 Joshua Hartley† '90
86 Chas. Hardy† '92
87 David Haggard† '98
1787 Geo. Hagerty† '92
87 Mathew Harris†' 91
87 Aaron Hutchinson* '91
88 Wm. Heath† '92
88 John Hill† '96
88 Andrew Harpending‡ '92
88 Hardy Herbert* '94
88 Thomas Hardy† '90
89 John Hut† '96
89 Rice Haggard‖ '93
89 Sylvester Hutchinson† 1806
90 John Hallida† 1793
90 Morris How† 1800
90 Thomas Hayman*(*b*) 1799
90 Daniel Hitt
90 Martin Hitt† '95
90 Robt. Hutchinson† '99
91 Abner Henly† '96
91 Henry Hill† '97
91 James Holley† '94
91 Sam. Hitt† 1800
91 Ezekiel Humphrey† 1794
91 Aaron Hunt† '95
92 Daniel Hall(*c*)
92 Edward Hardy† '96
92 Joshua Hall† 1801
92 James Hunter† 1797
92 Wm. Hardisty† 1801

(b) He located in 1796, but entered the travelling connection again a little before he died.

(c) He took a location in 1801, but finding his health returning, he took a circuit again after six months.

J

1785 Stephen Johnson† 1790
86 John Jarrall* '96
88 Jethro Johnson‖ '94
89 Jonathan Jackson
89 Wm. Jackson† '92
90 John N. Jones* '98
91 Joshua Jones† '97
92 James Jinkins† 1806
92 Jer. Jackson† 1795

K

90 John Kobler† 1801
91 Freeman Killingsworth† 1795
92 Zebulon Kankey†'98
92 Absalom Kensey†'96
92 Joel Ketchum† 1801

L

86 Jacob Lurton† 1795
86 Michael Lard† '92
87 Daniel Locket† '93
87 H Ledbetter† '95
87 Isaac Low† '95
88 Isaac Lunsford† '97
88 John Lee† '91
89 John Lindsey† '95
89 Wm. Losee† '93
90 Arthur Lipsey† '95
90 Wm. A. Lilley† '97
90 Joseph Lovell† 1800
91 Thomas Lyell‖ '04
91 Thomas Lucas

M

85. Jer. Mastin† 1790
85 John M'Claskey
86 John Merrick† '97
86 Lastley Matthews
86 Mark Moore† '99
87 Barnabas M'Henry† '95
1787 Jer. Mintor† 1791
87 John Milburn† '99
87 Thomas Morrell†'96
87 Nath. B. Mills
88 Bennet Maxey† '97
88 Wm. Moss† '99
88 James Meacham†'97
88 Peter Massey* '91
88 Wm. M'Kendree
88 John M'Gee† '93
89 Christopher S. Moring
89 Philip Matthews†'92
89 Wm. M'Dowell† '95
89 Wm. M'Lennahan
90 Geo. M'Kinney† '94
90 John Metcalf† '95
91 Geo Martin† '97
91 Jos. Moore† 1806
91 Levin Moore† '01
91 Robert M Coy
91 Wm. Moody† 1797
91 Simon Miller* '95
92 Law. M'Combs† 1806
92 Law. Mansfield† '03
92 Stith Mead

N

89 Jesse Nicholson† 1793
91 And. Nichols† 1801
91 James Nolly† 1794
91 Jon. Newman† '95
92 Jer. Norman† 1802

O

91 Wm. Ormond* '03

P

85 John Paup† 1792
87 Rich. Pearson† '90
88 James Parks† '95
88 Emory Pryer* '95
90 Geo. Pickering
90 Rich, Parriot† '94

1790 Francis Parker† 1794
90 John Pace† '95
91 Elisha Pelham† '96
92 Jacob Peck† '94
92 James Painter
92 John Page† 1804

R

85 Levin Ross† 1790
87 Ben. Roberts† '90
87 Benton Riggin* '99
88 Jesse Richardson† 1805
88 John Rowen† 1793
88 Eliphalet Reed* '91
89 John Robinson‖ '93
89 John Russill† '99
90 Evan Rogers† '95
90 Menzies Rainor‖ '95
90 Sam. Rudder† '97
90 Stewart Redman† '95
90 Stephen G. Roszel† '94
90 John Ragan* '97
90 Geo. Roberts† 1806
90 Fred. Roper† 1793
91 Isaac Robertson† '97
91 James Rogers† 1801
91 Josias Randell† 1799
92 Jordan Rexford‖ '95
92 Joseph Rowen† 1804
92 John Ray† '01
92 Levi Rogers† 1795

S

85 Robert Sparks† '96
86 John Simmons† 1807
86 Sihon Smith† 1792
87 Christ. Spry† 1804
88 Aquila Suggs† 1797
88 Lemuel Smith† '96
89 Nicholas Sebrell† '94
1789 Wm. Spencer† '97
89 Pem. Smith† 1802
89 Dan. Southall† 1797
89 Rich. Swain* 1808
90 Daniel Shines† 1795
90 John Sproul* '93
90 Matthias Swaim† '96
90 Daniel Stringer† '94
90 Thomas Scott† '95
90 Dan. Smith† '94
90 Hubbard Saunders† '93
91 John Scawell† '94
92 Philip Sands† '99
92 Sam. S Stewart† 1804
92 Solomon Sharp

T

85 Amos G. Thompson† 1796
86 Micajah Tracy† '91
86 Sam. Q. Talbott† '90
87 John Todd† '90
88 James Thomas† '95
91 Jas. Tolleson* 1800
91 Joshua Taylor† '06
91 Ben. Tarrant† 1796
92 Joel Tucker† '98
92 Wm. Talbut† '95
92 Joseph Totten

V

88 Albert Van Nostrand* (*d*) '97
91 David Valleau‡ '94

W

85 Mark Whitaker† '93

(d) He travelled one year and then stopped. Several years after he began to travel again and died in the work.

1785 Thos. Williamson† 1792
87 Edward West† '91
87 James Wilson* '93
87 Thos. Weatherford* '92
88 Sela. Weeks* 1800
88 George Wells† 1793
88 Sam. Wigton† '94
89 Joshua Wells
90 Ben. Wilson†(*e*)
1790 John West
90 John Wynn* 1794
90 Philip Wager† '98
90 Rufus Wiley† '94
92 James Ward
92 Smith Weeks† '99
92 Hugh Works† '95
92 John Watson

(e) He went to Nova Scotia in 1794, and after a few years located there.

In this list, from 1785 to 1792, there are 287 preachers; which being added to the former list, makes in all 412. About 30 preachers out of the last 287, have continued regularly in the travelling connection; and about 35 have died in the work.

It will be well for the reader to recollect that the account of the time when each preacher began to travel, and when he quit travelling, is taken from the annual minutes of the conferences; and in one case, two of the conferences which made up the minutes for the year 1792 were held in the latter part of the preceding year; of course, the preachers who were admitted on trial, with those who were located at the two conferences held in December 1791, are entered for the year 1792.

THIRD CLASS, OR DIVISION, OF METHODIST PREACHERS,

From the year 1793 *to* 1800.

A

1793 Francis Acuff* 1795
96 Wm. Atwood† 1802
97 Thomas Allen† '01
97 Abra. Andrews* '00
99 Wm. Avant† '05
99 Wm. Algood† '06
1800 George Armstrong† 1804
1800 Smith Arnold
1800 William Anson

B

1793 Robt. Bonham* 1800
93 William Ball‖ 1796

1794 Danl. Brumley† 1808
94 David Brown* 1803
94 John Brodhead
94 Jonathan Bateman† 1799
94 William Beauchamp† 1801
94 David Buck† '03
96 Moses Black† '07
96 Roger Benton† '05
96 Wm. Brittain† '02
96 Wesley Budd† '00
98 Elijah Bacheller† '04
98 Truman Bishop
99 Benjamin Bidlack
1800 Ezekiel Burdine† '04
1800 Joseph Baker
1800 Louner Blackman

C

1793 Moses Crane† 1796
93 Robert Cox† '97
94 Ezekiel Canfield
94 Josiah Cole† 1801
94 Rezin Cash* '03
94 Samuel Coate
94 Thomas Coop‡ 1797
95 Charles Cavender† 1800
95 Daniel Crouch† '04
95 Jacob Calbert† 1800
95 Michael Coate
95 Nathaniel Chapin† 1799
96 Zenas Conger† 1801
96 John Cullison† '04
97 Eber Cowles† 1800
97 Joseph Crawford
97 Wm. P. Chandler
99 Brittain Capell
99 Elij. Chichester† '07
199 Billy Corr† 1803
1800 Henry Clark† '06
1800 Jesse Coe† '07
1800 John Campbell† '07
1800 John Cox† '06

D

1793 Benj. Denton† 1797
93 Daniel Dennis† '97
93 James Douthit† 1803
93 John Durborough† 1795
93 Wm. Douglas† '96
93 Leonard Dyson† '96
95 Timothy Dewey† 1804
95 Wm. Duzan† 1798
96 Joseph Dunn† 1801
97 Johnson Dunham† '06
97 Samuel Douthit† '05
97 Thomas Dodson† '03
98 Thomas Daughaday† 1802
98 George Daugherty* '07
98 Hanover Donnon† '08
99 David Dunham† '06
99 James Denton† '04
99 Peter B. Davis† '06
1800 William Davis† '04

E

1793 Jacob Egbert† 1800
95 Edmund Ellis† 1799
96 Wm. Earley, jr.* '99
96 Benj. Essex† 1805
97 Llewellin Evans† '01
98 John Evans† '01
99 John Ellis, jr.† '03
99 Nathan Emory

1800 Henry Eames

F

1793 John Fountain† 1797
95 John Faulcom† 97
95 John Finegan
96 Archibald Foster† 1804
97 James Floyd† 1800
97 Loammi Floyd‖ 1800
99 Thomas Fletcher† '03
1800 Moses Floyd† '0.

G

1794 Lewis Garritt† 1806
95 H. M Gaines† 1799
97 Robert Gaines† 1801
99 John Garvin† '04
1800 John Gamewell
1800 Levi Garrison† '07
1800 Samuel Garrard
1800 Jacob Gruber
1800 John Gove† '07

H

1793 Wm. Hunter
94 Roger Hancock† 1800
95 Elias Hull‖ 1798
95 James L. Higgins 1801
95 Duke W. Hullum† 1799
86 John Harper†(*f*) 1803
96 Aaron Humphrey† 1799
96 James Hunter jr.
96 Solomon Harris‡ 1807
96 Stephen Hull‖ 1800

(f) He came to the United States from the West Indies, in the latter part of 1794.

1796 Hezekiah Harsman
97 Daniel Higby† 1807
97 Joseph Hill† '01
98 Asa Heath† '06
98 Billy Hibbert
98 Reu. Hubbard‖ '09
98 Samuel Hooser† '01
99 James Herron
99 Lewis Hunt* '01
1800 James Hunt† '04

J

1793 Hamilton Jefferson
94 James Jones† 1799
95 Aquilla Jones† '98
95 Joseph Jewel
96 Shadrach Johnson† 1800
97 Augustus Jocelin† '04
97 Thomas Jones† '06
97 Peter Jane* '06
98 Jesse Justice† '04
99 David James† '06
99 Nathan Jarratt* '03
99 Reuben Jones† '04

K

94 W. Kavanaugh† 1798
94 James King* '97
95 Sylvs Keeler† 1807
95 William Kenyon‡ '04
96 Caleb Kindall† '04
97 John King, jr.† '03
98 Epaphras Kibbe
99 Bent. Kendrick* '07
99 Jeremiah King† '05
1800 Gideon A. Knowlton
1800 William Knox

L

1794 Chs. Ledbetter† 1799
95 Benj. Lakin† '98
95 John Lackey† 1800
96 Jas. Lattomas* '06
96 Jeremiah Lawson† 1799
96 William Lambuth† 1800
97 John Leach* '02
97 Richard Lyon† '08
99 Edward Larkins
1800 Solomon Langdon† '05

M.

1793 Enoch Mudge† 1799
94 Jeremiah Munday† '99
94 Jos. Mitchell† 1804
94 Thomas Mann
94 Robert Manly† 01
94 James Moore
95 Archer Moody† 01
95 Benjamin Matthews† '03
96 Timothy Merritt† '03
97 Alexander M'Cain† '06
97 Bannister Meador† '01
98 Thomas Millegan
99 Alexander M'Lain† '06
99 John Moore† '05
99 Lewis Myers
99 Moses Matthews† '09
99 William Mills
99 Zachariah Maddux† '06
1800 Caleb Morris† 1803
1800 Samuel Munnett† '05
1800 Samuel Merwin

N.

1797 John Nichols† '04
98 Thomas Nelson† '03

O.

93 Daniel Ostrander
96 Anning Owen
1800 Joseph Osburn

P

1793 John Phillips, junior† '04
93 William Page† 1796
93 Zadock Priest* '96
94 Richard Posey† '99
95 James Patterson† 1804
95 Joseph Pinnell
96 John Pitts† '03
96 John Potts† '09
98 Josiah Phillips
1800 Daniel Pickett† '09

Q

1799 James Quinn† '07

R

93 Samuel Risher† '05
94 Edwd T. Rowzey† '97
94 Jacob Rickhow† 1800
94 John Robertson, junior† '05
97 John Ruth† 1800
1800 Daniel Ross† '08
1800 Daniel Ryan* '05
1800 Henry Ryan
1800 Jeremiah Russill† '06
1800 Isaac Robins† '04

S

1793 Anthony Sale† 1799
93 James Smith
93 JesseStoneman†1802
93 Richd. Stocket†1798
94 Henry Smith
94 Nicholas Snethen† 1806
94 Wm Storms† 1797
95 Cyrus Stebbins‖1805
95 John Seward† '01
95 John Shepherd†1797
95 Thomas F. Sargent
95 Roger Searl‖ 1805
96 James Stokes† 1800
96 John Sale
96 Joseph Stone
96 Obadiah Strange† 1799
96 Richard Sneath
96 David Stevens
97 Ebenezer Stevens† 1806
97 Joseph Snelling
97 Joseph Sawyer
98 Thomas Shaw† '06
99 Elijah R. Sabin† '04
99 Joshua Soul
99 Nathan Swain† '04
99 Thomas Smith
99 Comfort C. Smith‖ '06
1800 Joseph Shane† '04

T

1793 Anthony Turk*1803
94 David Thompson† 1797
95 Stephen Timmons† 1804
1796 Samuel Thomas
97 John Turner† 1801
97 William Thatcher
1800 Louther Taylor† '07

V

1793 JohnVanneman†1797
96 Peter Vannest
98 William Vredenburgh† 1808

W

93 Alward White†1797
93 Hezekiah C. Worster* '98
93 Elijah Woolsey† '97
93 William Wilkerson* '98
93 William Wells† '97
93 Thomas Wilkerson† 1808
94 ThomasWoolsey†'01
94 Samuel Walch† 1797
94 John Weeks† '97
95 Curtis Williams† 1805
95 Humphrey Wood
95 Joseph Whitbey† 1799
95 Moses Wilson† 1802
95 Nathan Williamson† 1799
96 Ralph Williston‖ 1806
97 Edmund Wayman* '02
97 John Wilson
97 Nathaniel Walker† '05
97 Bobert Wilkerson† '01
97 William West† '01

1798 Abner Wood‡ 1805
98 Daniel Webb
99 Barzilla Willey† '04
1800 Buddy W. Wheeler† 1806

Y

1796 Robert Yallely† 1799

In this third Class of preachers, there are 259 who have been admitted into full connection. About 20 of them have died in the travelling plan: and between 50 and 60, have continued to travel to the present time. Adding these 259 to the former numbers, make in all 671.

The reader will observe, that for the five first years, that is 1793 and 1797 inclusive, the conferences began in one year, and finished in the following year; and were all published as the minutes of conference for the year in which the last conference was held. For instance, in 1795 there were seven conferences; two of them were held in October, and November 1794, and five were held 1795. But they are all published together in a pamphlet, with this title, "Minutes taken at the several Annual Conferences of the *Methodist Episcopal Church* in America, for the year 1795."

The above dates, when the preachers began to travel, &c. being taken from these minutes, it will be understood that the time is according to the account published in the minutes

FOURTH CLASS, OR DIVISION, OF METHODIST PREACHERS,

From the year 1801 *to* 1806.

A

1801 George Askins
01 Luman Andrus
01 James Aikins
02 Thomas Adams
02 Joseph Aydelott
1804 Archibald Alexander† 1809
04 Abraham Amos
05 James Axley
05 Wm. Arendell† '07
06 Moses Ashworth

1806 Bridges Arendell
06 Thomas Asbury
06 Philip Ayer

B

01 David Best
01 Oliver Beal
01 Thomas Branch
01 William Brandon‡ 1805
02 David Bacheller† '09
02 John Billings† 05
02 John Bethell
02 Jeremiah Browning† '04
02 Mesheck Boyce† '07
02 Samuel Budd
02 Henry Boehm
02 Nathan Bangs
03 Dyer Burge‡ '08
03 John Ballew† '09
03 Luther Bishop
03 Mitchell B. Bull
03 Thomas Budd
03 Elisha Bowman
04 James Boyd, jr.
04 Dexter Bates† '09
04 Lewis Bates
04 Nathan Barnes
04 Robert Burch
04 Thomas Boring
04 William Barnes
04 William Blair† '09
05 Adam Burge
05 Francis Bird† '09
05 Plinney Brett
05 Thomas Burch
05 Warren Banister
05 Richard Browning
06 Robert Bolton
06 James Bateman

C

1801 Isaac Cook† 1806
01 Isaac Candee
01 James Chappel† '06
01 Joseph Cheuvront† '03
01 Joshua Crowel† '09
01 Seth Crowel
01 Labin Clark
01 Zenos Covel
02 Allen H Cobb† '09
02 Leonard Castle *'08
02 Nehemiah Coye
02 Robert Carter † '06
02 Thomas Church
03 Asa Cummings
03 James Crowder† '06
03 William Crutchfield† '06
03 Phenehas Cook
04 Gabril Christian† '06
04 John Collins
04 Samuel Cochran
04 Thomas Currin
04 Luther Chamberlain† '08
05 Amos Curtis† '09
05 Caleb W. Cloud
05 David Carr
05 Joseph Carson
05 Peter Cartwright
05 William Case
06 Abda Christian
06 Charles Callaway
06 James Charles
06 Jonathan Chaney

D

01 Thomas Darley† '06
01 Thomas L. Douglass
01 Samuel Draper

1802 Paul Dustin
03 Daniel Dudley† 1807
03 Gideon Draper
03 Caleb Dustin† '09
04 James Davidson† 09
04 Thomas Dunn
06 Samuel Dunwody
06 Benjamin Duvany
06 Abraham Daniels
06 Michael Dunn† '09

E

04 Datus Ensign
05 Benjamin Edge
05 William Ellington† '09
06 Thomas Elliott

F

01 Noah Fidler† '07
01 Nathan Felch‖ '07
02 Christopher Frye
02 Silvester Foster‡ '06
03 Ebenezer Fairbank† '09
05 John French
05 Joseph Fairbank† 09
05 Joseph Farrar† '08
05 William Fox
05 Hezekiah Field
06 Caleb Fogg

G

02 Wm. Goodhue† '06
02 John A. Granade† '05
03 John Gibbons† '08
04 Simon Gillespie
04 David Goodhue† '07
05 Charles Giles† '09
05 Nathan Gage† '08
06 Benjamin Gordon
06 James Glenn
1806 Job Guest
06 Alfred Griffith

H

01 Elijah Hedding
01 Joseph Hall† 1805
01 Wm. Hubbard† '09
02 James Hill† '06
02 John Hossilcus
02 Joseph Hays† '09
02 Samuel Hillman
03 Andrew Hemphill
03 Edmund Henly* '08
03 Reuben Harris
03 William Hoyer† '09
03 William Hill
04 Anthony Houston
04 Benoni Harris
04 John Holmes† '08
04 Silvester Hill
05 Erasmus Hill
05 John Hill, jr.
05 Miles Harper
05 William Houston
06 Thomas Hellums
06 Thomas Heathcock
06 Horatio E. Hall
06 William Hunt
06 Saul Hinkle

I

01 Benjamin Iliff* '05
04 Daniel Ireland

J

01 William Jones† '05
01 Benjamin Jones* '04
02 William Johnson‡ '04
04 James Jennings
04 Enoch Jones
05 Jeremiah Jeffries
05 William Jean
06 Hilliard Judge

1806 Amos Jinks

K

02 Asa Kent
04 Philip Kennerly† '06
04 Daniel Kelly
05 Joshua W. Kill-patrick† '09
06 William M. Kennedy
06 James Kelsey
06 William Keith

L

03 Ralph Lootspeich
03 Richard Lattimore
04 John Lattimore
04 Zalmon Lyon
04 Jeremiah Lumsden† '09
05 George Lane
05 Thomas Lasley
05 Timothy Lee
05 William B. Lacy
06 George C. Light† '09
06 Moses Lawrence† '09
06 Wm. G. Lowman
06 Benj. F. Lambord

M

01 Alexander Morton† 07
01 James H. Mellard
02 Alfred Medcalf
02 Andrew M'Kain
02 David B. Mintz† '07
02 Edward Matthews
02 Philip Munger
03 John M'Vain
04 Adject M'Guier† '09
04 Samuel Mills
1804 David M Masters† 1808
04 John M'Cluer
04 John Meek † 08
04 William M'Kinney
05 Thomas Madden
05 Hezekiah M'Lelland
05 Henry Martin* '08
06 William Murphrey
06 William M'Masters
06 Gerard Morgan
06 James Mitchell
06 George M'Crackin
06 John Miller

N

06 Greenleaf R. Norris

O

04 Joseph Oglesby
04 William Owen
05 Joshua Oglesby
05 Erastus Otis
05 John Owen
05 Richardson Owen† '08

P

01 James Polhamus
01 Phenehas Peck† '05
02 Asa Pattie‡ '05
02 Dan Perry† '09
02 Fielder Parker† '07
02 Hugh Porter† '07
03 Thomas Perry† '08
03 Gershom Pearce
04 Clement Parker† '08
04 Samuel Phillips† '07
04 William Pattison
05 John Porter
05 John Pinner† '09
05 Lovick Pearce

1805 Reddick Pearce
05 Robert Perry
05 Samuel Parker
05 Jesse Pinnell
06 Robert Porter
06 Thomas Pinnell
06 Andrew Prendle

R

01 Martin Rutter
02 Daniel Rickert† 1809
02 Thomas Ravling† '06
02 William Ryland
02 Robert R. Roberts
03 John Robertson 3d
03 James Ridgway
04 James Reed
04 John Richards‖ '08
05 Caleb Reynolds
05 James Russill

S

01 Asa Shinn
01 Griffin Sweet† '08
02 Frederick Stier
02 James Smith, jr.
02 William Smith
02 Thomas Stratton† '06
02 Thomas Skeel† '08
02 William Steel† '05
03 David Stimpson† '08
03 Joseph Stevens
04 Eben Smith
04 Henry Stead
04 Joseph A. Shackleford† '08
04 William Stevens
04 James M. Smith
04 Thomas Shands† '09
05 Joseph Sampson
05 James Saunders† '08
05 Joel Smith‡ '09
1805 Matthew P. Sturdivant
05 Joseph Scull
05 William W. Shepherd† 1809
05 William Shands† '07
06 Samuel Sellers
06 William W. Shepherd
06 John Swartzwalter
06 Oliver Sikes
06 Solomon Sias
06 Joel Steele
06 Theophilus Smith
06 William Snyder

T

01 Lewis Taylor† '07
02 Joseph Toy
02 Nehemiah U. Tompkins† '09
03 Noble W Thomas
03 Samuel Thompson
04 Eppa Tucker† '09
04 John Tinkum
04 Eli Town
04 Sampson Trammell‡
04 Joseph Tarpley
05 Benjamin Tradewell† '08
05 William Thompson† '07
06 Pleasant Thurman
06 Zadock B. Thackston

V

01 Matthew Vanduzan
02 Elias Vanderlip† '06
06 William Vermillion

W

01 Edward Whittle‡ '04

1801 Ebenezer Washburn
01 Joab Watson† 1806
01 Josiah Wilkerson† '06
01 Elijah Ward† '04
01 John Wiltbank
02 Ebenezer White
02 Frederick Woodward† '07
02 John Walker
02 Francis Ward
02 Joseph Willis
03 Elijah Willard† '07
03 George Woolley
03 Henry White
03 Jesse Walker
03 John P. Weaver
03 Joel Winch
1803 Nicholas Willis
03 Thomas Walker
03 Wm. Wright, jr.† '07
04 James Watts
04 Wiley Warwick
05 John Weaver
05 Nathan Weaden
05 Joseph Williams
05 John Williamson
05 Levi Walker.
06 Gray Williams

Y

01 Benj. Young‡ '05
03 Jacob Young
04 Dan Young† '09
04 James Young† '08
06 David Young

In this last Class of preachers, there are 317 who have been travelling in full connection: this number being added to the former numbers, make in all 988. Between 80 and 90 preachers from first to last have died in the travelling connection. I have set down the year in which each preacher died, although their death might not be published in the minutes till the following year: except in some cases where I could get no account of their death, only from the minutes of the conference. In that case I have entered them as I found them.

A LIST OF
METHODIST PREACHERS,
WHO WERE ONLY PROBATIONERS.
From the year 1773 *to* 1806.

The following preachers were admitted upon trial, but stopped travelling in a short time, and therefore were not admitted into full connection. I have inserted all their names in the following list, except those of a few who never went to their circuits. I have intentionally omitted such as came under my own observation. Several who began to travel, stopped through weakness of body, and some through discouragement; and many on the account of family concerns. Some of them however are now useful local preachers, and an honour to the Methodists. I have entered at the end of some of their names, the time when they died; and have put a mark at the end of a few names to shew that the person left us, or was expelled.

It has never been a practice among the Methodists, to publish any account in the minutes of the conferences, of those preachers who were only on trial; but in case they died, left us, or stopped travelling, their names have been omitted without further notice.

A

1778 John Atkins
79 Lewis Alfrey
79 Wm. Adams* 1779
89 Wyatt Andrews*'91
90 Edward Almond
93 David Abbott, jr.
1801 James Annis

B

1778 John Beck
81 Stephen Black*
85 Hezekiah Bonham
85 Shores Bright
86 Terence Burns
87 William Bradbury
88 Daily Beard
89 Joseph Benson
89 John Barker
1795 William Beck
95 Jeremiah Ballard
95 Charles Bonnewell
97 John Baker
1801 Banks M Burrough
02 Sharon Boothe
03 John Bell
04 James Brindle
04 John Brown
05 Benjamin Bishop
05 James Boykin
05 Joshua Barnes
06 John Brockington

C

1778 Carter Cole
82 Caleb Cole
87 David Combs
87 Daniel Combs

1789 John Childs
89 Julus Corner
90 Henry Christie
92 Charles Cook
92 Henry Crank
93 Frederick Curp
96 Thomas Curry
99 Nicholas Chambers
1800 Jesse Cole
01 Gilbert Carpenter
02 Solomon Covington
02 Thomas Carperter
04 Moses Currier
05 Adbel Coleman
05 Dempsey Clayton

D

1778 Daniel Duval
87 Thomas Davis
94 William Dawley
94 John Dickin
98 Lowrenzo Dow‖
98 Thomas Drumgoole
99 James Dillard
1800 Daniel W. Dickerson
1800 Robert Dier
02 Thomas Doxey
02 George Daugherty, junior
03 John Durbin* 1805
04 David Dannilly
04 George Dillard
04 Jesse Davis
04 John Dickins, jr.

E

1774 Philip Ebert
86 Aquilla Edwards
95 Thomas Edwards
97 Stephen Ellis
1803 Levin Edney
03 Ebenezer Easty
1804 Ira Ellis jr.
05 Seymour Ensign

F

1776 Adam Fonarden
85 John Freeman
92 Daniel Freeman
94 Rd. Furguson‡ 1796
96 John Fell
98 Elijah Fitchgerald
1802 Oren Fairbank
05 Nathan Fox
05 Richard Flint
06 Henry Fisher
06 George Fletcher

G

1779 Greenbury Green
85 Michael Gilbert
87 Lewis Grigg
89 Miles Green
92 Peter Gautier
94 Freeborn Garrettson, junior
94 Peter Guthrie
95 William Guiry
99 Daniel Gossage
1802 Samuel Gorsline
03 James Gwin
03 True Glidden
06 John Green

H

1779 Charles Hopkins
85 Eleazer Hatheway
85 Moses Hurley
86 William Hudson
86 William Harvey
92 Isaac Hammer
93 Samuel Hollis
97 Callier Hill* 1799
98 Cornelius Hill
1801 Dd. M. Hume* 1802

1801 Oliver Hall
02 Samuel How
03 Daniel Hudson
04 Benjamin Hill
04 Isaac Hall
05 William Hardwick
06 William Hitt
06 Nicholas Hill

J

1780 John James
84 David Jefferson
93 James Johnson‡
95 Daniel Johns
97 Hill Jones
97 William James
1800 Wiley Jones
02 Daniel Jones
04 John Johnson

K

1776 Henry Kennedy
82 George Kemble
1801 John Kewley
03 Andrew Kernegan
04 Samuel King

L

1786 Elijah Lumsdon
90 Joseph Lillard
91 Ricketson Lipsey
91 Thomas Lovell
93 William Le Masters
94 John Lindsey, jr.
96 Robert Leeds
98 Shubal Lamb
1802 James Lewis
06 Garnett Lee

M

1779 Thomas Morris
86 Caleb Maxey
86 John Mason
86 Robert J. Miller
87 Nathaniel Moore
1788 Lenox Martin
89 Lemuel Moore
91 Jeptha Moore
94 Matthew M'Gee
94 William M'Collom
95 Elijah M'Cay
95 Edward Millis
95 Nathaniel Munsy
97 Ebenezer M'Lain
99 John Merrick, jr.
1801 John Moody
01 William Marsh
01 Moses Morgan
02 Hugh M'Curdy
06 Charles B. Matheny

N

1785 George Noseworthy
92 Benjamin Northcot
92 William R Nichols
95 Nathaniel Norwood
1805 Obed Noland
06 William Neelley

O

1775 Richard Owen
86 Benjamin Ogden
91 James O'Cul

P

1784 John Phillips
87 Elijah Phelps
88 Richard Pope
90 James Powel
90 Nathaniel Pinkard
93 Jason Perkins
1800 Aaron Parvin
1800 William Picket
03 William Pettigrew
04 Parley Parker
05 George Powers
06 Thomas Paine

1806 George Phillips
06 Isaac Pease

R

1782 Hugh Roberts
89 William Ratliff
93 David Richardson‡
94 John Reynolds
1801 Samuel Rose
04 Henry Redstone
05 Joshua Riggin
05 Lawrence Riley
05 William Ridgway
06 Nathaniel Rider

S

1773 Robert Strawbridge
81 Charles Scott
85 John Street* 1786
85 William Steen* 87
86 John Stewart
88 Benjamin Snelling
92 George Streebeck
92 Jonathan Stephenson
92 Rezin Simpson
92 Elijah Sparks
93 Randolph Smith
94 Moses Spear
96 Ebenezer Smith
97 George Shanks
97 Asher Smith
98 John Saunders
99 John Stewart, junior
99 Nathan Smith
1800 Asa Smith
01 John Sweet
02 Lewis Sutton
03 Thomas Scott, jr.
04 Fletcher Sullivan
04 Nathan Smith, jr.
04 Manly Smallwood
05 Hollis Sampson
1806 Jesse Stansell
06 Thomas Stewart
06 Joseph Smith
06 Joseph Smith, jr.
06 Elisha Streeter

T

1785 James Thomas* 1786
90 Samuel Tucker
91 Joseph Tatman
93 Joseph Thrift
95 Charles Tankersly
95 Samuel Tar
1803 James Taylor
06 John Thompson
06 Stephen Thompson

V

1789 Henry Vanover
90 Nuwit Vick

W

1776 William Wrenn
77 Robert Worster
83 Joshua Whorley
83 Wm. Wright* 1784
89 Thomas Workman
89 William Ward
91 John Wood
92 Joseph Wainwright
94 John Worster
96 Michael H. R. Wilson* 1798
96 Solomon Wyatt
1800 William Williams
01 John Walls
02 Joel Weeker
02 Stephen G. Whitehead
04 Benjamin Watts
05 Edmund Wilcox
06 Charles Warfield

In the foregoing list, we have 251 preachers, who were admitted on trial to travel and preach. These being added to the former number, make 1249 who have travelled as Methodist preachers in the United states of America, including also that part of Canada which is supplied with preachers who are under the direction of our conference.

I have taken no account of the preachers who have begun to travel since the year 1806, as I could not in all cases tell whether they were yet on trial, or in full connection.

Thus far the Lord hath prospered us, and the number of preachers which have been raised up among us far exceeds our former expectation. It is now just 40 years since the first Methodist preachers were sent to America; they came over in 1769, of course it is now (1809) forty years. There have also been raised up amongst us in the course of the same time more than 3000 local preachers. This is the Lord's doing, and it is marvellous in our eyes.

CHAPTER XIII.

From the beginning of the year 1807, to the end of 1809.

In 1807, we had our conferences as follows:

The 205th conference was held at Ebenezer, in Tennessee, on the 15th of September 1806.

The 206th at Sparta, in Georgia, on the 29th of December 1806.

The 207th in Newbern, on the 2d of February 807.

The 208th in Baltimore, on the 2d of March.

The 209th in Philadelphia, on the 2d of April.

The 210th at Coeyman's Patent, on the 2d of May.

The 211th in Boston, on the 2d of June.

This year we took in several new circuits.—In the western conference we took in *West Point*, *Missourie*, *Oachitta*, *White River* and *Licking*. In the Southern conference we took in *Ohoopee* and *Savannah*. In the Virginia conference, *Iredel* and *Rocky Mount*. In Baltimore conference, *St. Mary's* and *Canestio*. In Philadelphia confeience, *Cumberland* and *Holland-Purchase*. In New-York conference, *Schenectady*. In New-England conference, *Stanstead* and *Conaway*.

At these conferences we admitted upon trial a few more than 100 young preachers; and lost out of the travelling connection thirty-seven. Thirty-two of them located, and three died: one left us, and one was expelled. Those who died were Richard Whatcoat, James Lattomus, and Peter Jayne.

1. Richard Whatcoat, was a native of England, born in Gloucestershire; he became a travelling

preacher, in the year 1769. He travelled extensively through England and Ireland; and in the latter end of the year 1784, he came to the United States of America; and at the Christmas conference, he assisted in the ordination of Mr. Asbury. He laboured among us after that, in various stations, in towns, cities, circuits and districts, until the year 1800, he was then ordained a bishop by the laying on of the hands of Dr. Coke, Mr. Asbury, and some of the elders: after which he travelled at large till he died. He travelled and preached in Europe and America 37 years. He attended the conferences in the south in the preceding year, that is in 1806, and continued to travel to the north as far as Dover in Delaware state, and there he yielded to his afflictions, and could go no further, and did not attend the three last conferences for that year. About three weeks after the last conference met he died, and of course there was no account of his death published until the following year.

His last affliction was very severe; he lay at the house of Richard Bassett, late governor of Delaware state, then residing in Dover, for 13 weeks, and then departed this life in the full assurance of faith, on the 5th of July 1806.

He was a pattern of piety and of patience; he let his moderation be known to all men. He was always serious and solemn, and seldom complained of any difficulties that he met with. He was an excellent preacher, sound in doctrine, and clear and plain in his explanations of the scriptures, with which he was particularly acquainted.

He might be ranked among the best of men, for meekness and patience, humility and sobriety; for watchfulness over his words, and for a smooth and even temper; and withal, for gifts and animation in preaching: especially in the latter part of his life. In his death the preachers have lost a pattern of piety, and the people have lost an able teacher.

He travelled 15 years in Europe, and 22 in America, which was 37 years in all.

He was born in 1736. Converted September 3, 1758.

Sanctified March 28, 1761. Began to travel and preach in 1769.

Came to America in 1784. Was ordained bishop in May 1800.

He acted as bishop 6 years, and died at Dover July 5, 1806.

2. James Lattomus, was born in Newcastle county in Delaware state; he began to travel and preach in 1796, and after six years he became a supernumerary, and continued so for four years before he died. He was a man of a feeble constitution, but was considered as a good pious man. He departed this life in peace in September 1806.

3. Peter Jayne, was a native of Marblehead, in Massachusetts; born in 1778, and was converted when he was about sixteen years old: he began to travel and preach when he was about eighteen years of age. He died in Boston on the 5th of September 1806. He had travelled a little more than nine years before he died; in which time he had been stationed in the province of Maine, Massachusetts, Connecticut and New-York states.

We added to the society 14020 members, which was a very great increase. The work of the Lord was very great during this year in most parts of the United States. Religion prospered greatly in the state of Georgia. At a camp meeting in Hancock county, about three miles south of Sparta, which began on Tuesday the 28th of July, and closed on Saturday following, there were 176 tents, and we calculated on 80 souls converted. There was another camp-meeting at Cold Water, after the former, where there were about the same number of souls brought into the favour of the Lord. Other meetings of the same kind were held in the state, where many souls were happily converted; but not as many as at the meetings before mentioned. The work spread greatly through the circuits, and some hundreds were added to the society in the course of a few months.

On the 19th of April this year we formed a society in Savannah, which was the first regular Methodist society we ever formed in that city. It was just 70 years from the time that Mr. John Wesley formed a society, and in the same place, which only continued for a short time, during his stay among them.

The accounts from various parts of the connection respecting the prosperity of religion was truly pleasing. The Eastern Shore of Maryland and Virginia and the lower counties in Delaware, were remarkably visited of the Lord; and many hundreds of people were truly converted, and made the subjects of grace. The holy flame of love ran from place to place, and from heart to heart. Ministers and people were remarkably engaged with God both in public and private, and their preaching and praying was followed with a blessing from the Lord.

In the course of the year 1806, there was a plan laid which would have overset and destroyed the rules and regulation of the Methodists, respecting the election and ordination of Bishops. It was said that the plan originated in the New-York conference, which was as follows: "To call a delegated conference of seven members from each conference, chosen by the conference, to meet in Baltimore on the fourth of July 1807, to choose superintendants, &c." This plan was adopted by four of the conferences, viz. New-York, New-England, the Western and South-Carolina conferences; and delegates were accordingly chosen. But when it was proposed to the Virginia conference, which met in Newbern, in February 1807, they refused to take it under consideration, and rejected it as being pointedly in opposition to all the rules of our church. The bishop laboured hard to carry the point, but he laboured in vain: and the whole business of that dangerous plan was overset by the Virginia conference. The inventers and defenders of that project might have meant well; but they certainly erred in judgment.

In 1808, we had eight conferences, the last of which was a general conference.

The 212th conference was held at Chilicothe, Ohio state, on the 14th of September 1807.

The 213th in Charleston, on the 28th of December 1807.

The 214th in Lynchburg, on the 2d of February 1808.

The 215th in George Town, on the 2d of March.

The 216th in Philadelphia, on the 20th of March.

The 217th at Amenia, on the 6th of April.

The 218th in New-London, on the 17th of April.

The 219th was the 5th general conference, held in Baltimore, on the 6th of May.

We took in several new circuits this year. In the western conference, *Duck River*, *Marymack* and *Wills Creek*. In the Southern conference, *Tom-Big-Bee* and *Fayetsville*. In the Virginia conference *Neuse*. In Philadelphia conference, *Antalany* and *Snowhill*. In New-England conference, *Smithfield* and *Palmira*; and a few more circuits were enlarged or divided.

At these conferences we admitted upon trial upwards of 80 young preachers, and we lost out of the travelling connection 36 preachers; 29 located, one was expelled, 2 left us and four died. Those who died, were George Daugherty, Bennet Kendrick, Henry Willis and Richard Swain.

1. George Daugherty was a native of South-Carolina. He lost one of his eyes when he was young by the small pox; he was tall and slender made, and had an effeminate voice. He was a sensible and useful preacher. He was very studious in private, and diligent and laborious in his ministerial labours. His piety and devotion was great. He travelled and preached 9 years, and was generally esteemed very highly for his work sake wherever he laboured. He was afflicted with the consumption some time before he died, which increased upon him till he died. He had his senses perfectly to the last, and retained his confidence in God, and a full assurance of eternal life. He died at Wilmington in North Carolina, on the 23d of March 1807, and was buried in the Methodist meeting-house.

2. Bennet Kendrick was born on the south side of Roan-Oak-river, in Mecklenburg county, Virginia. He entered on the travelling plan in 1799, and died on the 5th of April 1807 at Edward Crosland's, between the Chawraw hills and Long Bluff on Pee-Dee river in South-Carolina; having travelled from the time he was received at conference, within a few days of 8 years. He was a serious, pious young man; much devoted to God, and diligently engaged in the work of the ministry. He was generally esteemed, and

much beloved for his works' sake wherever he laboured. He was much engaged with God in his last sickness, and was comfortable and happy in his death.

3. Henry Willis was a native of Brunswick county, Virginia. He began to travel and preach the gospel in 1778, and located in 1790. He travelled 12 years only. Some time after he was located, he was again put on the minutes as a supernumery, and had some nominal appointments, but never after filled the place of a preacher in any circuit, but followed his own domestic business regularly; and preached on Sundays when he could conveniently. He was a sensible and lively preacher. He was greatly attached to the travelling plan, even when he was not able to fill a station. He was much devoted to God in the close of his life, and very happy in God at the last. The end of that man was peace.

4. Richard Swain was a native of New-Jersey. He began to travel in 1789, and after travelling about 19 years, he died on the 17th of January 1808. His ministerial labours were principally confined to the state in which he was born. He travelled a while in Connecticut, and then returned to New-Jersey. He was beloved by the brethren, and was useful in the ministry. The last years of his life he was very infirm, and much afflicted; and at last died in peace.

We added to the society 7,405 members this year. Although our increase was not as great this year as it had been in some of the preceding years, yet we had great cause to be thankful for an increase of so many thousands.

In the month of May we had our fifth and last General Conference, and as we made some alterations in our rules and discipline, it will be necessary to take notice of them at this place.

The first alteration is respecting the general conferences in future, and as the change is very considerable, I will insert the *rule* at full length.

Q. "Who shall compose the general conference, and what are the regulations and powers belonging to it?"

A. 1. "The general conference shall be composed of one member for every five members of each annual conference, to be appointed by seniority or choice, at the discretion of such annual conference: yet so that such representatives shall have travelled at least four full calender years from the time that they were received on trial by an annual confercnee, and are in full connection at the time of holding the conference.

2. The general conference shall meet on the first day of May, in the year of our lord 1812 in the city of New-York, and thence forward on the first day of May once in four years perpetually, in such place or places as shall be fixed on by the general conference from time to time: but the general superintendants, with or by the advice of all the annual conferences, or if there be no general superintendants, all the annual conferences respectively shall have power to call a general conference, if they judge it necessary at any time.

3. At all times when the general conference is met, it shall take two-thirds of the representatives of all the annual conferences to make a quorum for transacting business.

4, One of the general superintendants shall preside in the general conference; but in case no general superintendant be present, the general conference shall choose a president protempore.

5. The general conference shall have full powers to make rules and regulations for our church, under the following limitations and restrictions, viz.

1. The general conference shall not revoke, alter or change our articles of religion, nor establish any new standards or rules of doctrine contrary to our present existing and established standards of doctrine.

2. They shall not allow of more than one representative for every five members of the annual conference, nor allow of a less number than one for every seven.

3. They shall not change or alter any part or rule of our government, so as to do away episcopacy or destroy the plan of our itinerant general superintendancy.

4. They shall not revoke or change the general rules of the United Societies.

5. They shall not do away the privileges of our ministers or preachers of trial by a committee, and of an appeal. Neither shall they do away the privileges of our members of trial before the society, or by a committee, and of an appeal.

6. They shall not appropriate the produce of the book concern, or of the charter fund, to any purpose other than for the benefit of the travelling, supernumerary, superanuated and worn-out preachers, their wives, widows and children. Provided nevertheless, that upon the joint recommendation of all the annual conferences, then a majority of two-thirds of the general conference succeeding, shall suffice to alter any of the above restrictions."

Our connection having spread very extensively, and the number of our preachers being much larger than they were formerly, it was thought best to make some new regulations about our general conferences in future, and the foregoing regulations were agreed to, by which means each part of the connection would have a proportionable number of preachers in the general conference. The Baltimore and Philadelphia conferences will no longer include more than half the members of the general conference. At this conference was made the new rule for the ordination of local preachers. Formerly they were to have their recommendation signed by nine travelling preachers, before they could be ordained. The rule being changed, it now stands thus: "The bishops have obtained liberty, by the suffrages of the conference, to ordain local preachers to the office of deacons; provided their characters pass in examination, and obtain the approbation of the yearly conference, with a testimonial from the quarterly meeting of their respective circuits, after proper examination, signed by the president, and countersigned by the secretary."

There was a new regulation made at the last general conference in section 5th of the second part, in "raising annual supplies for the propagation of the gospel and for making up the allowance of the preachers." That part which is new is contained in these words, "Every annual conference has full liberty to adopt and recommend such plans and rules, as to them may appear necessary, the more effectually to raise supplies for the respective allowances of the preachers.

"If the respective allowances are not raised as provided for, the connection shall not be accountable for the deficiency, as in a case of debt."

Before that time we had but one rule in every place for raising money; but now each annual conference may choose a plan of their own for securing the funds necessary to meet the regular demands of the preachers within it's own limits.

At this general conference, it was thought best for Dr. Coke to be no longer considered as a superintendant of the methodists in the United

States. He had married in England, and taken regular appointments from the British conference, and of course could not attend to America according to his former engagement. We therefore concluded to enter him on the *Annual Minutes* thus:

"Dr. Coke, at the request of the British Conference, and by the consent of our General Conference, resides in Europe: he is not to exercise the office of Superintendant among us, in the United States, until he be recalled by the general conference, or by all the annual conferences respectively."

The General Conference elected another Bishop, and William M'Kendree of Virginia had a large majority of votes. On Wednesday the 18th day of May 1808, Bishop Asbury preached an ordination sermon in Light-street Church, from 1 Tim. 4, 16. *Take heed to thyself, and unto thy doctrine.* After sermon William M'Kendree was ordained a Bishop by the laying on of the hands of Bishop Asbury, and four of the oldest travelling preachers present, which were, Freeborn Garrettson, Philip Bruce, Jesse Lee, and Thomas Ware.

There was a good deal of peace and union among the preachers at that general conference; and there were 130 travelling preachers who were members of that conference. Mr. M'Kendree had been a travelling preacher just twenty years when he was ordained a Bishop. Most of the preachers returned from that conference well satisfied with what was done while we were together.

From all that I could learn from different parts of our connection there was a wonderful revival of religion after the Preachers returned from the general conference to their circuits. In the city of New-York there was a very great revival of religion; many souls were brought into favour with the Lord, and scores of members were added to the society. In the city of Philadelphia, there was a considerable stir of religion, and people were frequently converted, and joined our society.

The Camp-Meetings were greatly owned and honoured of God in different parts of the country; and very few if any were more favoured than one that was held at Boheamy, on the Eastern Shore of Maryland, where the slain of the Lord were many, and some scores of sinners were converted during the meeting. From that place many returned home happy in God, who had neither sought nor found religion before. Indeed we could hardly hear from any of our preachers or people who lived at a distance, without hearing of the prosperity of religion.

I will mention a revival which took place in the Penitentiary in Richmond Virginia, where there were about 130 prisoners at hard labour for a term of years. Some for murder in the second degree, and others for forgery, counterfeiting money, stealing horses, breaking open houses, &c. In Virginia *freemen* are not hanged for any thing except *murder in the first degree.*

In the month of April this year, Mr. Stith Mead, who was stationed in Richmond, began to preach in the penitentiary, and from that time he provided preaching for the prisoners on every Sabbath; some times he preached, and at other times he engaged other ministers to preach among them. Withal, he gave them some small books, and lent them others on religious subjects. In a short time the good effects were seen, and some of the prisoners began to weep freely under preaching, and the convictions of some were deep and lasting. At one time when there was a considerable melting among the people, the preacher proposed for all who were willing to offer themselves as candidates for heaven, to signify it by standing up: a few of them arose from their seats immediately. At another time it was proposed by the preacher for all of them, who were truly desirous of obtaining religion to come forward and kneel down and he would pray for them: several came forward and appeared to be much distressed on the account of their sins: and afterwards their number increased from time to time, until their convictions were accompanied with loud cries to God for mercy, while some were exclaiming against themselves as the worst of sinners, and labouring under awful apprehensions that there was no mercy for them. But in a short time some of them were happily converted to God, and gave a very satisfactory account of a real change of heart. The convictions of others were greatly increased, so that at times the greater part of the prisoners have been seen coming forward and kneeling down to be prayed for. Prayer was attended to by them, in their own rooms; and they were frequently engaged in singing psalms, hymns and spiritual songs, as well as in praying in their lodgings, until the whole circular building was made to resound with the praises of God. As the number of converts increased, the preacher advised the believers to form themselves into a society, to help each other on in their way to heaven; about twenty joined together at that time. Soon after that, they had about thirty of the prisoners united together, who were happily converted to God, according to their own profession, and the judgment of their preacher. I visited them myself, and talked with many of them, and could not doubt of the reality of their profession of faith in the Lord Jesus Christ.

In 1809 we had the usual number of conferences:

The 220th conference was held at Liberty hill, in Tennessee, on the 1st of October, 1808.

The 221st, at Liberty chapel, in Georgia, on the 26th of December.

The 222d, at Tarborough, on the 1st of February 1809.

The 223d, at Harrisonburg, on the second of March.

The 224th, in Philadelphia, on the 2d of April.

The 225th, in New-York, on the 10th of May

The 226th, in Monmouth, (Province of Maine) on the 15th of June.

We took in several new circuits this year; in the Western conference we took in 9; *Watauga, Tennessee Valley, Elk, Dickson, Green river, Fleming, Cold Water, White Water* and *Leading creek.* In the southern conference 4; *Alcovi, Ocmulgee, Congoree* and *Waterree.* In the Virginia conference 2; *Straits* and *Green Mountain.* In the New-York conference 4; *Courtlandt, Pownal, Detroit* and *Three Rivers.* In the New England conference 4; *Portsmouth, Booth Bay, George-town* and *Industry.*

We admitted 103 young preachers upon trial this year; and lost out of the travelling connection forty-four. Forty located, three died, and the other was expelled. Those who died were Edmund Henly, Leonard Cassell, and Henry Martin.

1. Edmund Henly was a native of Person county, North-Carolina. He began to travel in 1803, and after travelling and preaching for a little more than five years, he died in peace on the 26th day of August 1808.

For some time before his death he appeared to have an impression on his mind that the time of his departure was at hand. A few weeks before he died, he went home to his father's, erected a stage at the grave yard, and preached to his old friends and acquaintances. After his death he was carried home and buried there. He was about thirty years of age. He had professed sanctification for several years. He was very serious and very circumspect in his behaviour. He exercised great patience in his last sickness; and at times he would exhort and pray, shout and praise God, to the last of his life.

2. Leonard Cassell, was born in Frederick county in Maryland. He was of German parentage. In early life, through the ministry of the Methodists, he embraced the religion of Jesus Christ. He began to travel in 1802, at which time he was not 18 years old. He continued to travel and preach for upwards of six years before he died. His last station was at Fell's-Point, where he died of the yellow fever on the 26th of September 1808. He was respected for his gifts and piety, and his loss in the church was much lamented.

3. Henry Martin, was a native of New-Hampshire, a young man of a good character, both as a christian, and as a minister. He possessed a clear understanding, and a sound judgment in the holy scriptures. He was diligent, laborious, and persevering both in his private and public duties. He began to travel and preach the gospel in 1805, and continued therein about three years and a half, and then died on the sixth of December 1808, on Parker's Island in George Town, near the mouth of Kennebec river.

According to the returns of members in the minutes, we had added 11043 members to our society in the course of the year which ended at the conference held in June last, 1809.

Since the beginning of the present year we have had a pleasing prospect of religion, in various parts of the United States: and the accounts both verbal and writen from various persons, assure us that souls are coming to God by hundreds. At one camp-meeting held near Lynchburg in August, it was supposed that as many as eighty souls were converted to God from the beginning to the close of that meeting which lasted only a few days. Soon after that the work of God revived in the town of Lynchburg, and in the course of one week, it was thought that as many as eighty or ninety souls were born again. Such a wonderful display of the power and presence of God in the conversion of souls had never been known in that town.

On the 10th day of October, another camp-meeting began at Abner Early's about 18 miles from Lynchburg, where the people were more highly favoured of the Lord than usual. There was an account kept of 162 persons who professed to be converted during that meeting, which began on Tuesday and ended on Monday following. Many other meetings of the same kind have been held in Virginia, where there has been from twenty to fifty persons converted at a meeting. The work has prospered in many places at prayer meetings and class meetings. Some sinners have been brought to God in the fields, or in the woods, or when riding on the road. The christians themselves have been greatly quickened, and several of them have professed the perfect love of God, and have been able to *rejoice ever more, pray without ceasing, and in every thing give thanks.*

After the annual minutes for 1809 were published, Joseph Everit died. He was born in Queen Ann's county in the state of Maryland, on the 17th day of June 1732. He was converted on the 13th of June 1763, while alone in his own house. After a short time he became a backslider, and lost his religion. He remained in a backsliden state near 17 years. He became acquainted with the Methodists in Delaware state in the beginning of 1778, and by their preaching he was once more stirred up to seek the Lord, and on the 5th day of April in the same year, the Lord once more forgave his sins. After some time he joined society with the Methodists. It was not long after that, before he began to exhort in public meetings, and obtained license for that purpose. On the first day of October 1780, he left home and went to Dorchester circuit to preach, and travelled there four weeks. After a short time he returned to the same circuit again. He was ordained deacon at Abingdon on the 10th day of May, 1786. He was ordained elder in Philadelphia on the 25th of September 1788.—He was a travelling preacher for more than 28 years. The last five years he was entered on the minutes "a superannuated and worn out preacher." He was confined to his bed only a few days, the greater part of which time he was slightly delirious; but even then his mind was constantly in pursuit of the one thing needful. On Sunday morning, which was the last day of his life, when his pulse had entirely failed, he was quite recollected, and remained so to the last. At night, being sensible of his approaching dissolution, he took leave of some friends who were present; after which he slept some time. About midnight he awoke agitated from head to foot. He raised his hands as if he wished to clap them, and began and continued for about 25 minutes to shout Glory! Glory! Glory! till he ceased to shout and ceased to breathe. He died on the 15th of October 1809, in the 78th year of his age.

A List of the Numbers in Society in the United States, with the increase and decrease for each year, from 1771 to 1809, including 39 years, with the number of circuits and travelling preachers for each year.

The year	No. in society	Increase	Decrease	No. of circuits	No. of preach's
1771	316				
1772	500	184			
1773	1160	660		6	10
1774	2073	913		10	17
1775	3148	1075		10	20
1776	4921	1773		11	25
1777	6968	2047		15	37
1778	6095		873	17	29
1779	8577	2482		20	49
1780	8504		73	20	42
1781	10,539	2035		25	55
1782	11,785	1246		26	60
1783	13,740	1955		35	82
1784	14,988	1248		46	84
1785	18,000	3012		52	105
1786	18,791	791		56	118
1787	25,873	7082		65	134
1788	37,354	11,481		85	166
1789	43,265	5911		97	196
1790	57,621	14,356		116	228
1791	63,878	6257		129	252
1792	66,192	2314		136	267
1793	67,643	1451		149	276
1794	65,508		2135	150	298
1795	59,291		6217	164	313

The year	No. in society	Increase	Decrease	No. of circuits	No. of preach's
1796	56,664		2627	157	274
1797	58,663	1999		152	266
1798	60,169	1506		156	268
1799	61,351	1182		167	271
1800	64,894	3543		178	289
1801	72,874	7980		182	311
1802	86,734	13,860		210	358
1803	104,070	17,336		223	387
1804	113,134	9064		230	407
1805	119,945	6811		244	433
1806	130,570	10,625		261	466
1807	144,590	14,020		289	526
1808	151,995	7405		306	545
1809	163,038	11,043		324	589

Number of Members in the Methodist Society in 1809.

Total in Britain and Ireland,	157,921
in the West-Indies,	12,508
in the British dominions in America,	1121
Gibraltar and Africa,	40
in the United States of America,	163,038
Total number of the Methodist society throughout the world,	334,628

CHAPTER XIV.

The Conclusion.

AS I have frequently spoken of *Camp-Meetings* in the preceding pages, it may be of service to many of the readers of this work, who have never been at a meeting of this kind, to have a description of them.

1. With regard to the laying out the ground: we have two, three, or four acres of land cleared of the under growth, in an oblong square, sufficient to hold as many tents as will be erected. We then have the front of the tents on a line on each side, and at each end. Back of the tents we have a place cleared for the carriages to stand, whether they be waggons, carts, or riding carriages; so that every tent may have the carriage belonging to it in a convenient position. Just back of the carriages we have the horses tied and fed. Before the tents we generally have the fires for cooking, and to help in giving light at night to those who are walking about. But when it is not convenient to have the fire in the front of the tent, it is placed behind it.

2. We have one or two stages erected; if we have two, one is near the one end of the ground, and the other near the opposite end; but both within the lines whereon the tents are fixed. At each stage we have a sufficient number of seats to contain the principal part of the attentive hearers: who are requested to sit according to our form, the women on one side, and the men on the other. The stages are placed at such a distance from each other, that if necessity should require it, we might preach at each stage at the same time. Or in case there should be a great

degree of life and power among the people at one stage, we might without interrupting their devotion in singing and praying, withdraw to the other stage and preach to as many as might wish to hear.

3. We have the ground within the tents illuminated at night by candles, which we fix to the stage, the trees, and other places prepared for the purpose. These candles, with the light of the fires, keep the whole ground sufficiently illuminated. On some occasions, I have seen at these meetings as many as 120 candles burning at the same time. These lights in a dark night, when the evening is calm, add greatly to the solemnity of the meeting.

4. We generally appoint a guard, or watch, of a sufficient number of men, and request them by turn to walk all night through and around the incampment, to prevent disorderly persons from doing mischief, either in disturbing the people, or their property.

5. We proceed in our religious exercises as follows: soon after the first dawn of day, a person walks all round the ground in front of the tents, blowing a trumpet as he passes; which is to give the people notice to rise; about ten minutes after the trumpet is blown again with only one long blast; upon which, the people in all their tents begin to sing, and then pray, either in their tents, or at the door of them, as is most convenient. At the rising of the sun a sermon is preached, after which we eat breakfast. We have preaching again at 10 o'clock, and dine about one. We preach again at 3 o'clock, eat supper about the setting of the sun, and have preaching again at candle light. We generally begin these meetings on Fridays, and continue them until the Monday following about the mid-

dle of the day. I have known these meetings to continue without any intermission for two nights and a day, or longer. The people being continually engaged in singing, praying, preaching, or exhorting without any cessation.

But these meetings are varied, both with regard to the form and duration, according to the judgment of the preachers who attend them. I have known some Camp-Meetings to continue eight or ten days. Indeed these meetings have never been authorized by the Methodists, either at their general or annual conferences. They have been allowed of; but we, as a body of people, have never made any rules or regulations about them; we allow our presiding elders and travelling preachers to appoint them when and where they please, and to conduct them in what manner they think fit. Of course the form of a Camp meeting, as given above, is not the form of all the meetings of the kind, but of such as I myself have regulated or attended.

In this History there is such a collection of facts, and such a clear, plain, and full account of the *Methodists*, that he that runs may read, and he that reads may understand that the Lord has done great things for us, whereof we are glad.—It will here be seen, that from a very small beginning, we have grown to be a numerous people. In 1771 we had only 316 members in society; in 1780 we had 8504; in 1790 we had 57,621; in 1800 we had 64,894; and in 1809 we have 163,038.

In 1809 bishop Asbury collected the names of all the Local Preachers in connection with the Methodists; and, according to his account, there were 1610 local preachers in the United States.

I wish that we may increase in grace, as fast as we have in numbers.

FINIS.

INDEX.

SUBSCRIBERS NAMES.

Massachusetts.
Berzaleel Fuller Attlebo.
Calvin P. Fuller do.
Philip Fuller do.
Thomas Fuller do.
Zelotes Fuller do.
Polly Gazfield do.
Joseph Gould do.
Moses prentice Belchert.
Nathan Brownwell Brimf
Alfred Bliss Rehoboth
Benjamin Fuller do.
Timothy Perry do.
Stephen Hunt Taunton
Dier Pratt do.
Able Bliss Wilbraham
Abraham Avery do
John Kneeland do.
Persis Stebbins do.

Rhode-Island.
Henry Hawkins Cumberl.
Mathewson B. Lockwood
Nicholas Brown Gloucest.
Jeremiah Manton Johnson
Lloyd Beall Newport
Shubal Cady Providence
Wm. P. R. Benson do.
William Hinman do.
Mowry Randall North-Pr
Ezekiel Whipple do.
Thomas Whipple do.
James Brown Smithfield
Benedick Burlingame do.
Simon Irons Smithfild
Nathaniel Mowry do.
Lusina Windsor do.
Wm. Fletcher Warwich
Nicholas Gardiner do.
Nehemiah Jenks do.
Arnold Manchester do.
Thomas Slack do.
Resolved Wateaman do.

Connecticut.
David Balts Ashford
Cyrus Daw do.
Jeremiah Mumford do.
Joseph Work do.
Allen Barnes Bozrah
Ambrose Coleman Colech-
James Hammond Ellingt-
Sophia Steel do.
Amaziah Fillmore Frank.
Comfort D. Fillmore do.
John Howard Groton
Ralph Hurtbutt do.
Vine Stoddard do.
Elizur Bell, jr. Hartford
Rev. Elijah Hedding 6
Charles Treat do.
Gordon Wells do.
Dudley Birge Hebron
Daniel Burrows do.
Eleazer Puffer do.
Niel Robertson do.
Henry P. Sumner do. 12
John Beatty New-London

Isaial Bolles New-London
George Culver do.
Richard Douglass do.
Lodowick Fosdick do.
John P. Frett do.
David Frink, jr. do.
John H. Frink do.
Hezekiah Goddard do.
Erastus Hyde do.
Jirah Isham do.
David Johnson do.
E. Learner do.
James Lee do.
Isaac Regers do,
Asa Spencer do.
Isaac Thompson do.
Rev. Isaac Bonney Norw.
Noah Perrin Pomfret
Rev Nathaniel Chapen [Union
Alden Blodget Stafford
John Goodwill Willington
John Salter do.
Charles Beckwith Windh.
James Moore Waterford
Wait P. Green Pownal, [Vermont

New-York.

Thomas Kirk Brooklyn
Stephen Dando New-York
Abraham E. Brower do.
Israel Dissaway do.
Methodist Library do.
Abraham Russel do.
Rev. Daniel Smith do.
Joseph Smith do.
Robert Sands Rhynebeck
Rev. Freeborn Garrettson

New-Jersey,

Wm Mc'Collough Asb 6
Rev. Thomas Budd 36
Rev. Samuel Budd 12
Rachel Sandford Bergen
William D. Sandford do
Wm. S. Brooks Bridgct.
Gurtis Edwards do.
Rev. Michael Swing Cum.
Elias Howel Fairfield
Jeptha Abbott Gloucester
Edward Beaton do.
John Code do.
Rev- Moses Crane do.
James Elliott do.
Edward Hay do.
Malachi Horner do.
William Mitchell do.
Robert Newell do.
Restore Turner do.
Susannah Turner do.
Cornelius Wiltsce do.
Samuel Seagrave Mannin.
William C. Dorsey do.
Patrick Fields do.
Thomas Stevenson do.
Lewis Ashton Monmouth
Stephen Burkalow do.
Elihu Chadick do.
Eleson Covert do.
Lewis Garetson do.
Humphrey Jeffry do.
Michael Maps do.
Rev. James Moore 10
James Morris do.
Richard Rogers do.
Abner Tharp do.
John Thogmorton do.
John Borman Morri
George Dills do.
Ziba Hazen do.
Joseph Baker Penns neck

John Forton Penns-neck
William Gregory do
Benjamin Harvey do
Peter Hickman do
Vining Hill do
Joseph Jaquett do
Mary Popner do
John Price do
Joast Nieukirk, Pitts-gro.
Levi Alberson Salem
Andrew Alston do
John Ashton do
Daniel Clifton do
Sarah English do
Rev. Wm. S. Ferker 2
Isaac Ford do
George Horner, jr. do
Isaac C. Jones do
Amelia Lauderback, do
William Lummis do
John Mink do
Jacob Mulford do
William Mulford do
Thomas Murphy do
James Newell do
James Patterson do
William Pedrick do
Nicholas Peterson do
Joseph Price do
John Smith do
John Smith do
James Stiles do
William Strimple do
George Thomas do
William Treadway do
Michael Walker do
Enos Woodruff do
George Banghart, Sussex
Samuel Bradford do
Samuel Bradford do
John Cummins Sussex
Christian Cummins do
Matthias Cummins do
Philip Cummins do
James Drake do
James Egburt ditto
Conrad Emery ditto
Benjamin Freeman ditto
Nancy Green ditto
William Hillyer ditto
John Park ditto
Andrew Rose ditto
Joseph Tindall ditto
Samuel Tomlinson, Hope.

Pennsylvania.

John Widney, jr. Concord
Hugh Linn, jr. Franklin
Charles Widney, ditto
Rev. Thomas F. Sargent

Delaware.

Rev. Solomon Sharp, Mil-

Maryland.

Providence Baker, Balti.
Richard Colvin ditto
James C. Dew ditto
John Diddep ditto
George Earnest ditto
Rev. Daniel Fidler ditto
Robert Fisher ditto
Prudence Gough ditto
Levin Hall ditto
Samuel Harden ditto
William Hawkins ditto
Joseph Jamison ditto
Philip Littig ditto
Mary Ann M'Clure ditto
Gilbert Middleton ditto
Thomas Murphy ditto
Joseph Owens ditto
George G. Presbury, jr.

Daniel E. Reese, Baltimo.
Jesse M. Sherwood ditto
Richard A. Shipley ditto
Eli Simpkins ditto
Job Smith ditto
Rebecca Smith ditto
Rev. John Valiant ditto
Peregrine Welsh ditto
James Williams ditto
William Woods ditto
John Brown, Centre-Ville representative in Cong
Thomas Cecell, Centre-V
Luther L. Cox ditto
John Hackett, jr. ditto
Wm. Hackett ditto
Wm. Harper ditto
Benjamin Hatchison ditto
Daniel Morris ditto
John E. Spencer ditto
James B. Williams ditto
William Wren ditto
Samuel T. Wright do
Dr. Edw. White, Camb. 12
Wm. Harris, Chester-t. 6
Kidd Morsell, Prince-Geo.
Henry Wilson ditto

District of Columbia.

William Doughty
Andrew Mc'Kelden
Thomas L. Mc'Kenney
Rev. Richard Parrott
Rev. James Smith
Rev. James Saunders

Virginia.

John C. Cousins, Amelia
Thomas Coverly ditto
Henry H. Southall ditto
Elijah Brown, Albemarle
Ann Key ditto
Tandy Key, Albemarle
Walter Key ditto
Pleasant Dawson, Amhe.
Joseph Kennerly ditto
Hugh Norvill ditto
Benammi Stone ditto
Edmund Williamson ditto
Russel Goss, Bent-Creek
Henry M. Beddon ditto
Rev. John Belleu ditto
Dancey Perman ditto
Thom. Booth, Brunswick
Henry Abernathy ditto
Richardson Brown ditto
Frederick Burdge ditto
Jesse Coe ditto
Reuben Cooper ditto
Alexander Dameron ditto
Rev. Wm. Elliott ditto
John Fletcher ditto
Wm. Gholson ditto
James Gunn ditto
Richard Hall ditto
William Hammond ditto
Benjamin Johnson ditto
Benj. Johnson, jr. ditto
Rev. Edwin Johnson ditto
Henry Johnson ditto
John M. Jordan ditto
Benjamin Lashley ditto
John P. Malone ditto
Thomas Malone ditto
Judith Mason ditto
David Merideth ditto
William Merideth ditto
Rev. Henry Merritt ditto
Mathew Myrick ditto
William Palmer ditto
David Pilkington ditto
Rev. Josiah Phillips ditto

SUBSCRIBERS NAMES.

James Wyche, Brunsw.	Val. Winfree, Chesterfield
Rev. William Barnes do	E Boulding, Charlotte
Wm. Pritchett ditto	John Fennell ditto
Wm. Quarles ditto	Anthony Phillips ditto
Charles Ridont ditto	John Spencer, ditto
John Rogers ditto	Thomas Wood ditto
Henry Rose ditto	Jacob Bransford, Cumber.
Rev. John Shell ditto	Benjamin Bransford ditto
Phebe Rhodes ditto	Noton Goodman ditto
Thomas A. Stroud ditto	Rev. Wm. Spencer ditto
Lucy W. Weaver ditto	Edmund Brown, Campb.
William Wilkerson ditto	Rev. Abner Early ditto
Peter P. Wyche ditto	George Jude ditto
Rd. Anderson, Buckingh.	James Lashells ditto
George Christian ditto	George Martin ditto
William F. Davis ditto	John Porter ditto
Samuel Du Vall ditto	Benjamin Cook, Franklin
Wiatt R. Gilbert ditto	Richard Mitchell ditto
Zadock Lackland ditto	Rd. Cornet, Culpepper
Henry Lewis ditto	Wm. Booth, Dinwidie
Robert Pattison ditto	Robert C. Booth ditto
William Staples ditto	David Browder ditto
John M. Walker ditto	Wm. Crowder ditto
Jesse Walton ditto	Paton Daniel ditto
Richard Anderson, ditto	Peter Epes ditto
Susannah Ishell, Caroline	John Fraiser, jr. ditto
Richard Petross ditto	Thomas Leach ditto
Elijah White ditto	David Miller ditto
Edw. Burnett, Chesterfi	John Mitchell ditto
Rev. Thos. Anderson, jr.	John Perkins ditto
Rev. John R Bradley do.	John P. Pool ditto
Henry Bridgewater ditto	Peter Pride ditto
Thomas Cheatham ditto	Baker Rather ditto
John J. Kleinhoff ditto	Enoch Rather ditto
Levin Landrum ditto	Rev. Henry Reese ditto 6
Rev. Hezekiah Mc'Lel	Matilda Reese ditto
[land ditto	William Rivers ditto
P. Poindexter ditto	C B. Rives ditto
Joseph Prince ditto	Rev. Richard Rives ditto
James Winfree ditto	Dennis Steel ditto

Wood Tucker ditto
John Watkins ditto
Joseph Whitehead ditto
Wm. Blake, Gloucester
Richard C. Jones ditto
John Stubbs ditto
Edwin Clark, G.eensville
James Clark ditto
Edwin Cook ditto
Foster Cook ditto
Uriah Cook ditto
Williamson Bonner ditto
Mathew Davis ditto
Lewis Dupree ditto
Thomas Dupree, Greensv.
James C. Fennell ditto
Edmund Heath ditto 3
Rev. William W. Hen-[drick ditto
Irvin Mayes ditto
Rev. James M'Kendree
Edward Moore ditto
Kinchen Peterson ditto
Thomas Spencer ditto
Fred. Whittington ditto
Lewis Whittington ditto
Henry Wyche ditto
Fanny Leak, Goochland
J. B. Ferguson ditto
David Anderson, Hanov.
John M. Anderson ditto
Pines Allen Henry
William F Mills ditto
John Travis ditto
William Moore, Halifax
Asa Barnes, Lunenburg
Rev. Thomas Adams do
John Blackwell ditto
Jeremiah Burnett ditto
John Burnett ditto
Mary Davis Lunenburg
Rev. John Christian ditto
Vincent Inge ditto
Rev. John Pritchett ditto
Betsey Smith ditto
Winnifred Wallace ditto
Rev. Stephen Jones ditto
Thomas Jordan ditto
John Marshall ditto
Sterling Niblett ditto
John Ogburn ditto
Samuel Peace ditto
Wm. Burd, Lynchburg
Shubal Barnard ditto
Thomas Cohen ditto
Wm. Goss, Lynchburg
Christopher Drummond
James Gilliam ditto
Rev. William Heath 4
Rev. S. K. Jennings ditto
John F. Lamb ditto
Rev. Wm. P. Martin do
David Mason ditto
James C. Moorman ditto
Benjamin Mosby ditto
Owen Owens ditto
John Pointer ditto
Henry Priddy ditto
Philip Rhor ditto
Robert Rutherford ditto
George See ditto
William Sumpter ditto
Rodirick Taliaferro ditto
William Tardy ditto
John C. Taylor ditto
Townsel Trustlow ditto
John Wiatt ditto
Thomas Wiatt ditto
Culwell Williamson ditto
Christopher Winfree do

John H. Word Lynch
Parson Wright ditto
Rev. Thomas P. Ander-
[son, Louisa
Rev. Henry Fry, Madison
John Algood, Macklin
[burg
George R. Edwards ditto
Samuel Holmes ditto
Rev. Charles Ogburn do
John Ogburn ditto
Samuel Simmons ditto
Edmund Taylor ditto
Cornelius Buck, Manches
Edward D Diggs ditto
Nathaniel Quarles ditto
Nicholas Mills, Manches.
Henry W. Wills, Isle of
Vincite Hart, King & Q.
John Hemingway ditto
Barbary Edwards, K. W
William Nunn ditto
James Powell ditto
Henry Timberlook ditto
William G. Waters ditto
John Curle, New-Kent
George Rugland ditto
Samuel Keiningham ditto
Gilliam Booth, jr. Notta
Rev. Peter Robinson do.
Littlebury Royall do 6
James Carney Norfolk
David Duke, Nancymond
Abraham Norfleet ditto
Jane Meridith, New-G. 2
Benjamin Payne, Nelson
William Murrill ditto
William L. Watts ditto
Spotswood Garland do 6
Rev. William Wright 6

Joel Brown, Petersburg
Rev. John Cox ditto
Rev Benjamin Devany do
Joseph Gray ditto
Clement Hawks ditto
Edward Lee ditto
Edward Lee, jr. ditto
Nathaniel Lee ditto
Peter M'Colock ditto
Jones Mitchell ditto
Mathew Murray ditto
Burwell Rossell ditto
Rev. Pleasant Thurman 6
William Weeks ditto 6
Wm. Ligon, Prince-Edw.
Rev. Robert Carter do 6
Francis A. Martin ditto
Robert Vanable ditto
Tho's Lewis, Prince-Geo.
James Perkins Prince-G.
Rev. Augustin Heath do
Christopher Procter ditto
Nathaniel Raines ditto
Peyton Rives ditto
Jeduthen Carter, Pittsyl.
Reuben Smith ditto
Rev. Elisha Maxey, Pow-
[hatan 6
Rev. Jesse Nicholson,
[Portsmouth
Peggy Sanford, Prince W
John Spindle, Spotsylvan.
Eneas Foster, Richmond 6
Rev. Charles Callaway do
Mosby Pulliam ditto
Enoch Sullivan ditto
Richardson Taylor ditto
Joshua West ditto
Jesse Battle, Southampton
Benjamin Barrett ditto

SUBSCRIBERS NAMES.

Elizabeth Cary Southam.
John P. Richardson ditto
Jesse King Surry
Rev. James Hill ditto
David Graves, Sussex
William Graves ditto
Rev. William Burge do
Benjamin Chappell ditto
George Dillard ditto
Rev. James Gibbons ditto
Patsey Gilliam ditto
Wm. C. Goodrich ditto
Wilkins Harper ditto
Rev. Joseph Hill ditto
Thomas Hunt ditto
Thomas Hunt, jr. ditto
Ann Huson ditto
George Jones ditto
Rev. Booth Malone ditto
Wm. Malone ditto
Robert Moore Sussex
John Massenberg ditto
John Parham ditto
Thomas Parham ditto
John Pennington ditto
Marcus Pennington ditto
Rev. Thomas Porch ditto
George Rives ditto
Rev. James Rogers ditto
Augustus Shands ditto
Rev. Tho's Shands ditto
Rev. Tho's Shands ditto
Wm. Shands ditto
John Smith ditto
Wm. Thornton ditto
Rev. John Weaver ditto
Wm. Wilburn ditto
Reuben Williams ditto
Benjamin Huley Essex
Philip Mann ditto
Wm. Parry ditto
Gidion Ratcliff, Williams-[burg

North-Carolina,

John Robins Bertie
Tho's Windsor, Caswell
Gabriel Lea do
Duke W. Davis, Franklin
Benjamin Odam Gates
Winburn Jinkins do
Richard Stanford (member of Congress)
Rev Daniel Southall do
John Gullett Guilford
James Hanner do
Levin Kirkman do
Andrew M Gee do
Edmund Taylor, Granvill
Robert Jones, Jun'r do
William Moore, Hertford
Elisha Lawrence Hert.
Willafred Horton do
Jesse Yeates do
Isaac Foster, Murphris-[borough
Patrick Brown do
Edward Kelbee do 6
Thomas O Dwyer do
Joseph G. Rea do 6
Rev Samuel Wells do 6
Seth Peebles, Northampt.
James Barrett do
Isham Fennell do
Benjamin Fox do
Charles Harrison do
Thomas N. Hosea do
Rev John Moore do
Richard Putney do
William Richards do
Revd Humphrey Wood,

Sterling Ruffin, Rocking
[ham
John Seagroves Surrey
William Smith do
Charles S. Tucker do
James Tucker do
William Tucker do
Joseph Finney do
Jacob Harris do
John Kelley do
John Day Stokes
Wiley Jane do
James Kelley Wilks
Nancy Reynolds do
Polly Reynolds do
Henry Robinson, Warren
Joseph F. Dickinson,
Winton 6
James H. Keys Warren
William Matkins, Orange
Eli Terry Rutherford

South-Carolina

Gates Gaff Darlington
Cornelius Cook do
Demsy Dowling do
Benjamin Dubose do
Joseph S. Edwards do
Alexander Fleming do
Dreury Flowers do
Cornelius Grantham do
Spencer Harrell do
Jeremiah Heath do
Richard Horn do
George Huggins do
John Huggins do
Rev Thos. Humphris do
James Hutson do
William Hutson do
Edwin James do
Enos James do
John M'Crea Darling.
John Stewart do
Anthony Windham do
Daniel Windham do
Elias Windham do
James Wright do
Thos. Boone Geo Town
Archibald Brown do
John T. Green do
John T Green do
Richard Green do
Jas Bland Sumter Dist.
George Bird do
William Byrd do
John Campbell do
Samuel Fraser do
Thomas M'Cree do
John M'Donald do
Zachariah Norwood do
Charles Williamson do
R. Witherspoon (repre
sentative in congress)
Williamsburg
Stephen Miller do
Thomas Lane do
James Graham do
John Hickson do
James Holland Marion
James Myers do

Georgia

S. Lark Augusta
Abner M'Gehee Elbert
William Wilkins, Eatont.
W. Devereux, Milledge-
[ville
Solomon Betton do
Abraham Borland do
Joseph Cowen do
Richard W. Ellis do
Mickleberry Ferrell do

SUBSCRIBERS NAMES.

John Herbert, Milledgev
Howell Cobb, (representative in congress)
Abner Flew-Ellen

Tennessee

Robert Hill do
Henry Johnson do
James Kenan do
Thomas H. Kenan do
John Mathews do
Alex'r M'Millian do
Anthony Porter do
John H Posey do
Hubert Reynolds do
Robert Rutherford do
William Rutherford do
Dennis L. Ryan do
Francis Smith do
Samuel S. Steel do
Benjamin Tarver do
Thomas Taylor do
William Turner do
Charles Williamson do
Tho's Old, Williamson-county 6
Lewis Ashman do
Robert Davis do 6
Sterling Davis do
David Dunn do
John Gholson do
James Goely do
Abraham Maury do
Frederick Peebles do 6
Turner Saunders, Williamson county
Stephen Smith do
Isham R. Trotter do
John Watson, jr. do
Edward Washam do

Ohio

Revd. Joseph S. Collins, Chillicothe
Revd. Samuel Monet do
William Rutledge do
Revd. Edward Scott do
Revd. Thomas Scott do
Samuel Williams do

ERRATA.

Page 13, line 32, for 1792, read 1729.
121, 17, for Bee, read Pee Dee.
156, 34, for Tite, read Tait
318, 16, for Micajah, read Michael.

PEOPLE

PLACES

THE UNITED STATES
FROM THE
CLOSE OF THE REVOLUTION
TO THE
PURCHASE OF LOUISIANA.
1783–1803.

CIRCUITS

DISTRICTS

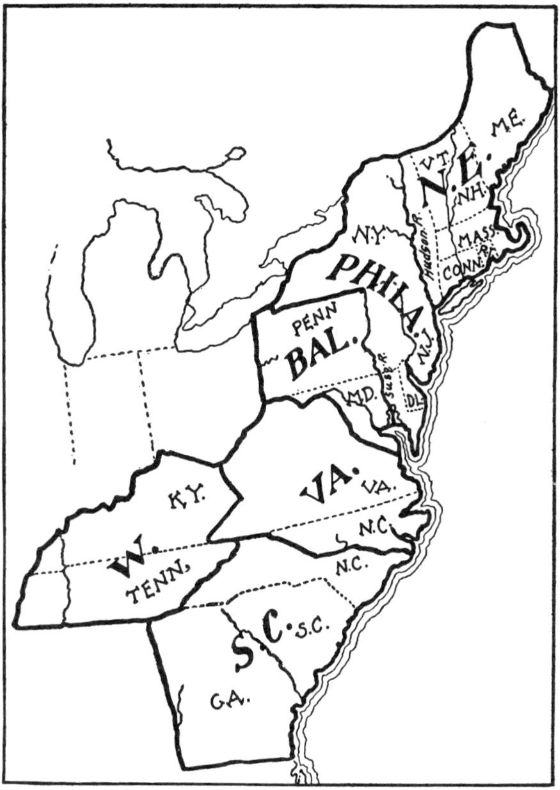

The Original Six Annual Yearly Conferences.

CONFERENCES

Prior to 1796, annual conferences had been called district conferences (names & sites), in future would be called yearly (annual) conferences.

The project of reprinting Lee's "Short History" has been going on for a number of years. The stimulus that lead us to move forward came through inspiration of the late Dr. Jacob S. Payton and the assistance of Rev. Edwin Schell, executive secretary of the United Methodist Historical Society of the Baltimore Conference and Lovely Lane Museum, Baltimore, Maryland.

If we were to dedicate this publication, these two men deserve the recognition.

The Publisher

Monuments to Jesse Lee, Robert Strawbridge, and Bishop Asbury, George, Emory and Waugh at the Mount Olivet Cemetery, Baltimore, Maryland, the Jesse Lee stone is no longer in the Bishops' lot as depicted, but has been separated from Lee's sarcrophagus (still in Bishops' lot) and installed in its own circle on the opposite side of the cemetery.

W. M. MERRICK

JESSE LEE PREACHING UN

The topography of this *fac-simile* drawing is a good r